Unfading Light

Unfading Light

The Sustaining Insight and Inspiration of Abraham Lincoln

Richard Fritzky

Hamilton Books

Lanham • Boulder • New York • Toronto • London

Published by Hamilton Books
An imprint of The Rowman & Littlefield Publishing Group, Inc.
4501 Forbes Boulevard, Suite 200, Lanham, Maryland 20706
Hamilton Books Acquisitions Department (301) 459-3366

6 Tinworth Street, London SE11 5AL, United Kingdom

British Library Cataloguing in Publication Information Available

Library of Congress Control Number:

ISBN 9780761872375 (pbk. : alk. paper)
ISBN 9780761872382 (electronic)

∞™ The paper used in this publication meets the minimum requirements of American National Standard for Information Sciences Permanence of Paper for Printed Library Materials, ANSI/NISO Z39.48-1992.

With heartfelt appreciation to the 45 contributors whose lifetime love affairs with Abraham Lincoln colored this work.

And to Richard Branca, my extraordinary friend, for his kind support in making this possible.

And most especially, to my Maggie, for her relentless and sustaining love and to our 12 children, the loves in their lives and 22 'light up the life' grandchildren. May all of their lives be lived in the light of this humblest of gentle souls who dreamed oh so very big dreams for them.

Figure 0.1.   Here Lincoln stands, firm, inspired, determined, about to lay down the ax, pick up the pen, raise his voice and change the world. *Source:* The Resolute Lincoln, New Salem, Illinois - by Avard Fairbanks 1954. Photographed by Dave Wiegers.

Above all, there are these simple truths. We need Abraham Lincoln back on the ground with us. We need his voice and his aspirations. We need his light, his humility, his empathy, his "Better Angels." We need to reclaim our national soul and to rededicate ourselves to the "Vast unfished work that he so nobly advanced."

Contents

Foreword

John C. Waugh

No president is as firmly fixed in the imagination, memory, and esteem of his countrymen today, a century and a half after his service to us all, than Abraham Lincoln.

Fifteen presidents preceded him. Twenty eight have succeeded him. Yet, of them all, he is the most intensely favored, remembered, written and read about of any in American history.

Lincoln emerged from the American West of his time, from Illinois, from relative political obscurity, just when the young Union was lethally imperiled by rebellion and civil war. On paper, he came to this nation-destroying crisis, totally inexperienced and unprepared to carry so heavy a load—the enormous task of then reuniting and saving the planet's first and unprecedented experiment in representative democracy. At stake was the salvation of a republican government "of the people, by the people, and for the people," a wholly new concept to the nations of the world. This people's nation had lasted "four score and seven years" up to Lincoln's time. Would it now live or die?

Lincoln had not a day of executive experience. He had been but a lawyer and a politician in what was then a frontier state. Because he was a humble man, he understood his limitations.

He told Lot M. Morrill, the newly elected senator from Maine: "I don't know but that God has created one man great enough to comprehend the whole of this stupendous crisis and transaction from beginning to end, and endowed him with sufficient wisdom to manage and direct it. I confess I do not fully understand and foresee it all. But I am placed here where I am obliged to the best of my poor ability to deal with it." In short, there may be one man great enough in this country to do all that, but he ain't here, so I have to do it.

But Lincoln brought with him to the task a set of intangible qualities that most men and no other president possessed to the degree that he did. And these qualities would go far in making him what he turned out to be, the savior of the nation. They are the qualities that a century and a half later have made him perhaps the most admired and written about figure in world history. They are the qualities that have attracted him to the forty-five admirers testifying to his greatness in this compelling book. They are the qualities that have helped make him an "Unfading Light."

Lincoln possessed humility, a rare, yet extraordinary trait in a powerful man. It is a difficult characteristic to develop and hold on to in the face of high achievement, celebrity, and acclamation, but as tall as he was, he never looked down on anyone.

Horace Greeley, the influential editor of the influential New York Tribune, who clashed repeatedly with Lincoln throughout the war, finally said of him: He remained to the last "simply, absolutely, alike in heart and manner, one of the people. . . . There never yet was a man so lowly as to feel humbled in the presence of Abraham Lincoln; there was no honest man who feared or dreaded to meet him."

Lincoln was kind. Despite having to commit thousands of men to their deaths to save the Union, he knew it had to be done. And it tore at his heart constantly and often brought tears to his eyes. Yet kindness is a characteristic of great and good men. The novelist Henry James said, "Three things in human life are important: the first is to be kind; the second is to be kind; and the third is to be kind." Lincoln might well have agreed.

Lincoln was gentle. This is often the trait of a man—or an animal who is big physically. One of the most gentle of dogs is a St. Bernard. Lincoln was big, six feet four inches tall, towering for his time, and yet he was gentle. At the end of the war, he wanted the Confederates to be "let up easy." He wished this for Jefferson Davis, the president of the Confederacy and the other leaders of the rebellion. It was his will that surrender terms for Confederate soldiers be lenient.

Gentleness and kindness are, of course, primary components of reconciliation. From the inception of the war and the massive suffering it inflicted, it was Lincoln's determination that it be followed by a reunited Union, the reconciliation of the two warring parties, and by a reconstruction wherein former slaves and free citizens peacefully coexist as equals.

These were but three of the key personal traits, among the many, that Lincoln was endowed with as a person. He also was noted for being truthful, thoughtful, and compassionate. He was strong and firm, but willing to rethink and change as necessary.

Lincoln was a politician, one of the most effective and successful in our history. Despite his lack of executive inexperience, he became a master of it—and despite his clodhopping ways, he became one of our greatest statesmen—and despite his lack of formal schooling, he became a giant of American literature.

His vast repertoire of intangibles and all they embodied were major elements in his winning the war and becoming the beacon of light we still turn to. They were the traits that drew people to him, traits that have made these forty-five testifiers in *Unfading Light* so fascinated in and admiring of him.

We have had presidents whose lack of these intangibles have rendered them failures. Our 45th president is a striking example. Every fine quality Lincoln possessed, Donald Trump lacks. Where Lincoln was humble, Trump remains a self- aggrandizing narcissist who visualizes himself as the greatest of presidents. Where Lincoln was kind, Trump radiates mean-spiritedness, even hatred. Where Lincoln was gentle, Trump runs roughshod over people, demeaning them, insulting them. Where Lincoln was a healer, Trump constantly wounds people. Where Lincoln was truthful, an "Honest Abe, "Trump is a constant liar, who every day clocks an average of six outright lies, misstatements, or unsubstantiated facts.

Karl Marx, a contemporary of Lincoln, said of him, that "he was one of those rare men who became great without ceasing to be good." And that has enabled him to live abundantly in the American memory for more than 150 years and the kind of man we can turn to in times of chaos, the one man great enough.

Firmly believing this, Rich Fritzky has probed the minds of these forty-five good souls who have devoted much, if not the all of their lives, to Lincoln—a wide array of celebrated historians, scholars, artists, impersonators, curators, animators, professors, presenters, teachers and more. Fritzky has taken their offerings and insights to heart, to mind and to pen and dove deep into the nooks, crannies, and crevices of the great constellation that was our 16th President.

Together, these testifiers to Lincoln's greatness movingly respond to all who would dare equate the 45th president with him. They compellingly argue that we need to get right with Lincoln and look to his light and his resolve to raise up all in the race of life and see our way through the madness and turbulence of our own time. What would Lincoln have us do? Fritzky asks. With unbridled passion and conviction, what would Lincoln, 155 years removed, have us do?

Fritzky's book is a fresh, unique and compelling look at Lincoln whose greatness was secured by the fact that he also was good, humble, compassionate, gentle, and more than kind enough.

Figure 0.2.   Here, our own George Buss ate lunch in Grade School and here,
there would be no ascension to the Senate, but one innocent question of his
gave rise to the Freeport Doctrine which would open up the very door to the
presidency. *Source:* Lincoln the Debater, Freeport, Illinois - by Leonard Crunelle
1929. Photographed by Dave Wiegers.

Preface

We Must Go to Lincoln

My life with Abraham Lincoln began on my tenth birthday. As childhood stories go, it's not a bad one, but I won't dare tell it until later. A Lincoln man for 60 years, I have never tired of reading the latest book about him or about the war he fought or about the slaves he freed, the world he imagined, the jokes he told or the tears he shed. I have long walked where he walked. I have taught so very many classes in which he starred. Ever inspired, I have never stopped searching for him. And now, 60 years after my March 12, 1960 epiphany, I throw my own 'two cents' or Lincoln pennies worth of sentiments onto the vast sea of Lincoln scholarship.

I do because the times demand it. I do because all that is at issue in a fractured America today demands it. I do because I will internally combust if I don't. For we need him back in the field and on the ground today. And should you have eyes that see, a heart that beats and a soul that bleeds, I trust you understand why.

With the help of some great Lincoln historians, scholars and Lincoln devotees of all shapes and stripes, we'll probe the depths and meandering tributaries of their thought provoking and moving responses to these simple questions about our Lincoln, in the belief that the simplest of questions evoke the profoundest of responses.

THE FIVE QUESTIONS

1. What was it that first drew you to the study of Abraham Lincoln? When did you know that you were going to have a relationship with him? Was it a book, an event, a conversation, an image, an issue, a class, a teacher-professor, a trip?

2. What, for you, is the Abraham Lincoln "fixed mark," the quality that inspired, moved and drove your relentless study of and interest in him?

3. Were you to have an actual conversation with him, what would you most want it to be about and why?

4. What words of his never cease to inspire you and why? Please share as many quotes and corresponding thoughts as you like.

5. What stands and actions taken by Lincoln and/or words both written and said by him do you feel most inspire us to question and challenge the administration of our 45th president today? Please be as specific as you can.

These are not frivolous questions and while you will be the ultimate judge, I was overwhelmed and moved by the profound that they evoked.

There in the midst of the worn, beleaguered but still 'better angels' of our own nature, Lincoln's spirit still thrives. For grace was given him and grace he extended and grace suffers neither the darkness nor demise. Grace endures.

I believe this.

An existential force, Abraham Lincoln, our sixteenth president, continues to shine a light upon the ideal America or at least an 'America true to its creed,' the one, despite our rigid divide, that might make us all proud to be Americans again. Despite the passage of time and our stormy present, there is something so very powerful in the vast reservoir of ideas and ideals, dreams and deeds and soaring words of Lincoln's to which we are bound, all replete with potency and power.

I also believe this.

Well aware that I step upon territory that has for long been intensely explored by tens of thousands, the more than 16,000 books about Abraham Lincoln speak loudly.

More than 16,000 books and growing, abundant and prolific is our romance with and our belonging to. So some argue that the Lincoln wellspring is drained. Books have again and again been written about his childhood and the early loss of his mother and sister, the impact of his Step-Mom, the strained relationship with his Dad and those "short and simple annals of the poor," his retentive mind and self-education and his love of Anne Rutledge, his life in New Salem and his life in Springfield, his marriage to Mary Todd, his skills as a lawyer, his political genius, his legislative years, his races for the United States Senate, he and his sons and his mourning them, his melancholy and depression, his pre-occupation with mortality, his fatalistic poetry, the Douglas campaign, the great debates, the presidential campaign, his humor, his leadership, his administrative genius, his suspension of the writ of habeas corpus, his cabinet, his growth on the slavery issue, his honor, his ethics, his relationship with and search for the right Generals, his great proclamation and fight for the 13th amendment, his speeches, his family, his relationships with Seward and Stanton and his Generals, his letters, his migraines, his dreams, his courage, his God, his doubt, his faith and ever so much more.

The Great Emancipator, he has been mythologized, revered, examined, re-examined and examined again. He has been debunked, criticized, humanized, championed, placed on a pedestal and, very likely, quoted more often than anyone with the possible exception of Jesus of Nazareth or Shakespeare.

Enough, they argue. I disagree.

There will never be enough and so I am raising my oars with the intention of piling on. Holzer, Burlingame, Goodwin, Waugh, Gramm, White, Egerton, Brookhiser, Brewster, Boritt, Williams, McPherson are among the many who have only recently released perfect books on Lincoln and dozens more did so immediately before them and dozens more are working to do so now and I am hungry for all of them.

In one of those books that never leaves my desktop, *November – Lincoln's Elegy at Gettysburg*, Kent Gramm bled out in an extraordinary reflective work.

With a vast historical and literary treasure chest in head and heart, he soulfully and spiritually dwelled upon the gifts handed down to us by our 16th president as he placed and considered Lincoln in the vortex and heart of an ancient and long running historical drama that has yet to run its course. With dry humor, he discussed the then 'raging' debate as to the actual site where Lincoln stood when he gave the *Gettysburg Address* (where the monument is or in the Evergreen Cemetery or at the Selleck site on the lower slope, below rather than above the graves). He suggested, in both jest and in all seriousness that this simply could not be, for after all, if we can't find Lincoln, we are lost.

If we cannot connect with and continue to be inspired by Lincoln, we are lost.

"We need conversations with him," wrote Gramm. We need to reconnect with his vision for America, his 'new birth of freedom' and the wisdom and perpetual meaning of his 'of, by, and for the people.' We need his 'last full measure of devotion' and his prolific reminder that nations and people advance only in so far as its citizens are willing to sacrifice, pick up the cross and carry each other. Something that far too many of today's political leaders sadly seem to have forgotten.

Movingly, Gramm was in Gettysburg when he wrote, "Lincoln addressed their grief, why not mine. He gave his generation purpose, why not ours"?

I rather feel that Lincoln both can and does try to assuage our grief and elevate us in that the words of his immortal *Second Inaugural*, letters of consolation and so many other documents attending to loss and to his nation of suffering live in us as well. The very life he lived, his presidency, his words, his faith, his devotion and his character, the meaning, essence, force and spirit of it all are not buried somewhere on our bookshelves but rather in us, in we broken and despondent yet still aspiring Americans in 2020 as one of the most critical presidential elections in our history awaits.

Lincoln's purpose in life, to the extent that it remains unfulfilled in his death, is still in play and we the living, more than 155 years removed, must strive, as best we can, to pay forward what he so blessedly paid in the heart of the 19th century.

The work on the ground today is ours. So will it be the ruin of all of our sacred ideals or new life?

Not long ago, I came across a Ronald C. White (author of *The Eloquent President, A Portrait of Lincoln through His Words* and many other works) interview that struck me. He was relating Aristotle and the Greek word, ethos to nineteenth-century rhetoric and to Lincoln specifically. He said, "Although Lincoln was a lawyer and very much believed in rational logic, he came to understand that persuasion took more than getting the audience to agree with your argument. Persuasion, in fact, could and would only be effected, in so much as they came to trust his character."

To Lincoln, to speak was, in words, truth and faith, to quite literally transform the audience and to construct a belonging to them. In short, there had to be that something real behind the words. There had to be character and value and wisdom and truth. He had to earn it. He had to be worthy of both it and of them. Otherwise, they were just words.

In his book, Billy Herndon, Lincoln's faithful law partner, wrote about a newspaperman from Galena, Illinois who was particularly impressed with Lincoln's forthright manner. After hearing him speak at Freeport, often regarded as the greatest or the most important of the 1858 Lincoln-Douglas debates, the reporter filed this article in the local newspaper, *The Daily Advertiser*. It clearly speaks to the manner in which Lincoln's truth manifested and inevitably fashioned that belonging to and covenant with the people in his audience.

And so too and mysteriously, as we here assert, still with us today.

> His voice is clear, sonorous and pleasant and he enunciated with distinctness and his style of address is earnest, not bombastic, but animated without being furious and impresses one with the fact that he is speaking what he believes. His manner is neither fanciful nor rhetorical but logical. His thoughts are strong thoughts and are strongly jointed together. He is clear (and) reasoned and has the faculty of making himself clearly understood. He does not leave a vague impression that he has said something worth hearing; the hearer remembers what that something is. The sledge hammer effect of the speech results from the force of the argument of the logician, not the fierce gestures and loud rantings of the demagogue.

He was speaking what he believed, connecting, persuading and effecting that belonging.

Lincoln's words were neither empty nor static nor for that moment alone. His contagious faith and heartfelt belief in the promise that America's destiny was to elevate all for the good, to raise up all in "race of life" and to lift the burdens of mankind gave way to covenants.

Lasting covenants, both then and not for that moment alone or that day or the mere lifetime of his administration, but rather with and on behalf of you and me, here and now.

As such, we do not study Lincoln in a vacuum, quiet and alone, just for the sake of learning. No, we rather do so because he feeds our souls and our spirits and still mysteriously responds to our longings.

Above all, we rendezvous with him in the hope of advancing what he longed for America to be.

Yes, this belonging, this ethos that he fashioned with ancient audiences also was fashioned with us; and it is for us the living, is it not?

So whoever the next president of the United States is, they will need both Lincoln's spirit and ideals in tow. Thy will need to take the best in our history into the fray with them.

I do not believe that oil or gas or any mineral on earth or even our vast technology to be our greatest resource. I believe history is our greatest resource and I feel that the true glory and greatness of our American story has neither passed by nor faded. Jefferson's Declaration, Thoreau's Civil Disobedience, Teddy's "Big Stick," FDR's New Deal, Kennedy's Camelot, Ike's honesty, Carter's human decency, Martin's dream, Bobby's empathy, Obama's dignity and Reagan's love of America rather live in us. Lincoln, the meteor that he was, lives in us, steeling and girding us always for what lies ahead.

"We must believe in our history in order to believe in ourselves," added Gramm.

He further suggested that "What withstood the German advance at Bastogne and drove us through the barbed wire at Dachau and into Berlin," what moved us through Brown versus Topeka and beyond the evil of separate but equal and what restored our soul after days like 9/11 was the faith that Lincoln instilled in us at Gettysburg and throughout his presidency.

"Were it not for him, we would be an entirely different people," Gramm argued.

For it was a visionary Lincoln, who gave "Flesh to our hope and to our faith"! It was a visionary Lincoln who defined our national character. Out of the fiercely burning crucible of Civil War, his spirit and passion gave rise to our irrepressible national soul and to the very sinew and marrow of the American Ideal.

Ultimately, the more important question to me is, have we been true to the faith Lincoln had in us? He left us a re-consecrated, rededicated, reborn America and 630,000 or more laid their costly sacrifice down upon his "altar of freedom" then and hundreds of thousands have done so since and still unto this very day, and yet we fritter away the goodness and greatness of his legacy and even more importantly, their extraordinary sacrifice.

Tainted and tarnished, these sacred ideals have so sadly been tossed to the vagaries of the wind in the America at risk today.

As Lincoln traveled from Springfield to Washington, D.C. in the winter of 1861, the nation he went to lead was crumbling around him and he would speak of being in the very "*Garden of Gethsemane*" itself. A great darkness had descended upon the nation born of his beloved founding fathers, "*the proposition that all men are created equal*" and a government where a people ruled and not despots. Slipping away in the darkness was what he then believed to be the "*Last best hope of earth.*"

To Washington and to it, he would bring his "*stand firm like a chain of steel*" and the light of new birth. Under him and throughout the fiery storm, a new nation with a firmly rooted and re-consecrated ideal would rise.

It takes no quantum leap to suggest that America in 2020 is being threatened by a different darkness, born of a political leadership that celebrates the worst in us and dares to war with both its own people and so very often with truth, basic human decency and civility. Today, forever twitter tormented, presidential lies, as verified by the Washington Post, are soon to pass the 18,000 mark. There is that and the bullying, the demeaning, the raging, the incoherence and the surprising.

It is, in the face of this, that 'we the people' must still keep faith with October 5, 2016 and that which was pledged to 159 sovereign partners to meet the greatest threat our world faces—with July 21, 2010 and Dodd Frank—with December 2, 1970 and Environmental Protection—with July 9, 1965 and Voting Rights—with July 21, 1964 and Civil Rights—with December 20 thru 27, 1944 and the Bulge and Bastogne where 89,000 Americans fell and 19,000 died—with June 6, 1944 and Utah, Omaha and Normandy Beaches where 10,000 fell and 2500 died—with October 28, 1886 and "*Give me your tired, your poor, your hungry, your struggling masses yearning to breathe free, send these the tempest tossed to me*"—with December 15, 1791 and our Bill of Rights—and with July 4, 1776 and "*All men are created equal and endowed by their creator.*"

We must keep faith with April 4, 1968 and Martin, with June 6, 1968 and Bobby, with November 22, 1963 and John.

We must keep faith with April 14, 1865 and Abraham.

We must keep faith with March 4, 1865 and that most sacred of inaugural addresses and "*with malice toward none, with charity for all,*" with November 19, 1863 and "*their last full measure of devotion,*" "*a new birth of freedom"* and *"of, by and for the people"* and with July 1 thru 3, 1863 and Gettysburg and its 50,000 either dead, wounded or missing and with the more than 630,000 who *"laid so costly a sacrifice upon the altar of freedom."*

Yes, we must keep faith with Lincoln if we are to take the high ground back from the forces of mean-spiritedness and selfishness and back from the denizens of darkness and extreme wealth.

We must, as Lincoln once suggested, *"disenthrall ourselves and so save our nation,"* which is 'to get right with him,' which is to go towards his light.

As bright today as it was in 1861, my collaborators and I believe that Abraham Lincoln's Light endures, inspiring one generation unto the next, inviting all to see what he saw, to value what he valued and to pay forward a political system that would strive to do justice for all and to open up the doors of opportunity for all, the opportunity that began with the freedom for all that he long fought for and finally bled out for on April 14, 1865.

This is not, make no mistake, the by-product of any manipulative desire or determination, in desperation or fear, to further idealize or mythologize in order to fashion or lay claim to a true or quintessential American hero who we can turn to. That ship sailed a long time ago, for he became larger than life or mythical long before I was even a glint in my parent's eyes. He is what he is and just as Senator Ted Kennedy so movingly said of his brother, Bobby, who was wired a lot like Lincoln, at his funeral in 1968, *"He need not be idealized or enlarged in death beyond what he was in life."*

A subject for another tome or time, I often dwell upon the fact that their two assassinations, divided by a century and monumental change, exacted incalculable tolls upon futures that became so very much poorer for their loss.

Game changers, the death of each bitterly altered the historical dynamic in the latter parts of both the nineteenth and twentieth centuries. As hard as it is to imagine, it is now more than 52 years for Bobby whose death is still mourned by many. Compassionate to a fault, the same angels and saints nestled in the souls of both of these men and while Bobby went to Aeschylus and the realism of his "Pain which cannot forget falls drop by drop upon the heart until, in our own despair, against our will, comes wisdom through the awful grace of God," and Lincoln to Knox and the romance of his *"Tis the wink of an eye, tis the draught of a breath, from the blossom of birth to the paleness of death,"* both, in the dead of their sleepless nights dwelled long and hard upon the eternal verities and mysteries and in their suffering, weighed down by great trial and loss, determined to give their all to bless and to heal.

No, there is no need to manufacture nor manipulate.

Lincoln is the real deal and he remains, as Whitman wrote, *"As complete a man as America has ever produced."*

Whitman, ever volunteering at the hospitals in D.C., also wrote about a Confederate Captain from the 2nd Virginia Regiment who startled him on May 28, 1865 when he said of Lincoln, *"Take him altogether, he was the best man this country ever produced. It was quite a while I thought very different, but some time before the murder, that's the way I have seen it."* Whitman reflected upon his earnestness' and his sadness, for this rebel and enemy had heard the words of the *Gettysburg* and *Second Inaugural Addresses* and seen the light (see *The Sacrificial Years*, edited by John Harmon McElroy).

As to his words, which we continue to rely upon, and his purpose and policy, Lincoln was the straight arrow who would save the union and who would free the slaves and who would secure the perpetuity of representative government not only for America but also for a weary world. Underlying and driving the all of this, there was his own 'fixed mark,' his primary objective and end game, the elevation of all *"in the race of life."* A people's president, he truly believed that the United States was to become a great land of unlimited opportunity. Yes, opportunity was at the epicenter of his thinking. It was the Holy Grail, the difference maker (see *A Just and Generous Nation: Abraham Lincoln and the Fight for American Opportunity* by Harold Holzer and Norton Garfinkle).

Truly, it was and so, my apologies to those this might offend, but our first Republican president was, without question or doubt, clothed in 21st Century liberal and progressive garb.

I love Lincoln, above all, because he was driven by compassion, empathy, kindness and decency. As naturally humble and *'You before I'* as it was possible for any human being to be.

In the dark depths of his awful war, he saw the big picture and envisioned what these United States could be. So, he would hold tight, with his iron grip, to render that vision a reality and to forge a nation where no man, however low, has to bow and where all could rise and thrive. Through the great benefit of a representative and free government, providential resources, American ingenuity, industrial modernization and fair and reasoned national policies, this would, he firmly believed be achieved.

He well may have shadow-boxed with God but not with this. As to the prospective growth and advance of economy and opportunity, he suffered no doubt. America's great witness to the world, as to the blessings of representative government would, he believed, be clearly demonstrated.

However besieged and pre-occupied by the awful war, he never let go of his ties to Alexander Hamilton's un-adopted *Report on Manufactures*, a report that was later picked up and adopted by Lincoln's political ideal, Henry Clay, whose "American System" was devoted to investing in the infrastructure that would drive economic growth and jobs, jobs, jobs. The opportunity or the pursuit of the same drove Lincoln to champion the raising of the waters of the Sangamon River for navigational purposes, when first elected to the Illinois State Legislature. While unsuccessful then, the intercontinental railroad that he set in motion as president indeed would be. *"Tried by War"* as he was, he never took his eyes off the prize.

And so it is on that truly cared and gave a damn' scale, where Lincoln earned his place on the pedestal.

Above all, the light to which we look was channeled by the man himself, via his own poetic prose and that vast and extraordinary body of work that he bequeathed to American Literature.

While the world well knows his 'Greatest Hits," the *Gettysburg Address* and the *Second Inaugural*, there is in all he penned, from letters to proclamations to silent 'Messages to Congress' to the earliest of pronouncements, a genius and a spiritual force in words that brilliantly soared then and continues to soar as if on angelic wings today. They demand to be read again—lifting—elevating—expanding the mind—exuding faith, hope and light (see *The Annotated Lincoln,* Harold Holzer & Thomas Horrocks).

Oh how he dwelled upon the God and reason dichotomy, the nature of man and emotion and love and the essential questions of either immortality or the abyss. He and doubting were old friends.

"But it is only in the doubting," as Father James Carroll suggested in his book, *A Terrible Beauty,* *"where we truly find our belief."* Tennyson, in his *Ode on Intimations of Immortality* takes this faith-doubt equation to another dimension with his, *"Primordial sympathy which having been must ever be."* Likewise, this notion rises in Lincoln, the thinking that we are indeed driven not merely by the reality and struggles of our own day and our own questions, but more so by our belonging to others, by our heritage, by intrinsic and enduring values and by principles that compel and, consequently, by our own duty to posterity.

We pay the grace and goodness by which we live forward, our life's blood, our failings, our hopes and achievements. Over the broad span of life, past to future, we do this. We give while recognizing, the doubting notwithstanding, that we owe both our ancestors and our descendants, our own humble efforts to advance the line for good.

Taking this one step further, Todd Brewster, author of *Lincoln's Gamble*, in an extensive and moving response to one of our questions, wrote, *"I am reminded of the Episcopal prayer book's Confession of Sin, the plea for forgiveness for "what we have done and what we have left undone." There is, in that, a quality of collective responsibility for the iniquities of the world and I think it is similar to what Lincoln felt and felt quite keenly."* To my, we take and we give or we receive and we pass on, Brewster here interestingly and appropriately adds the weight of sin and guilt. It is no easy thing to carry the weight of the world, but that is what Lincoln did and as such, he keenly felt the need to cleanse and to heal and to strive to be of good, so as not to pile more on an already beleaguered posterity.

Inside this vortex of musing and questioning and guilt and philosophizing and striving to identify the essentials of life and giving it all to purpose, Lincoln lived. He dove deep into this morass, and maybe as deep as anyone can or should without going mad.

Indeed, he wildly tested these boundaries.

He also read and read and read and, more importantly, remembered what he read. These five forces then combined to make him so great a writer and so great a man:

- The constant diving deep and painstakingly grappling with both the mysteries and the essentials of life.
- The inexhaustible appetite to, via reading, grow and improve.
- The fact that everything entering his mind stayed right there. Like the elephant, he never forgot, which is why he had a story in mind for everything.
- Genius – plain and simple - unadulterated Genius.
- He brought to all of the above, a rare and extraordinary combination of humility, compassion and kindness, along with an unbridled determination to serve, to be of good and to *make his mark.*

Of particular importance to me and my placing so much faith in Lincoln's light is that it just seems driven by a power greater than. There is, I feel and intensely so, a divinity lurking in him and in his words.

Having already addressed an '*only in the doubting, does one find their belief'* thesis, I pile on and note that God is on full dress parade in Lincoln's writing and referenced even more than the immortal "*All men are created equal and endowed by their creator.*" Whatever problems he may have had with God, and we could begin with the deaths and the mourning that accompanied his youth and the likely irrationality, bombast, hellfire and brimstone of frontier ministers, God, in his work, certainly appears to have had no problem with him. And neither did the deaths of Eddie and Willie, nor the 630,000 preclude God from being front and center in his *sacred effort* or *Second Inaugural.*

I once read a biography of Thomas Jefferson by Fawn Brodie that moved me. She suggested that however rational he tried to be, the right hand of God took hold of him and the very fire of the "*Spirit of Jehova trembled within him,*" whenever he wrote. So too with Lincoln, our oh so rational, logical and often despondent inspiration who so struggled to get right with life, the '*Enigma*' (Gabor Boritt) who was destined to forever change the lives of untold millions and, if you buy into my thinking, arguably billions for the better.

As to this duty to his own and to posterity, purpose, faith, God, doubt, belief and even these musings as to the relationship between his writing and his God, here's just a purposefully small sampling of insight from Lincoln himself:

July 10, 1858 – *Lincoln-Douglas Debates*

"Sir, my concern is not whether God is on our side; my greatest concern is to be on His side, for God is always right."

"Surely God would not have created such a being as man, with an ability to grasp the infinite, to exist only for a day! No, no, man was made for immortality."

September 27, 1841 – Letter to Mary Speed

How true it is that "God tempers the wind to the shorn lamb," or in other words, that He renders the worst of human conditions tolerable, while He permits the best, to be nothing better than tolerable.

March, 1846 – Illinois State Journal (appeared about a week after his son, Eddie's death)

Sweet Eddie, we bid thee adieu – Affection's wail cannot reach thee now – Deep though it be, and true – Bright is the home to him now given – For of such is the kingdom of heaven.

Believed to have been authored by Lincoln (see Burlingame, *A. Lincoln, A Life*, p. 359)

February 11, 1861 Springfield, Illinois – *Farewell Address*

Trusting in Him, who can go with me, and remain with you and be everywhere for good, let us confidently hope that all will yet be well. To His care commending you, as I hope in your prayers, you will commend me, I bid you an affectionate farewell.

February 13, 1861 – To the Ohio State Legislature

I turn, then, and look to the American people and to that God who has never forsaken them.

Early 1863 – Day of Fast & Thanks Proclamation

We have been the recipients of the choicest bounties of Heaven. We have been preserved, these many years, in peace and prosperity. We have grown in numbers, wealth and power, as no other nation has ever grown. But we have forgotten God. We have forgotten the gracious hand which preserved us in peace, and multiplied and enriched and strengthened us; and we have vainly

> *imagined, in the deceitfulness of our hearts, that all these blessings were produced by some superior wisdom and virtue of our own. Intoxicated with unbroken success, we have become too self-sufficient to feel the necessity of redeeming and preserving grace, too proud to pray to the God that made us.*

This, one of my favorite passages of his, has been read every year at our Thanksgiving table.

Sept 4, 1864 – Letter to Eliza Gurney

> *The purposes of the Almighty are perfect and must prevail. Meanwhile we must work earnestly in the best light He gives us, trusting that so working still conduces to the great ends he ordains.* (see Burlingame, *Abraham Lincoln – A Life, p. 259)*

Late in the war, Joshua Speed, Lincoln's best friend, was visiting and he witnessed a meeting that Lincoln had with two women, a wife whose husband and a mother whose son had both been arrested for resisting the draft. They came without the required written petition as neither of them could write nor afford to pay someone to prepare the documents for them. Waving it off, Lincoln excused the pre-requisites (he always did), listened and, as always, predisposed to pardon, said, *"I believe I will turn out the flock."*

That is just what he did.

One woman got on her knees. Uncomfortable, Lincoln urged her to get up saying, *"Don't kneel to me. Thank God."* The other woman said, *"Mr. Lincoln, I shall never see you again till we meet in heaven."* Deeply moved by her, he took her right hand in both of his while escorting her to the door. He said, *"I am afraid with all my troubles, I shall never get there, but if I do, I will find you. That you wish me to get there is the best wish you could make for me."*

What Lincoln shared with this woman was that he was taking personal responsibility for the appalling death tolls. He saw the all of it as his sin and penance, rendering him unworthy even of a heaven.

Then alone, as these two old and close friends considered one another, Speed softly said, *"With my knowledge of your nervous sensibility, it is a wonder that such scenes as this don't kill you"* upon which Lincoln responded, *"It was the only thing I did all day that gave me any pleasure."*

It was a drama of mercy, snatched from the torrents of horror, as he did what one wired to lead with compassion and kindness does.

March 4, 1865 – Washington, D.C. – *Second Inaugural*

> *With malice toward none, with charity for all, with firmness in the right as God gives us to see the right, let us strive on to finish the work we are in.*

Discovered after His Death – *The Meditation on Divine Will*

The will of God prevails.

No faith. No God, no way. Prayer was how he breathed and transformative grace dripped from his words.

Lincoln's light also is channeled through everything from the monuments we have built to the historical sites we visit - to the many Lincoln Associations and Forums and Institutes we join - to the classrooms where professors profess and teachers teach - to the wide array of historians who keep on digging deeper to the endless array of faiths and political parties and candidates and refugees and even our new brother and sister citizens who only just today, I pray, placed their hands on their hearts and took the oath of citizenship - for all are enjoined by the claim that Lincoln is their own.

Picture the light of the Lincoln Memorial itself. In the dead of night, it beams out of that prodigious and imposing structure, illuminating the mall in Washington D.C., overwhelming, compelling and even demanding that *attention must be paid*. No matter if it is 3:00 a.m. or 5:00 a.m., it silently asks all who pass to pause. For it is, after all, not about the light that radiates but rather the all of the values, faith, determination and vision of the one for whom it shines

No, no one passes by it without being moved in some way as each is subliminally invited by Lincoln to be a better, more complete citizen. Always the subliminal message, *"Come on in, take stock, it is your government and you lead, so take charge and please, please, Ask Not"*?

The iconic, 16,000, 3-story book tower in the lobby at Ford's Theatre bears physical witness to just how vast the Lincoln literature is. While there is indeed reason to shake one's head at the likes of *Abe & Fido* and *Abraham Lincoln: Vampire Hunter*, so many unanswered questions still remain and today's historians and others yet to come bring their own passions, insights and ever challenging points of view.

The thing about history is that there is always, always more. To conjecture about an end is silly. There are no ends.

As to my own belonging to Lincoln, discovery was advanced by his partners, friends and personal secretaries like Billy Herndon, Ward Hill Lamon and the inimitable Hay and Nicolay, but the torch passed over the years through the Carl Sanburgs, Lord Charnwoods and Dale Carnegies and on to the Richard Nelson Currents, David Herbert Donalds and others. As for today, there are, first and foremost the generous contemporary historians, who so kindly contributed their best thinking to this work, Harold Holzer, Jack C. Waugh, Douglas Egerton, Edna Greene Medford, Richard Brookhiser, Todd Brewster, Rabbi Jonathan Sarna, Frank J. Williams, Michelle Krowl and my old friends, Tracy Power and Kent Gramm. Gramm's profoundly moving *November – Lincoln's Elegy at Gettysburg*, as already noted, is the spiritual impetus of this effort.

Two additional contributing authors include Rebecca Morris *(A Low Dirty Place)* of the Anne Arundel Historical Society in Maryland and Eileen Patch *(This From George)* of the Broome County Historical Society in Binghamton, New York. Many others who study Lincoln closely and advance our understanding and appreciation of him also contributed. They include the leaders and members of The Lincoln Forum, the Abraham Lincoln Association, the Lincoln Group of New York and Civil War Roundtables that span the country, everyone from Henry Ballone to Steve Koppelman to Kathryn Harris to Bob Willard to Bill Grandstaff to Mike Movius, Mel Maurer and Joe Truglio. They include celebrated Lincoln artists, like Wendy Allen and Rich Thompson and a generous collector of Lincoln art, Jim McGrath, impersonators like George Buss, Gettysburg's own, Dave Walker and Mel Maurer, animators like Chris Oakley, curators like Anne Moseley, presenters like Paula Hopewell, professors like Al Azinger, teachers like Matt Lakemacher, Robert Brugler, Win Anderson and beautiful, prayerful souls like Karen Hawbecker, Paula Hopewell, Darla Moe and Marilyn Krowl Rexilius.

There is Joan Chaconas, History Specialist at the Surratt House Museum and Dave Wiegers, a photographer on a quest to capture every monument to Lincoln. There are lawyers and students and enthusiasts like Paul Mellen, Steve Raymond, David Sullivan, Michaela Wieties and Angela Mayer who travels from Germany to the Annual Lincoln Forum in Gettysburg each year.

Living vestiges of Lincoln's light, I am blessed to be able to share their passions about Lincoln with you as well of my own.

Beyond the bloated and exaggerated tomes of some of the aforementioned 'oldies but goodies' and the mighty contributions of our 11 contributing historians, all of whom I revere, there also is the recent and contemporary scholarship of James McPherson, Ronald C. White, Doris Kearns Goodwin, Eric Foner, Mark Neely, Fred Kaplan, Gabor Boritt, Catherine Clinton, Peter Carmichael, Gary Wills and Michael Burlingame, who represent but a smattering of the wide universe of Lincoln biographers who have educated and moved me. All are gifted, but I must admit that 'Hail to the Chief' reverberates whenever we touch the Harold Holzer collection, Burlingame's *Abraham Lincoln: A Life* or Goodwin's *Team of Rivals*.

In their individual historic explorations and discoveries, they widen the scope of the narrative. Each new take or slant or point of information or word spoken or written or action of never until then shared conspires to keep paying forward the same enduring values and principles that drove Lincoln to "*disenthrall*" our nation and to render it a land where all might share in its promise.

In response to the final question asked of my contributors, the one which focused upon our politics and our governance today and Lincoln's light,

Steve Koppelman, formerly the president of the Lincoln Group of New York, pulled this memorable passage from Lincoln's *First Inaugural Address* -- *"While the people retain their virtue and vigilance, no administration, by any extreme of wickedness or folly, can very seriously injure the government in the short space of four years."* Having shared this, he added, *"Fondly do I hope, fervently do I pray,"* that he is right.

But the truth is that things moved much slower 155 years ago. There is now more reason to pause, because everything moves at the speed of light today. Consideration, deliberation and thoughtfulness are remnants of the past as news and information instantaneously beams in from all sectors, tossing everyone up against the wall, turning us upside down and demanding our visceral and immediate response. It is so seethingly maniacal that all it takes for President Trump to serve the rich and mighty and powerful alone is to feed his cult-like base a steady diet of rage, misinformation and vitriol, for it is, he contends you and me against them. Blinded by an endless array of lies, bullying and dissonance, they sadly and almost robotically respond. In truth, he actually abuses his base by not lifting a finger for them practically. He doesn't have to. So long as they are constantly stroked and assured that they fall under the umbrella of the *'great again.'*

That's all they get, the invitational wonder of wallowing in his greatness.

Into our ever-advancing robotic and technological futures, we rush, faster and faster, and ever more perplexingly, with information and communications tools that astound and yet, in the end, ironically and sadly, only invite us to communicate less and less and get 'dumbed down' versions of that which we absorb. Faster and greater somehow sadly seems to evoke less and less. We stare into our cell phones, computers and gadgets as we instagram, post, tweet and text our lives away. Less thought, less personal, less substance, less real. Increasingly, we live on the snippets rather than the substance.

Demagoguery and hate thrive on this and ignorance has no better friend than social media. Truth, knowledge, understanding, even basic human decency and honor, have been and continue to be wildly threatened by this. And while ignorance may well be born of innocence, it is no less destructive.

Lincoln ever lived in the light of July 4, 1776 as do we, but we also live in the light of November 19, 1863 and March 4, 1865 when that light was to grow all the brighter. It shined when Teddy busted the trusts and when FDR quelled the fear and when Americans stormed up Hacksaw Ridge and freed the emaciated and the dying at Buchenwald. It shined the day Ike warned us about that Military Industrial Complex and John Kennedy introduced a Civil Rights Bill that LBJ brought home. It shined when Martin spoke so eloquently of a dream in front of Lincoln's own memorial and when Bobby spoke of pain and suffering upon his death. In his *Audacity of Hope,* Obama looked to it and Occupy Wall Street, however unfulfilled, was driven by it and Bernie and his millennials basked in it and all who are tired of the hate and the division and the injustice and the egregious disparity and the erosion of honor are now being warmed and steeled by it, as the promise and hope of change, new beginnings and the ascension of justice never fades.

In 1863, Lincoln responded to his nation's doom and despair and he put both it and its resilient promise on his broad shoulders. Today, however extraordinarily different, we look to the same. We look to spiritually climb upon those same broad shoulders and take *"increased devotion"* from his *"last full measure of devotion."*

Again, this is not a 'What would Lincoln do' exercise alone. It is rather an exercise in applying Lincoln's ethics, values, compassion, ideals and humility to an overarching contemporary morass and threat. Oh yes, as to policy, we can well make reasoned assumptions, but as to the application of principle, we need have no doubt.

Harold Holzer, in a piece he contributed to the *Huffington Post* on October, 16, 2016, addressed the manner in which Lincoln was used and abused in a then only recent presidential debate. In it, he excoriated one candidate and upheld the other while more broadly investigating how it is that Lincoln has been used by presidents over time. As Lincoln is revered, all seek to identify with him to enhance their own standing. While valid and illuminating, my attention was and remains drawn to his concluding sentence.

It read, "Whether a wish, a hope, a prayer, the moral lights are flickering again. Perhaps Lincoln, if truly understood, can illuminate the right path again."

There you have it—that is exactly what we are after here. What myself and 45 good and generous collaborators or *'Lights of Lincoln,'* including Holzer, are after here.

He focuses upon three key words - *wish, hope, prayer*. They give way to two prospective outcomes - *moral lights flicker again* and *illuminate the right path again.* Such is the very premise of *Unfading Light.* Like the presidents he then wrote of, Holzer also and so very clearly looks to Lincoln, America's moral light.

A fan of the once TV series, Aaron Sorkin's *West Wing* and the life and struggles of its fictional President, Jed Bartlett, there is one episode that especially resonates that I allude to now.

The 100th episode, it was entitled The *Stormy Present.* It revolved around the death of a former conservative President Lassiter who was, in his final days, clamoring to make contact with Bartlett. Dark and brooding, he was apparently searching for some kind of reconciliation, redemption or understanding, traveling the world, visiting every spot where American lives had been sacrificed, bringing home canisters of dirt to memorialize every field or patch of dirt. Reflective, this once bombastic, 'blowhard' of a president was pictured, in his demise, in a mysterious and certainly different light, given his passionate and almost desperate pilgrimage.

Set against a backdrop of sub-plots that included *Arab Spring* like Democratic revolts in the Middle East, a White House mediation of a Civil War generated battle over whether South Carolina or Connecticut rightfully owned an original copy of the *Bill of Rights,* intelligence gathering miscues and residual impacts upon privacy and civil liberties. Yet the primary focus and spotlight of the show remained and shined upon the former and now deceased president.

In the closing scene, Mrs. Lassiter takes a shot at Bartlett for not taking her husband's last calls, before handing him a handwritten note that Lassiter, in one of his final acts, drafted and left for him. The episode reaches its crescendo as the camera zones in on that note alone. Difficult to read, it clearly has to do with conflict in the Middle East. Muddled, it is the last line alone to which your attention is drawn.

It read, "You must go to Lincoln, Jed"!

In crisis, to Lincoln.

One president to another, upon the conclusion of an impassioned pilgrimage, "You must go to Lincoln."

An end of life crisis, the lonely visits to fields where oh so many laid their costly sacrifices down, a sacred and final pilgrimage, a last word of advice and Lincoln. The end game, the muted enlightenment. In the wilderness and in hope and prayer and on pilgrimage whenever marching to reclaim our national soul, we go to Lincoln, who entrusted that re-consecrated soul to our keeping in the first place.

With the stark exception of early 1861, we are more polarized and more a house divided than we have been at any other time in our history; and as to whether or not there is a crisis or a great American political meltdown, there is no doubt. All, no matter where they stand, share a profound sense of loss and fear

That sense of loss and fear is our common denominator and it is in that loss, that longing and that hurting where Lincoln can and will, I pray, help lift us up again. Save for the 1 percent plus, the neo-Nazis and the irredeemable racists, we have more in common than the noise and the screaming and the vitriol.

Much like 1861, when there was no taste for even discussion much less compromise, we are enjoined by our pain, our sadness, our longing. Deeply divided, yet bound. That is where Lincoln lived, spot on where he lived and no one in our history has ever been better able to bridge great divides than he.

In a blog, Nathan Raab shared his "*This is an Abraham Lincoln Revival.*" He addressed the celebrity that accompanied the unveiling of a recent bust of Lincoln, sculpted by Frank Porcu, in April of 2013 at the New York Historical Society. Star studded, it drew the likes of Tony Bennett and Judy Collins and the toast of Manhattan.

Why Lincoln, he asked?

"George Washington exists in our historical memory as stoic and dispassionate. But Abraham Lincoln seems closer, more human, tortured, vulnerable, but moral, powerful, and transformative." He suggested that we respond personally to Lincoln, as if he is the friend with whom we can open up. "We all know a different Abraham Lincoln," he suggested, "and we love him."

Here, you will meet the Lincoln that many who have spent their very lives in his company know and love. We will consider their intimate and individual belongings to him and what we call the *Fixed Mark* or character trait or value in him that sealed their bond. There, the values and ideals that we desperately need to bring back into vogue today. We will then discuss the conversations that they would most like to have with him and the words of his that most move and forever inspire, before weighing in, with truth and not vitriol, on Lincoln's Light and the scars and wounds in the life of our nation today that must be healed.

Holzer, in his introduction to *Lincoln on Democracy*, a book he co-authored with the late Governor Mario Cuomo, also referred to Walt Whitman who, like my Cavalry of collaborators, enjoyed a unique bond to Lincoln.

"Years later," he wrote, "As Whitman looked back, he pronounced Abraham Lincoln still 'the grandest figure yet, on all the crowded canvass of the nineteenth Century.' To Whitman, whose own life's work seemed to one contemporary "imbued with the spirit of democracy," the explanation for Lincoln's unwavering appeal was obvious. He had been "Dear to democracy, to the very last."

Well, we here take the liberty of pronouncing Lincoln still "the grandest figure on the crowded canvass" of the all of the American Experience.

Every day, I look into his deep-set eyes and wrinkled face, one tortured by the horror of war, on the walls surrounding me and find renewed inspiration and devotion to be of good and to make some small difference. For I look into the face of a man, an extraordinary man, who forever made great differences and invited posterity to build upon the gifts he passed down to us.

Whitman, for the record, described his face as "so awful ugly, it becomes beautiful. Of technical beauty, it had nothing, but to the eye of the great artist, it furnished a rare study, a feast and fascination. His personal magnetism came to life through the ear and not the eye."

A beautiful face, a beautiful man and more than 155 years after his death, we, my Cavalry and I, keep faith with him as he does with us.

A "feast and a fascination" indeed.

Acknowledgments

Acolytes of Abraham Lincoln, these 45 good and caring souls who channel him every day of their lives, kindly took time out to contribute directly to this work. They shared, upheld, drove and inspired me with their insights and their belonging to our *One Man Great Enough*. Thanks is too small a word, but it is extended with rich reverence and heartfelt appreciation.

PUBLISHED HISTORIANS

- Todd Brewster, Former Senior Editor of Time & Senior Editorial Producer of ABC News
- Richard Brookhiser, Senior Editor of the *National Review*
- Douglas Egerton, Professor of History at LeMoyne College
- Kent Gramm, Faculty Member at Gettysburg College
- Harold Holzer, The Director of Hunter College's Roosevelt House Public Policy Institute
- Michelle Krowl, Civil War & Reconstruction Specialist/Manuscript Division, Library of Congress
- Edna Greene Medford, Chairwoman of the History Department at Howard University
- Tracy Power, Professor of History and Director of Archives at Newberry College
- Rabbi Jonathan Sarna, Professor of American Jewish History at Brandeis University
- Jack C. Waugh, Accomplished Journalist & Historian
- Frank J. Williams, Past President of the National Lincoln Forum & Chief Justice of the Supreme Court of Rhode Island

ARTISTS/IMPERSONATORS/CURATORS/ANIMATORS/ PROFESSORS/TEACHERS/ASSOCIATION LEADERS

- Wendy Allen, Celebrated Lincoln Artist
- Winifred Anderson, High School Teacher
- Al Azinger, Professor & Department Chair, Illinois State University
- Henry Ballone, Treasurer of National Lincoln Forum
- Mel Berger, Business Executive, National Lincoln Forum
- Robert Brugler, High School Teacher
- George Buss, Renown Impersonator, Gettysburg's Own Lincoln
- Joan Chaconas, History Specialist, Surratt House Museum
- Bill Grandstaff, Civil War Enthusiast
- Kathryn Harris, Past President, A. Lincoln Association of Springfield, Illinois
- Karen Hawbecker, Lawyer – U.S. Department of the Interior
- Paula Hopewell, Lincoln Presenter & Enthusiast
- Steve Koppelman, Past President, Lincoln Group of NY
- Matt Lakemacher, American History Teacher
- Mel Maurer, Past President, Cleveland Civil War Roundtable
- Angela Mayer, Lincoln Enthusiast, Germany
- Jim McGrath, Lincoln Enthusiast
- Paul Mellen, Lawyer, A. Lincoln Association
- Darla Moe, Lincoln Enthusiast
- Rebecca Morris, The Anne Arundel Historical Society
- Anne Moseley, former Curator of Lincoln Heritage Center Museum
- Mike Movius, President, Puget Sound (Seattle) Civil War Roundtable
- Christopher Oakley, Professor and Director of Lincoln Project, UNC
- Eileen Patch, Author/Impersonator of Mary Todd Lincoln
- Dennis Perreault, American History Teacher
- Steven Raymond, Lincoln Enthusiast
- Marilyn Krowl Rexilius, Descendant of the Virginia Lincolns
- David Sullivan, Lincoln Enthusiast
- Rich Thompson, Celebrated Lincoln Artist
- Joe Truglio, President, Philip Kearny Civil War Roundtable, NJ
- Dave Walker, Impersonator of Jefferson Davis
- Dave Wiegers, Photographer of Lincoln Monuments in US
- Michaela Wieties, Collegiate student of History, Lincoln Forum Scholar
- Bob Willard, Past President, A. Lincoln Association of Springfield Illinois
- Cover Art, courtesy of Rich Thompson
- Photographs, courtesy of David Wiegers

Among the above, these acclaimed historians and founders and leaders of Lincoln Forums and Associations, went above and beyond to offer these kind comments, as to what *Unfading Light* achieved. And for these words of theirs, I also am especially grateful:

Harold Holzer wrote, "In a time of precarity and anxiety, Abraham Lincoln still offers hope that the best hope of earth is yet to come. Author Rich Fritzky, who has overcome more challenges than most, offers inspiration of his own—and in using Lincoln to unlock the better angels of our nature, he has provided a rich, valuable, and deeply moving work."

Great men and women leave great legacies," suggested *Jack C. Waugh.* "No great man has left a legacy greater, wider, deeper, more lasting, more penetrating, more infinite than Abraham Lincoln. In this original, innovative, and beautifully woven book, Rich Fritzky has brought proof—the powerful testimony of two mighty handfuls of eminent Lincoln historians and dozens of buffs as to how Lincoln has enriched their lives. It is testimony that could be compounded by the testimony of many thousands more. *Unfading Light* is a superb addition to the vast Lincoln literature."

"In *Unfading Light ,* Rich Fritzky elegantly weaves together reflections and insights about our greatest president from the nation's leading Lincoln scholars." writes *Douglas Egerton.* "No reader interested in our sixteenth president will want to miss this fascinating, beautifully crafted volume."

"Rich Fritzky's book is the reason why Abraham Lincoln remains the paradigm of leadership," suggested *Frank J. Williams.* "In this complex world, the simple traits of Mr. Lincoln's shine through here and set the standard for leadership. With many Lincoln scholars contributing—and I am proud to be one of them—the author demonstrates anew that Lincoln is "our man for all seasons."

"Abraham Lincoln, more than any other American president, and more than most figures in recorded history, is instantly recognizable. We all know Lincoln: born in a log cabin, Honest Abe, the rail-splitter, the war president, the Great Emancipator, the man of the people, by the people, for the people. But do we really know him," asks *Tracy Power*? "Rich Fritzky believes that we can, we should, and we must—now more than ever. So he asked a host of people who have studied and lived with Lincoln five searching questions about their efforts to appreciate and understand him. Their answers, some from the head and some from the heart, but most from both, illuminate Lincoln the man and Lincoln the icon. The author's mission to compile their thinking and to add his own lifetime of reflections on Lincoln, the Civil War, and the great "So What?" question that we demand of history, will reward any reader who seeks to "get right" with Lincoln and his legacy.

"If interested in the wonder of Abraham Lincoln," wrote *Richard Brookhiser*, "you'll find a great deal to chew upon in Rich Fritzky's illuminating *Unfading Light*."

"Truly inspiring! This is a much needed and most-timely addition to the field of Lincoln studies," wrote *Steve Koppelman*.

"The endless stream of character traits that defined our sixteenth president come alive in *Unfading Light*," wrote *Kathryn Harris*, "a book that is, at once, informative and inspirational, touching and transformative."

Chapter One

The Cavalry Responds

Lincoln was the spiritual and soulful sojourner, who would end slavery, save the Union, win the devastating war, but more importantly, shine the brightest of lights upon enduring and sacred ideals, while giving rise to our National Soul. Ever since, we have lived in Lincoln's America, where I long to remain. And so, in the face of a contemporary madness, my epiphany was not merely to go to Lincoln but to loudly celebrate and suggest that we bring him back onto the ground and in the field today.

And not only my Lincoln, I thought, but why not that of others who have devoted the all of their lives or the better part of it to him as well? Why not go big and share the mystery of myriad belongings to him? Why not do our bit and maybe our best to turn the Lincoln lights back on, so as to help a battered and sleeping America reclaim and resurrect.

And so, the plan—to reach into the minds and hearts of good souls who have long belonged to Lincoln, in the hope of bringing him alive for others and reminding even more of what greatness actually is. I am blessed to be in this with my 45 collaborators. What a wonder they are and oh, the power of their insights. They have no skin in the game, save their own love of Lincoln and the strength that comes from knowing just how much he ought to mean to you.

Of the many I contacted, of course, far more begged off, a few of them even nicely, while most simply ignored repeated appeals. But hell, 45 good sons and daughters of Lincoln, and this 45, my 45, proved to be spot on perfect.

That truth notwithstanding, permit me just one anecdotal regret. Born in Jersey City, New Jersey, it is the land of my fathers and mothers, so I was delighted to discover that its *Abraham Lincoln Association* was in 1868, the very first to be established. While their website peculiarly failed to identify

1

either officers or members, I was able, with considerable effort, to get the names of five prominent members, who I, a son of Jersey City and kindred spirit, pressed hard.

I worked them, implored them but no matter the extent of my pitches, promises or prayers, only the sounds of silence came back to me.

As to Question 1 and that which first brought my 45 collaborators to Lincoln, I couldn't help but think about the twists and turns of life that fascinate and so too the odds, ends and even the coincidences that lead us to our great passions, to the loves in our lives, our vocations and most certainly our avocations. As such, each of us had portals to Lincoln that were circumstantially unique. Yet all were of one, fervently bound in their devotion to, reverence for and endless study of; and not a one could conceive of laying down or putting aside this passion.

There were two inviolable common denominators: the love of and the endless study of. Among the whole, there are those who do the primary research and keep advancing the scholarship, others who reflect upon all that has been discovered and enhance our understanding and insight, still others who channel both of the above as artists, curators, animators, impersonators, teachers and presenters.

Among them are celebrated historians, leaders of national and regional Lincoln Forums and many Civil War Roundtables. There also are extraordinary homemakers who make detailed presentations about him to local organizations and there are teachers of history, social studies and political science who were first inspired by him. There are husbands and wives who have, for decades, impersonated Abe and Mary. There is one who impersonates Jefferson Davis, another who is on a mission to photograph every Lincoln monument in the country, another who helped open a museum, still another who brings him to life at a major museum and yet another who holds a birthday party for him on every February 12.

They all cling to the softly reverberating promise of Lincoln's "*Last Best Hope*." By their service, even this service here, they do this. Through them and in them, the goodness and grace that was Lincoln is paid forward and I am in awe of each of them.

Unless and until, no one remembers and we are severed completely and forever from the historical epics and tidal waves and heroes of our past, the lights do not go out on us.

We live, hope lives, the dream lives, America lives. The light shines on.

They said yes. They trusted me with their Lincoln and allowed me, in a rather unique way, to present him to you in a moment in time when Americans so need to hear from him. So, we begin, here, with personal stories relating just how it was that these good men and women came to be Lincoln Men and Women.

Highlighting these tales may ultimately be less important or meaningful than the more substantive material that is to follow, but this is the fun stuff, the chance happenings, the moments that lit the spark, the odd ball stuff.

Above all, it's the falling in love with stuff.

You never know what's going to light the fire within or send you flying off in an unexpected direction and, maybe just maybe, to Lincoln, as these 45—my 45—certainly discovered.

HOWEVER DESERVING, JUST WON'T LAY CLAIM TO LINCOLN

Tracy Power is a respected historian and professor of History at Newberry College, South Carolina. He also is the Director of both the State of South Carolina's and Newberry College's Archives. He has authored a number of books that include *Lee's Miserables: Life in the Army of Northern Virginia from the Wilderness to Appomattox* and *I Will Not Be Silent and I Will Be Heard: Martin Luther King.*

A good friend, he is a giver, so after apologizing for how busy he was and how little time he had, he naturally responded in great detail. He endorsed the effort as both a wonderful opportunity and a significant challenge and then asserted, "*I am no Lincoln scholar, by even the most generous measure!*" Then, he humbly piled on further, suggesting, "*I don't believe I even belong in the conversation with the other scholars you're addressing.*"

While truly, there is no conversation related to Lincoln or to the Civil War that Tracy Power does not belong in.

"I was born in Atlanta in 1958, and grew up in its suburbs," he wrote. "I first encountered Abraham Lincoln at the age of 5, in February 1964 before my sixth birthday. The assassination of President John F. Kennedy the previous November had a dramatic impact on all of us, and I vividly remember my parents talking about it that Friday and throughout that weekend. My mother saved the Atlanta Journal from that November 22 thru 25 and I still have those newspapers."

"We celebrated Lincoln's Birthday in our class at Skyland Methodist Church. Our teacher reminded us of President Kennedy's assassination, and of how sad everyone felt. She told us that President Lincoln had been assassinated almost a hundred years before and that many Americans were sad then too."

Soon after that, Power, early reader that he was, came across Clara Ingram Judson's *Abraham Lincoln* (1950), and one paragraph, especially, stuck in his imagination. He remembered it still and one imagines that he must have read it over and over again. The line was:

"It was a very dreadful war, because it was between people who had been friends. It was often brother against brother and father against son."

The *very idea* conveyed in that line had an enormous impact on him, leading him to read everything he could get his hands on about the Civil War in his early grammar school years. Tracy Power was indeed one precocious, young student.

"Sometimes when I give Power Point presentations today," he continued, "I show a photo of me at age 5, and the front page of the Atlanta Journal for November 22, 1963, and that particular page of Judson's book, to illustrate why I am a historian, and even more, why I am a Civil War historian. It probably didn't hurt that this was during the Centennial, either. My mother claims to this day that I loved Lincoln so much that I became quite upset when I found out that he was on the "other side" and even the "wrong side" from the point of view of my native Georgian South. I'm not sure I believe her, but it is a good story all the same."

A few of the more memorable Lincoln books that he then read back in the 1960s included Earl Schenck Miers's, *Abraham Lincoln in Peace and War* in the American Heritage Junior Library series; Dorothy and Philip Kunhardt's vivid *Twenty Days* on Lincoln's assassination and its aftermath; and Carl Sandburg's *Lincoln* which he read over and over again. He noted that Sandburg's work was oft-maligned but still dramatic and compelling biography. He then devoured many, many books on Lincoln specifically and the Civil War generally, from history and biography to fiction. Naturally, given the above, he had very quickly graduated from children's books to adult books. By 1966, when he was in the third grade, his teachers reported to his parents that they should try to get him interested "in something, anything*"* besides the Civil War. He protested, writing, "I was interested in other things: astronauts and space, baseball—the Atlanta Braves came to town that year—rock 'n' roll and other music, rocks, arrowheads, and stamps, for example, but Lincoln, and the Civil War, and history, were my first love."

They still are. They always will be.

"I was especially honored, many years later, when I was awarded Second Place in the 1999 Lincoln Prize given by the Lincoln and Soldiers Institute at Gettysburg College for *Lee's Miserables: Life in the Army of Northern Virginia from the Wilderness to Appomattox"* he noted. Being asked to give a talk on Lee's soldiers and their reactions to the Election of 1864 at *Lincoln 2000* at the Lincoln Forum Symposium in Gettysburg also meant a great deal to him. His essay on that subject was included in *Rediscovering Abraham Lincoln*, the Lincoln Forum volume edited by John Y. Simon, Harold Holzer, and Dawn Ruark.

"I have also taught a course on *American Biography in History, Memory, Myth, and Popular Culture* that featured Lincoln as one of 16 notable American historical figures," he continued, "and the next time I teach it, I plan to focus on eight figures: four chosen by me (Thomas Jefferson, Abraham Lincoln, Frederick Douglass, and Martin Luther King, Jr.) and four chosen by my class from a list of 25 choices. I am confident, based on my first attempt with the course that Lincoln will continue to be a compelling choice for my students to examine, for he is at the very heart of what America is and what it strives to be."

I too, for the record, was glued to the TV those 4 days in November of 1963 as well, rushing around like a mad man to complete my paper route each day, so as not to miss anything. I witnessed the rider-less black stallion, the caisson, Jacqueline's black veil, Bobby's sadness, Oswald's murder, 3-year-old John's salute, the mass and the lighting of the eternal flame. I too saved 4 newspapers including the New York Times and all the *Look* and *Life* magazines and the book *Four Days* and even the *Warren Commission Report*, which did not satisfy, only to lose them all forty years later in a devastating 2003 house fire.

What remained in November of '63 was the overarching sense of loss, the sadness, the fact that it was so personal and so intimate and the realization that, for a moment in time, all people seemed to be on the same page. Thanksgiving, but a few days later, was not the same but that Christmas, I received a bust of John F. Kennedy from my parents and an 8-volume set of the *Collected Writings of Abraham Lincoln* edited by Arthur Philip Lapsley from my sister, Joan. I received the gifts of both Lincoln and Kennedy, the gifts of unfading light and eternal flame. They inspired and gave me hope.

Douglas Egerton, a great historian, scholar, professor and now friend, teaches at LeMoyne College in Syracuse, New York. Great works of his include *1860 Year of Meteors: Stephen Douglas, Abraham Lincoln and the Election that Brought on the Civil War* and *Thunder at the Gates: The Black Civil War Regiments That Redeemed America*. Like Power, this humble man also insists that he too cannot lay claim to a Lincoln pedigree, as his contributions have long been focused upon the mid-nineteenth-century intersection of race and politics.

But that's where Lincoln lived, making escaping him impossible.

"Actually, I have never regarded myself a Lincoln scholar," he wrote, "at least not in the way that skillful biographers such as Ronald C. White or Michael Burlingame are. My interests have always been focused upon the issues of race and politics in early America." Earlier books of Egerton's have been about politicians involved in the colonization movement or highly politicized slave rebels, such as the Virginia blacksmith, Gabriel. Note, of course, Lincoln also dipped his oar into the colonization movement, up and until late 1862 that is.

"I also prefer to write about topics that have not previously been covered," he continued, "and my books on Congressman Charles Fenton Mercer, Gabriel, and Denmark Vesey were the first studies of those individuals. I also found it strange that for all of the small mountain of Lincoln books, the previous study of that critical election of 1860 was more than a half century old, perhaps because until the Chicago convention, William Henry Seward, and not the former Illinois congressman, was the clear front runner for the Republican nomination."

He then noted that his 2010 sesquicentennial book about 1860, *Year of Meteors*, actually has Lincoln's name behind that of Stephen A. Douglas in the subtitle, because up and until he received the nomination, the story was not really about him. "If one were alive in January 1860 and asked any seasoned politician or journalist what was about to happen that year, he would have assured you that the two major party candidates would be Douglas and Seward," he continued, "and that if the Democrats could put aside their squabbling long enough to focus on the Republican threat, Douglas, like James Buchanan before him, might well pull out a close victory. In the end, of course, Douglas came in second in the popular vote and fourth in the Electoral College, so midway through the book, Lincoln finally took over the narrative."

Egerton also observed that Lincoln's 1860 election was the presidential election that had more to do with race than any other in our history. That was up until 2008, when a handsome man by the name of Barack Obama, who also hailed from Illinois, entered the fray.

In Egerton's *He Shall Go Out Free: The Lives of Denmark Vesey*, you meet a man who fortuitously bought his freedom and did well as an artisan in Charlestown, South Carolina. A man who could have lived relatively comfortably by distancing himself from the life he knew and slavery itself, but he had a moral compass. Rather than secure his personal economy and standing, he determined to use his freedom as a platform in the struggle to advance the liberation of brother and sister slaves. Other slave insurrections in America in the early nineteenth century that failed seemed rudderless while Vesey, at least, had an actual plan. Focus was upon the poorly guarded arsenal and a seized ship with which to sail away to Haiti in the end. Can you shoot holes in it? No doubt, but at least, it afforded a chance and a hope. Betrayed by his own, it was not to be and he and his band of brothers paid with their lives.

He did not have to make the sacrifice that he did, but he saw suffering and tried to stop it. He lived on the high ground where the saints and the visionaries roam.

It would be about two years later when Lincoln would first go to Vandalia as a member of the Illinois State Legislature. In short order, he voted against a resolution that upheld the "sacred right of slavery" and condemned the outrage of creeping abolitionism. Five other brave souls would join him and opposed, while 77 voted in favor. Joined by one other legislator, Lincoln issued a formal protest of the resolution. Once in a most distinct minority, many years would pass and he would come to end the ghastly practice and render those Denmark Vesey hoped to liberate "once and forever" free.

"There have been men who have proposed to me to return to slavery the black warriors of Port Hudson and Olustee to their masters to conciliate the South. I should be damned in time and in eternity for so doing so." So said Lincoln, upon being urged to win over the supremacists and the copperheads when prospects for victory seemed dim.

Todd Brewster is an American author, historian, journalist and film producer. For some time, he was the editorial producer of ABC News. He co-authored with Peter Jennings of ABC News, three bestselling books, *The Century*, *The Century for Young People* and *In Search of America*. He has lectured and taught at a number of universities, most recently Temple and Mount Holyoke, and he has written expansively on twentieth century American history.

"My experience," he wrote, "may be different from others whom you have asked this question. I am not a Lincoln specialist. I devoted only a single six-month period to Lincoln. My exploration began when a friend alerted me to the coming sesquicentennial (2013) of the signing of the Emancipation Proclamation." He explained that an anniversary is an artificial reason to revisit any historical moment, but it is something that authors do nonetheless.

> As I considered the Proclamation, my interest was piqued by the way that so many of the paths to understanding the Civil War including the military strategy, the moral and legal dimensions, the understanding of American identity, the testing of Lincoln, our greatest president, the testing of the Constitution and more appeared to come to a head in the six-month period outlined by the July 1862 carriage ride when Lincoln first tells Seward and Welles of his intention to free the slaves and the moment on January 1, 1863 when he signs the Proclamation itself. I saw not only an episode of historical curiosity, but a very personal story as well. In these six months, we witness a man struggling mightily with competing truths. I felt as if there was a lot to learn by excising this period and examining it in detail.

In this, his *Lincoln's Gamble*, the all of what he synoptically pinpoints above is perfectly crystallized.

A gentleman of the first order and a historian with a probing and incisive mind, the issues probed by Brewster were indeed vexing ones for Lincoln. While it is my own take that the constitutional war powers put him and his Emancipation proclamation on solid ground, Lincoln would consistently question himself, not as to what he had done but as to whether or not he had the right to do so (we will dive deep into this later). More importantly, he worried so about what might become of his *"Henceforth and Forever Free"* after the war and without him, which is what drove him to press so very hard for passage of the 13th amendment as the war was winding down.

CAN'T QUITE RECALL

Lincoln people alright, I am so taken by them.

Take *Bob Willard* who is next on our hit parade, whose own praises must first be sung. I found his fascinating 'Facebook' page and I loved the many Lincoln images, paintings and monuments, as well as the personal pictures from his 'Walk with Lincoln' from Knob Creek onto Springfield. It also heralded the anniversary dates of major historical events, along with inviting pictures or images or quotes or short reflections. I was moved by his encounter with one of the greatest justices in the history of the United States Supreme Court, William Brennan and his calling out of our current president with images of *Alternative Fact Free Abe* or that of Lincoln in tears on the day after the 2016 presidential election. And so too, his public thank you to David Rubinstein for the great gift given to refurbish the Lincoln Memorial and finally and most especially, although I could well go on, his sharing the haunting picture of Bobby Kennedy with tears glistening in his eyes as he stood at the podium at the Democratic National Convention in Atlantic City in 1964 as that spellbinding 22 minutes of applause elapsed before he could even utter a word to introduce the film about his brother.

14 years old then, it was the *"Take him out and cut him up into little stars and he will make the face of heaven so fine that all the world will be in love with night and pay no worship to the garish sun"* night. Fifty-six years removed, that image and my fierce belonging to Bobby still haunt.

While memory is foggy, Willard suggested that it was back in those halcyon days of fourth grade, when he was cast as Lincoln in a school play that was performed for every class that his great interest in Lincoln may have dawned. At least, it represented his first conscious interaction with him.

"What actually led to my lifelong obsession is lost to memory, but something struck in 1958," he wrote. "I had a hobby of collecting old postcards (that's deltiology for crossword fans) and I remember that 4 commemorative Lincoln stamps were issued that year in keeping with the celebration of the 150th anniversary of his birth. I was proud of having learned the word, Sesquicentennial and the Centennial of the Lincoln-Douglas Debates as well."

"It's highly likely that Jim Bishop's book, *The Day Lincoln Was Shot*, was the first book I ever read on Lincoln; I actually wrote to Bishop and his response is one of the earliest personal mementoes in my collection," he continued. "I also wrote to Richard Boone who played Lincoln on Broadway in Norman Corwin's *The Rivalry*, and got a letter back on *Have Gun Will Travel* and Palladin stationery from him." He even recalled standing outside the stage door with his 59-year old grandmother to get their autographs on his playbill.

Silly I know, but the show's theme *"Palladin, Palladin, where do you roam? Palladin, Palladin, far-far from home,"* still echoes in the deep recesses of my mind.

At the reenactment of Lincoln's First Inaugural, Bob got to meet and shake the hand of Carl Sandburg, while at the Second, he recalled watching Bobby and Teddy Kennedy walking back into the Senate Office Building together as the program concluded.

"My interest in Lincoln," he concluded, "began early and has given me the opportunity to be involved in amazing and memorable events. But can I point to a single thing that started it all? No." Blunt and clear enough.

All that and more and yet, *Kent Gramm*, my Inspiration in Chief, could not answer Question 1. Try as he might, he could not, but he did have a deep-down 'maybe' lurking and that 'maybe' was Walt Whitman whose love for Lincoln lives in me as well. It is as good a 'maybe' as possible—a perfect maybe.

Just for the record, Gramm is a poetry/literary maven first, so why not Whitman. History both poured out of that love and inevitably, I think, the two became one. Not for nothing, but having taught both American Literature and American History and even the Political Tradition in American Literature, I'm a double-dipper too.

Rebecca Morris, a gentle woman who hails from Annapolis, Maryland, also found it difficult to pinpoint a single event. She wrote, "I suppose it just grew over time. as I began to learn more about the Civil War and started to attend conferences and lectures that deepened my interest in this man who led the nation through its greatest crisis."

"To many people," she added, "Lincoln is an icon or figurehead, the marble statue in a museum, the monument downtown, but then the more you learn about him, the more you begin to understand his frailties, his failings, his sorrows and the many trials that tested him. It all becomes personal to you, as he comes to life, this man with all the flaws of any mere mortal, but flaws that were to be surmounted with passion and genius."

JUST THE RIGHT BOOK OR CLASS OR FRIEND OR EVENT

"Fortuitously, unbelievably, I picked Lincoln and then I had the equal good fortune of choosing Richard Nelson Current's *The Lincoln Nobody Knows* as my source," this most relentless of Lincoln historians wrote. *Harold Holzer* explained that his inspiration to pursue a "Lincoln Life" came early in 5th Grade as it did for so many others, just as the Civil War Centennial in the early sixties was starting to gain traction in the popular mind and among young people especially.

"That year," he wrote, "my terrific teacher brought a hatful of folded-up papers into class one day--each containing the name of a historical giant (no giantesses as I recall)." Holzer and his classmates had to stand in line, take their turn, blindly pick a piece of paper out of the hat and then proceed directly to the Library to select a book about their giant of history. He further explained that he was then attending an experimental elementary school that was blessed with a great library and, therefore, a number of books from which to choose.

That Current's *The Lincoln Nobody Knows* was among them mattered so, but that he had the grace to select it may well have been the tiny step that led to his unparalleled and brilliant Lincoln Life.

"It took only a few pages of Current's book for me to fall under Lincoln's spell, a spell that has retained its grip ever since," he continued. Given the magnitude of Holzer's contributions to Lincoln scholarship, one necessarily cannot help but think of what might have been lost had he picked John Quincy Adams or Alexander Hamilton who were, of course, great men, but lesser giants.

As it happened, he would later get the opportunity to tell Professor Current this story and enjoy what he described as the "blessing of his friendship and continued inspiration" for decades to come.

Holzer closed by observing that his friend, Professor Current, lived to be 100. As such, he caustically suggests, *"I think all Lincoln scholars should live to be 100."* And why not?

Now *Jack C. Waugh*, the author of so many books that I treasure like *One Man Great Enough: Abraham Lincoln's Road to Civil War, The Class of 1846: From West Point to Appomattox – Stonewall Jackson, George McClellan and Their Brothers* and *Lincoln and McClellan: The Troubled Relationship between a President and His General* is a friend. I first 'fell in like' with him when I viewed his website quite a while ago, where he personally introduced himself to me in a classic, down-home and folksy manner. And truth be told, down-home and folksy and kind, he is. He took time out to read the manuscript of my *What Must Needs Come*, a journey through the mind, heart and soul of Robert E. Lee on the 3rd Day at Gettysburg, after which he so very generously identified a couple of factual errors and then supported me with a heartfelt review and reflection.

I had the great privilege of personally meeting and chatting with him a few times at the 2016 symposium in Gettysburg, which he had to leave early, by the way, due to an annual and extended Thanksgiving celebration with his family. That Jack's family gathers not just for a day but rather for days to give thanks for each other each year tells you just what kind of loving family he has.

"I believe that from the moment I became conscious that the past was fantastic drama, I was drawn into history, and in particular to the Civil War era and to Abraham Lincoln, its central character. I was drawn to his craggy looks and to everything I was reading about him—to his magnetic greatness," wrote Waugh.

Very early in life, Jack just knew that he wanted to be a writer. "I thought I had a feel for it," he continued. "I saw that the past was teeming with passion, drama, and larger than life figures. And the Civil War, the most dramatic and critical passage in American history, became my passion. My longing was one day to write about it and particularly about Lincoln, its chief protagonist. But it would take me thirty years of contributing to 20th century journalism before it would happen."

Books mainly, combined with what he called "*the increasingly sharp image of Lincoln emerging*" from his reading then sealed the deal for him. The one special book that first fired him up was Carl Sandburg's essential *Lincoln*. But there also was one special professor whose field had nothing to do with either the Civil War or Lincoln, who also mightily inspired his work.

It occurred during a summer course on the Bible as Literature. "The professor was simply retelling the story of Abraham, who upon God's command, took his only son, Isaac, up to the mountain to sacrifice him. As the Professor so movingly related the story, tears welled up in his eyes and ran down his cheeks. If a story well written and well told can so move tellers and listeners and readers to tears—or to laughter—over and over, that was the kind of writing I wanted to bring to the Civil war and Lincoln."

He has movingly done so, giving readers both the tears and the laughter and the considerable wonder of it all as well.

David Walker has enjoyed many a thoughtful conversation and so too, raucous debates with Abraham Lincoln these past fourteen years. For once a Lincoln impersonator himself, he realized that a Jefferson Davis might do well to accompany him, as there were others in his Van Wert, Ohio region who would be more than delighted to play the part of Lincoln. While every inch a Lincoln man, whenever he becomes Davis, he is both true to the life he lived and true to the views that he espoused throughout the Civil War.

He does this because he believes that the debate itself ought to be framed and that the all of our history ought to be presented and that as wrong as their arguments and positions may have been, they need to be understood in the living context through which they were articulated. Not all who supported the Confederacy, after all, were inhumane scoundrels or cruel racist bigots, who deserve to have their monuments and memorials removed or their names and stories suppressed and forever forgotten. David Walker simply believes that we need the all of our history. And not for nothing, but our Lincoln, after all, looked to forgive in 1865, which necessarily begs the question, why then do we, 155 years after he forgave, seem so hell bent on condemning anew.

Don't get me wrong, I understand and fully appreciate what drives this, but the words of that "*sacred effort*," his *Second Inaugural*, after all, were his, so his unofficial but privately expressed policy was to tread softly and pray that the traitorous leaders escape. He wanted nothing to do with trials, tribunals or vengeance. Robber Barons in the north, textile manufacturers, bankers, insurance brokers, shipping magnets, etc., as well as the southern lords of slavery, after all, had together gotten rich on King Cotton and slavery.

To remove memorials of any and all servants of the south simply because they fought for the Confederacy, while well intentioned, might also be misguided. The true haters, the vile, the cruel, the fierce defenders of slavery, have at it, but if you must go down that road, be sure to put Andrew Jackson and Woodrow Wilson at the top of your list. I just hope that we let the complicated, in whom there also was good, rest in peace in their marble and bronze.

Walker ordered his first book on Lincoln at the age of 9 while in the 3rd Grade in 1962, the Civil War Centennial rising again days. "I just fell in love with the man," he wrote, "and I had the good fortune of having both a father and older brother who were history buffs as well, so whenever we traveled, a stop at a historical site was always in order." Two years later, they drove the 6 to 7 hours to the Land of Lincoln in Springfield. "We went to the Lincoln Home, the Old Statehouse, his tomb and New Salem and my love of books only grew as I began to read everything on Lincoln that I could get my hands on."

"I can actually remember the librarian trying to get me to check out a book about trees or anything other than Lincoln and I also can recall telling her that a tree was not a person and that it would not contribute to my knowledge of history," added Walker. But his 8th-Grade teacher supported him and he went on to study History in college and Graduate School at Wright State University. After that, it was the Lincoln Colloquiums, the Lincoln Forum and the Civil War Institute at Gettysburg College.

"I started impersonating in 1987 and made the lateral move to Jefferson Davis in 2005. My goal is to teach the period with accuracy as a historian. When I am Davis, I share his views which are, to say the least, much different than my own."

Next on our hit parade is *Al Azinger*, who is the Dean of the College of Education at Illinois State University. He noted, interestingly, that his entry into the Civil War and inevitably Lincoln all began because he read The *Widow of the South*, a book that a friend recommended to him. About the Battle of Franklin, it piqued his interest and he began reading more books on the battle itself; and then fortuitously, a trip to Nashville afforded him the opportunity to detour to the Franklin battlefields and the Carnton Plantation.

He had been hooked alright and once hooked on the Civil War, you are hooked forever, because there is always more to discover. Soon thereafter, he learned that Doris Kearns Goodwin was going to be coming to campus to speak about her recently published, *Team of Rivals*, which he determined to read before her appearance. From Franklin to Lincoln, he had so casually journeyed and ever deeper into Lincoln, he would go. "From that point on," Azinger wrote, "I was hooked on learning more and more about Lincoln. I was intrigued and fascinated by his political insight and ability to flourish under extreme pressure and by the courage demonstrated in appointing cabinet members and advisors who had the most to offer, no matter their divergent viewpoints or political aspirations."

Over time, I believe that I have used every positive adjective and adverb in the English tongue to define Lincoln, but in dwelling upon Azinger's comments, the word undaunted came to mind. For undaunted, he was. Despite the intense pressure, despite the fear and the unknown, despite great loss, defeat and depression, despite the political madness, he went forward. His truth and faith in hand, forward. "*I might walk slow,*" he is alleged to have said, "*but I never walk back.*" Undaunted indeed!

After Goodwin, it was Ron White and still others for Azinger, but there was to be a second wave for him that would drive his immersion into Lincoln further forward and it came in the form of a friend, Roger Bridges, a historian, who just happened to attend the same church. "In casual discussion with him one day, my wife told him of my growing interest in the Civil War and Lincoln. So, we began to enjoy discussions about Lincoln and he introduced me to the Lincoln scholars (of whom he is one). It was Roger who talked me into joining the Association and Forum where I became involved with so many others who forever study Lincoln."

I never cease to be amazed. Here, the busy Dean of a College of Education gets carried away by The *Widow of the South* and before he even blinks, he finds himself immersed in a new, demanding and impassioned avocation. One that comes with no end in sight.

Rabbi Jonathan Sarna is the Joseph H. & Belle R. Braun Professor of American Jewish History at Brandeis University, the Chief Historian of the National Museum of American Jewish History in Philadelphia and the author of the groundbreaking *Lincoln and the Jews* and many other books.

"While I had long been interested in Abraham Lincoln, it was only when Benjamin Shapell introduced me to his private collection regarding Abraham Lincoln and the Jews that I realized, notwithstanding the thousands of books on Lincoln, one more, *Lincoln and the Jews*, needed to be written."

The all of this prompted the long lasting exhibit at the National Lincoln Library and Museum in Springfield.

His book is a revealing and moving effort that speaks to the many ways in which Lincoln rejected the Anti-Semitic bias and bigotry of his time; and rather welcomed them into the full fabric of a free America. It also makes the case that American Jews truly impacted both Lincoln's path to the presidency and the very policies that he implemented as president. While you will meet quite a number of Jewish friends of Lincoln's within, it is the very immediacy of Lincoln's countermanding of General Grant's infamous General Order #11, where Sarna's history takes flight and soars.

Grant's 'war zone' at the time ran from the Mississippi to the Tennessee River and from Northern Mississippi to Cairo Illinois. General Order #11, therefore, effectively ordered all Jewish sutlers, peddlers, traders out of Kentucky, Tennessee and Mississippi. Prompted by the widespread illegal trade of cotton north, the Jews were an easy target and they were being made to take the hit for all. Upon learning of this, a delegation of Jews visited Lincoln at the White House and their spokesman was the colorful Cesar Kaskel. I so enjoy the exchange that followed Kaskel's presentation of grievances.

"And so the Children of Israel were driven from the Happy Land of Canaan," said Lincoln, showing off his near photographic knowledge of scripture.

"Yes," replied Kaskel, *"That is why we have come unto Father Abraham's bosom, seeking protection."*

"And this protection they shall have at once," roared Lincoln. (*Lincoln and the Jews*)

Lincoln's compassion, empathy and inert decency never failed. Never.

MORE BOOKS

Michelle Krowl is a scholar, historian, author of *Women of the Civil War* and the Civil War and Reconstruction Specialist in the Manuscript Division of the Library of Congress. She handles thousands upon thousands of sacred documents with reverence, of which her favorite is Lincoln's August 23, 1864 *Blind Memorandum*, which he wrote when prospects for re-election were looking rather bleak. It was his last ditch prescription as to how to save the Union between the prospective November 1864 election of a Peace Democrat and his last day in office in March of 1865. It is his 'assuming the worst' document, one that was glued closed to make its own envelope and then signed by all members of his Cabinet, who faithfully trusting in him, did so. Just where this hard-edged Brooklyn moxie of Lincoln's came from remains a matter of mystery, as they all respectfully signed even though its contents were not revealed --- even to them --- until he won re-election.

Interestingly, he does proceed to come very close to achieving total victory within that same timeframe. As it turns out, the pressure of a hard date added no more pressure than that which he had already placed upon himself.

The book that Krowl most reveres is a 1965 Children's Book authored by Barbara Cary, *Meet Mr. Lincoln.* "Fascinated by Abraham Lincoln's life," she wrote, "I read it over and over again, but by the second grade, I graduated to Stefan Lorant's photographic biography of Lincoln." Her interest continued to grow and as the years passed, expanded to all things related to the Civil War. Still she insists that Lincoln forever remained at the epicenter of her studies. "Just as it was after my first introduction to him, through *Meet Mr. Lincoln*, he remained my favorite historical figure to study," she concluded. *Meet Mr. Lincoln*, the original copy, is still reverently displayed in her personal library today.

Richard Brookhiser, an acclaimed author of many books on America's founding fathers, not long ago made what he called a "lateral move" and a "natural progression" to Lincoln with *Founder's Son*, his first, major work on him. He also has, for long, served as the editor of the highly respected *National Review.* He was pointed, direct and deeply committed to his response. My problem was that my ignorance of both of the books that he alluded to forced me to read, to dive deeper and to fashion what has become a keen interest in the depths of his thinking.

His response to Question 1 was, "Two authors and two books: First, *The Ethics of Rhetoric,* by Richard Weaver, specifically the chapters "*Edmund Burke and the Argument from Circumstance*" and "*Abraham Lincoln and the Argument from Definition.*" And so too *The Crisis of the House Divided*, by Harry Jaffa. These planted the seed. Twenty years of writing about the founding fathers prepared me for a lateral entry to Lincoln."

He noted that he had worked for and served as the Editor of *National Review* magazine for some forty years and that Richard Weaver wrote for it before his time. On the other hand, Harry Jaffa was there and very much alive when he first came to the *Review*, so he claimed to have "read both of these books as if it were by osmosis."

Weaver is interested in the eternal verities, transcendent truths, the higher plane, the ideal and the ability of the masters of rhetoric, via the use of poetic imagery and language, to relate abstract political truths and ideas directly to the people. He is interested in language that wins an audience over, the kind of language that convinces, moves and inspires. Language, he insists, that has the power to fashion tangible responses and to so impact people as to make them want to strive to make a difference themselves. Language that is a 'call to action.' The all of which reminds me of Ron White's ethos and Lincoln's own fashioning of belongings and covenants.

In Weaver's "*Two Orators*," he goes on to suggest that Senator Robert Hayne of South Carolina gets the better of Senator Daniel Webster in the famous Hayne/Webster Debate in the United States Senate during the Jacksonian era Nullification Crisis Debate of January 19, 1830. He so argues, despite Webster's stirring, *"Liberty and Union, one and inseparable, now and forever."*

Most History books, given the negativity and unacceptability of Nullification itself, almost universally quote Daniel Webster and seem to give him the nod as the unassailable victor. My guess is that Weaver, being among that rare breed to have actually read Hayne's speech, saw it differently. As Weaver had me necessarily dwelling upon this firebrand of a Senator from South Carolina, I came across a reported conversation that Hayne was said to have had with Thomas Hart Benton. He asked Benton if he believed that President Andrew Jackson was serious about his threats regarding John C. Calhoun's nullification doctrine and what he intended to do to Charleston if federal laws were disregarded. Benton responded, "I have known Andrew Jackson for quite some time and I can tell you one thing, if Jackson starts talking about a hanging, it's time to get a rope." (Shi & Tindall, America – A Narrative History, p.361)

Note that Lincoln praised Webster as the ideal speaker and his speech as the greatest of speeches, suggesting that "a man who can make such speeches as that ought never to die." (Shi & Tindall, America – A Narrative History, p.363).

It is interesting that Weaver then praises Lincoln as the "ideal conservative." He also praises both Lincoln's philosophy and his oratory and yet goes on to accuse him of having assumed virtually unlimited power during the war and of having established very dangerous precedents "which any future 'strong man' could use for his own purposes." He seems to blame Lincoln for setting the stage upon which New Deal liberalism rises and sees both Roosevelt and Lincoln as great idealists. No New Deal liberal himself, Weaver then holds up Lincoln despite his assumed failings.

As to Harry Jaffa and his *The Crisis of the House Divided*, his thesis was that the events of 1860 and 1861 were literally shaped, forged if you will, two years earlier, as a direct result of the Lincoln/Douglas Debates of 1858, those gut wrenching debates and specifically Douglas' seemingly innocent reply to a fair question of Lincoln's, which gave way to his *Freeport Doctrine*. Through this, Lincoln, Jaffa maintains, forever destroyed Douglas' preordained role as the prospective leader of a national political coalition. It was in 1858, Jaffa insists, that the South's interests and those of the nation that would rather be true to the faith of its fathers and to the espoused political philosophy of its Declaration irreconcilably severed. The fact that the Democratic Party was to be split in two, along a north-south sectional divide, had been rendered inevitable.

The war that was to be unexpectedly long and horrific and the nation's anguish, both north and south, was but a reckoning rendered unavoidable and inevitable, given both the issues and the ideals that had a light shone upon them in that one campaign in Illinois in 1858.

Richard Brookhiser and his two 'making of a Lincoln Man' books educate and take you to new vistas of insight and to a better understanding and appreciation of both the highly impactful debates of 1858 and the extent of the impact of Lincoln's strong leadership. Just for the record, I believe Lincoln would have been just fine with having been linked to FDR as Weaver insists.

Mel Maurer wrote, "There was not one moment either when or where I made a decision to study Lincoln in depth. It was simply a case of discovering that the more I came to know about him, the more I wanted to know," he wrote. "I do clearly recall taking out my first library book on Lincoln at roughly the age of 11. That simple children's biography made him my childhood hero. Now there was someone I wanted to be like and I must admit that the Horatio Alger components of his life powerfully lured me in."

Even though Maurer describes himself as having had the benefit of good schools as a child, sadly no teacher ever impacted. Again and again, he emphasized that it was no one moment, no one particular book, but rather the compilation of the whole that resulted in making him want to have a personal and intellectual relationship with Lincoln.

Having read Maurer's work, I can personally attest to the rich devotion and distinctive detail of his National Lincoln Forum Annual Symposium's reviews, the ones that got posted on the website of the Cleveland Civil War Roundtable. In this regard, he channels all of the contemporary Lincoln scholarship, all of the latest findings and insights and theories for his friends.

Mike Movius , the president of the Puget Sound Civil War Roundtable, came across a paperback copy of a book displaying the Battlefield Photographs of the Civil War era artist, Mathew Brady as a boy. That book and its stunning and numbing pictures were his portal to the study of the Civil War and, via a quick and natural progression, to the study of Lincoln. "This all took place for me, over the course of the Civil War Centennial in the early 1960s just as it did for so many of our collaborators," he noted.

Swept up into the Civil War itself, he found himself reflecting upon the fact that the very issues that the war had been fought over were still very much on the table and unresolved as the country looked back upon it during the early sixties. One hundred years removed but still unresolved.

"So very many issues were intersecting with commemorating the Centennial of the Civil War for Civil Rights was everywhere at issue," he wrote. In dwelling upon it all, the long arm of Abraham Lincoln may well have seemed to reach across the ugly divide of 100 years of Jim Crow. Where Lincoln had Frederick Douglass, Kennedy and Johnson had Martin Luther King, where Lincoln had an Emancipation Proclamation and the 13th amendment, they had Brown v. Topeka, the 1964 Civil Rights Act and the 1965 Voting Rights Act. On one end, the madness of war and reconstruction and on the other, the inner city riots of 1966 and 1967 as 100 years of justice and equality denied erupted into flames and chaos.

It was then that Langston Hughes' "Dream Deferred" no longer festered or ran or sank but rather 'exploded.' And one is left to wonder just how great was the price our nation paid for the loss of Lincoln when the time came to begin "binding up" rather than tearing down.

For *Dennis Perreault*, an American History and Civics High School teacher from Manchester, New Hampshire, the journey to and the inevitable embrace of Lincoln was driven by two moments that were separated by many years. "I was drawn to the writing and world of Abraham Lincoln when my High School English teacher saw me reading a book of Bobby Kennedy's speeches and recommended Paul Angle's Lincoln Reader *to me*."

The idea of Lincoln complementing Bobby Kennedy and vice versa has already been engaged, via Kent Gramm's *November – Lincoln's Elegy at Gettysburg* and my own musings. Just mentioning them in a single sentence gives me a rush as they collectively represent my 'beaux ideal' of American statesmen, just as Henry Clay did for Lincoln. Spliced together, they epitomize the very best of us to me.

Lincoln had won the great and bloody war and ushered in the historic and game-changing 13th amendment, but his greatest work, his 'magnus opus' might well have been and certainly should have or could have been, the peaceful reconstruction of a broken and divided nation. For its failure contributed to another 150 years of racism, cruelty and insufferable injustice.

As for Bobby, allow me this brief tangent. He had been there for his brother, Jack, in the thick of it all, on Civil Rights and Nuclear Disarmament and, certainly, he appeared to have saved us all during the October of the Cuban Missile Crisis when *"We were eyeball to eyeball"* with the USSR during the Cold War. Yet the great work that demanded his heart, compassion and love was never to be attended to either. In my now 52 years of mourning, I hold tight to the supposition that his having been the 37th president of the United States, which was not to be, may have precluded the nation's current and appalling leadership from ever having been.

Indeed, the vagaries and mystery of way leading unto way are out there to ponder.

Bobby, like Lincoln, brought disparate parties and factions and people together. And what Murray Kempton, celebrated journalist, once so tellingly said of Bobby could just as well have been said of Lincoln: ''God, he's not a politician! He's a character in a novel!'' They had that rare and special gift and students of history cannot help but see the parallels between Bobby's train and Lincoln's train, however shorter the journey of the former. Everywhere along the routes, people stood vigil, the dispossessed and the marginalized to great degree, they were living testaments to the impassioned service and great sacrifice of two American saints. Two, separated by a century and the contours of their day, but one in their desire to see that every American be given the sacred opportunity to *"rise up in the race of life."* People mourned simply because they knew that these two actually gave a damn. Personal and intimate, they felt it in their bones and in their souls.

That Dennis connected these dots moves me and so too, his wife's inspiration in bringing it all full circle for him by giving him the gift, so long ago recommended, of Paul Angle's *Lincoln Reader*. He read it and more, but he clearly noted that his relationship with Lincoln truly began when he went directly to the source. "When I stopped reading secondary sources and started reading the *Collected Works of Abraham Lincoln* and discerning for myself the many important lessons Lincoln offers, I finally became a Lincoln Man."

A TEACHER OR A CLASS

Nine, the largest class of respondents to Question 1, linked the epicenter of their relationship with Lincoln directly to the classroom.

"Unlike many of my colleagues in the Lincoln world, I did not grow up with a burning interest in our 16th president. My heroes were more immediate. It was the 60s and 70s, and the nation was in the midst of the Civil Rights Movement," wrote *Edna Greene Medford*. "I was smitten with the leaders of that movement, as were many young people of color at that time."

As it happened, her interest in Lincoln only began to develop when she was pursuing her Masters in American History at the University of Illinois. She noted the influence of Robert Johansen, a Douglas biographer, but above all, there was Vernon Burton whose course on the *History of the South* took her to greater heights. "It was in his classes," she wrote, "that I discovered Lincoln's complexity. My interest in exploring that complexity grew in the 1990s when C-SPAN invited me to participate in their programming on the Lincoln-Douglas Debates."

She added that her fascination with him has only continued to increase over the years. "The more I learn, the more questions I have. I know there will never be a time when all my questions are answered, but it has been academically rewarding to study him," she concluded.

Her testimony bears witness to the fact that once one bores into Lincoln at all, it becomes nearly impossible to stop probing and exploring. Medford also and most interestingly wrote of his 'mystery.' What a great word to reference and consider and what a different light it sheds. For mystery indeed abounds.

Frank J. Williams wrote, "When I was about eight years old, my dear Mother, Natalie Williams, read me a story about Lincoln and I was very intrigued. But the seminal moment for continuing engagement was in the sixth grade in public school." He explained that the class was oh so typically alphabetically seated and that his 'W,' as usual, took him to the last row where he had the good fortune to be seated right next to a portrait of Abraham Lincoln.

"I could not keep my eyes off his forlorn and pine cone face," he added; and his teacher, Mrs. Taylor, who he remembers fondly, took notice and continually encouraged him to study American History. It was at that point that the tide turned completely for him, as he used his then all of a quarter for lunch to buy used books about Abraham Lincoln instead. "It was these books that sealed the deal and rendered me a Lincoln Man," he added.

From his Mother to Lincoln's portrait to Mrs. Taylor to getting to read more and more about him, he was freely taken by and fully committed to the study of Lincoln. "I even decided to be a lawyer, because Lincoln was one and a very good one at that," he concluded.

Wendy Allen's response to this question was exquisitely extensive. She began by focusing upon the pain that came when watching her Mother suffer so with terminal cancer. She was dying at the same time that the words of Dr. Richard Selzer, one of her Professor's kept echoing in her ears. "Delicate durability," that was it. Nothing more and nothing less, just "Delicate durability." He was speaking of the human body but given her Mom's condition and the vulnerability, sadness and transformation at issue, Wendy realized just *how Delicate* she was, but also, and most importantly, *how Durable.*

To get beyond the loss, the emptiness, the mourning, the fear that accompanies such a profound loss, would certainly test that durability. Yes, the body, but also the spirit and the soul, the *delicately durable.*

She then turned to another professor who influenced her, a Dr. Michael Autuori, a Biology professor, who challenged her class to consider this question, "What most distinguishes human beings from other animals"? There were, she maintained, no shortage of responses but he dismissed them all and eventually said, "Only humans have a sense of history."

That answer inspired.

She then detailed her journey as a young artist, describing her early work as amateurish and suggesting that the problem lied in identifying the subject that might truly inspire

"Finally, it hit me," she wrote. "Modern art contained no history, the very subject I had grown to value the most. Artists had turned their backs on history! How, I wondered, could they ignore the very thing that defines us as human"?

Defining herself as an artist required separating herself from the pack and then, in the summer of 1983, she attended the very first conference of the Civil War Institute at Gettysburg College with her now dear friend, Dr. Gabor Boritt. "That experience" she noted, "changed the course of my life."

But it wasn't until she put the brush to the canvass back in her small, Mountain View, California apartment that she would find release. Absorbed and moved, she worked all night long and came out whole. "I had gone into Merlin's cave," she wrote, "and emerged with the secret of my universe. I had painted my first portrait of Abraham Lincoln. The very moment that Elaine, my beloved lifetime partner, first saw it, she cried out, "That's it! That's it!" She didn't hesitate. She was moved. I was thrilled. I had discovered my passion and my purpose and I knew that I would never tire of painting him."

She wondered how he had eluded her for so long, as she had carried him with her since childhood. In him, like her, a softness, gentleness, kindness, humility or that which was delicate. In him, a rare strength and inspirational determination or that which was durable. In him, the 'delicate durability' of her artistry. Both it and she had come full circle.

"To me," she concluded, "he represented the best of humankind, the best of our story; and, through my art, I would give the world new ways of both perceiving and seeing Abraham Lincoln."

Like our friend, Frank Williams, *Christopher Oakley*, a highly accomplished animation artist, had a direct and pointed response.

While he discovered Lincoln in his 1st Grade classroom, he too, just like Frank Williams, did so after having been fascinated by the Lincoln painting that hung in the room. The image and the lure of that face, one that spoke volumes stayed with him as he journeyed through life. He too would make his way home to Lincoln at the University of North Carolina, come to isolate and identify an image of Lincoln in a November 19, 1863 photograph that had never before been recognized and give rise to his exciting *Virtual Lincoln Project* at the University of North Carolina.

A gentle man, he loves his students and the great work that they did together to, via animation, recreate the Gettysburg of November 19, 1863.

Some found their belonging to Lincoln in the mere painting of him in a classroom, but not *Eileen Patch*. She rather found hers in a 5th Grade assignment. At the Longfellow School on Pennsylvania Avenue in Binghamton, New York, all 5th- graders were assigned to make a speech about a figure in history and it was her good fortune to get Lincoln. She recalls only that her presentation was a factual speech that began with, Abraham Lincoln was born in Hardin County, Kentucky. "I was much too intimidated by public speaking then to remember the teacher's name or the audience reaction," she wrote. "All I know is that I got a good grade and that Lincoln never left me."

Note that her labor of love, *This From George,* is focused upon one man and one regiment in the war. But he was a Lincoln Man.

Robert Brugler actually recalled details of a 1st Grade birthday party, for it was there where he first learned of Abraham Lincoln. The Party just happened to be on February 12, which was but a day before his February 13 birthday. "So, in my young mind," he wrote, "I naturally assumed that the party was for me. First grade was so much fun, I thought." But his teacher burst his bubble when she announced that the party was actually a celebration of the birthday of a once great president, a man named Abraham Lincoln.

"She read a story about him, we colored pictures of him and we had cupcakes and Kool-Aid," he added. "All in all, I wasn't at all disappointed that my party had actually been for someone else. I liked this guy" and hey, he said to himself, "Maybe, I'll grow up to be President one day."

He has never stopped liking him.

Mel Berger first met Lincoln, up close and personally, because his American History class professor just happened to be a Lincoln expert, *Winifred Anderson* did so through what she called, "Her own great love of history in general" and *Steve Raymond* via the blessing of attending a single lecture by Don Fehrenbacher, the late Stanford University Lincoln scholar.

Berger notes that his professor was a founding member of the Lincoln Group of Boston and that he assigned him to read Bruce Catton's work, books which captivated him. Anderson explained that she undertook a personal and intense study of Lincoln's views on Union, Slavery, Kansas-Nebraska and what was, to Lincoln, that ever and always living *Declaration of Independence*. Steven Raymond elaborated upon the fact that he was a lifelong student of the Civil War, who, naturally, kept encountering Lincoln along the way.

These three gave brief but substantive responses that got to the point and then hammered them home. Mel Berger wrote, "It was the 200th Birthday Symposium sponsored by Harvard's Houghton Library that turned what had been an interest into an avocation." As for Win Anderson, she wrote, "None of my work was original, of course, but I had the chance to immerse myself in Lincoln scholarship and history." In having come to understand the mind of Lincoln, she explained, she simply wanted more and more.

Steven Raymond returned again and again to that great Fehrenbacher lecture and to a question that someone in the audience asked him. Yes, just this question, "How could Lincoln speak and write with such wonderful eloquence when he had so little education"?

"*Genius*," that was the answer. Just Genius

"That one word, Genius and it inspired Raymond to begin a serious study that has known no end."

A TRIP

I have yet to have the pleasure of meeting *Rich Thompson* personally, but I know him and much of what has to be in his heart and soul, having long looked upon the five mesmerizing paintings of his Lincolns in my small home office. Frequent flyer visitors to Gettysburg, as we are, my wife enjoys the Gallery 30 store on York Street by Lincoln Square, where his art is featured and where Maggie has generously secured these greatest of Christmas presents for me in years gone by.

Thompson's work has been displayed in the Lincoln Collection at the Abraham Lincoln Library and Museum in Springfield, Illinois, the Lincoln Museum in Hodgenville, Kentucky, The Lincoln Library and Museum in Harrogate, Tennessee, as well as Ford's Theatre in Washington, D.C.

"The earliest memory of being drawn to the study of Lincoln occurred when I was 9-years old and a special guest of my grandmother on a trip to Washington, D.C.," he wrote. "She was a member of a Women's Club and she made arrangements for me to join her and her friends on a 1-day bus trip from New Jersey to Washington. The day was packed as I ran from one monument to the next and I remember feeling tired when the bus pulled up to Ford's Theatre as the sun was setting."

Ford's Theatre, he explained, wasn't quite what it is today, but upon entering it, he was taken by a powerful feeling that was just electric. By the time the park ranger finished explaining the events of April 14, 1865, he was captivated.

Growing up, he felt that he could relate to Lincoln and a number of his qualities and he tried to emulate his perseverance, honesty and mirror his sense of humor. "As an adult," he added, "I immersed myself in the study of Lincoln and as a self-taught artist, decided to express my connection by painting him. I was so drawn to the ravaged skin under Lincoln's eyes, which I have always viewed as a cypher for the soul-searing, wear and tear of the war and personal tragedy. But even more moving, I think, is the light and sensitivity in his eyes. In them, compassion, honesty and humor."

Just as Wendy Allen suggested, so too is it for Thompson, a spiritual and soulful experience—an avocation.

For *Steve Koppelman*, the former president of the Lincoln Group of New York, there was a marked and defined progression of events that rendered him a Lincoln Man, but given his witness, I believe that he was just predisposed, wired genetically if you will, to be a lifelong student of history.

"By 9, history was my favorite subject. Every name encountered seemed to be larger than life," he wrote. "In those days, as you might recall, everyone you met in the history books either did great things or thought great things or somehow changed the world in some way; and you probably recall, you got none of the infamy, cruelty, deceit or subterfuge in the early primary grades," he explained.

"It was the good stuff only, where you were introduced to adventure and courage and glory and determination and daring and love of the idea or ideal or dream. Those you met and hitched their lives to the stars of possibility, promise, and hope. As you advanced, you could not help but realize that ever so much more remained, the mysterious and the unknown."

We journey both forward and back into that unknown. We know so very much, but vast universes are always waiting to unveil their secrets.

Intuitively, Koppelman felt the all of the above in his bones at the age of 9. It was the source of the 'can't sleep, can't wait' excitement that preceded a family trip to Washington.

"It was all I could talk or think about," he wrote. "When we finally got there, the Washington Monument did not turn out to be all that special to me. Perhaps I had built it up too much in my mind, but the Lincoln Memorial which we visited at night truly affected me, as I stood there and looked up at that wonderful Daniel Chester French sculpture and read those immortal words carved in the walls, though I little understood what they actually meant at the time. A souvenir purchase of a small Lincoln bust sealed the deal."

Later, sometime in his early teens, he acquired the *American Heritage Picture History of the Civil War* by Bruce Catton. He was especially moved by the Alexander Gardner February 24, 1861 photo of Lincoln, the first taken in Washington D.C., which pictures him deep in thought and with an apparent awareness of all that lies ahead.

It was more than 20 years ago when he first attended a meeting of a scholarly organization, The Lincoln Group of New York. "Within and through this wonderful organization, I truly came to have a relationship with Lincoln." His leadership of that organization for long kept it humming and on the cutting edge of the advance of Lincoln scholarship. Only a recent move to Virginia necessitated his severing this deeply valued relationship.

Oh yes, as Steve powerfully reminds us all, we are left to wonder, which is why we write or paint or impersonate or study or present or set up exhibits or teach or research or animate or guide or join, so as to ever remain in awe.

Karen Hawbecker is many things. She is an attorney who graduated from the J. Reuben Clark Law School at Brigham Young University and she was named Prince William County, Virginia's *Most Influential Women of 2017*. She serves as the Associate Solicitor for the Division of Mineral Resources in the Office of the Solicitor, U.S. Department of the Interior and is a deeply faithful and spiritually driven woman for whom service is paramount.

Despite her close proximity to the Land of Lincoln from her home in Iowa in her youth, she knew very little of Abraham Lincoln or the Civil War when she was growing up and she now insists that she wasted her childhood in not visiting Lincoln sites when she had the opportunity to do so back then.

She has since more than made up for any childhood lapse. At the age of 20, she had the opportunity to visit the Andersonville Prisoner of War Camp in Georgia, which woke her up, she suggests, to the harsh realities of the Civil War. After that, she went on a pilgrimage, a passionate and deeply spiritual search for the deeper meanings and inspirations to be extracted from communing with the Civil War and with Lincoln. Out of this communion came her commitment to pay the good in her own life forward.

"When my husband and I moved to Virginia," she wrote, "we began to tour Civil War battlefields and I started to read Civil War history books. Over the years, I found that, in studying the Civil War, all roads lead to Lincoln. Books about specific battles, biographies and memoirs about and by generals and other luminaries of the era. All, in some way, cast light on Lincoln. So it didn't take long for Lincoln to become my primary focus."

She sought out Lincoln books, Lincoln lectures, and Lincoln symposia. She first discovered the Lincoln Group of Washington, D.C. and then the Lincoln Forum and then again and, maybe just maybe, much to the chagrin of her husband, she began to tour Lincoln sites. That's tour with a great big capital T. So much so that her husband has long since referred to himself as a "Lincoln widower."

"One of my best solo trips was all Lincoln," she wrote. "My starting point was the old Lincoln Family Cemetery in the Shenandoah Valley in Virginia, followed by all of the major and some of the minor Lincoln sites in Kentucky, Indiana, and Illinois. At the Lincoln property in the Shenandoah, I could not tell where the cemetery was, but a young man noticed my distress, got out of his car, came to my aid and graciously hiked down the road with me and through an open field to show me where the cemetery was. It wasn't until I returned to my car that I saw that his license plate read, "L'il Abe."

"Similarly, in Kentucky," she continued, "upon learning of my plans, the man staffing the gift shop at the Lincoln Homestead State Park asked if I was interested in seeing Uncle Mordecai's house." She told him that she intended to but was disappointed to hear that the house was not open to the public, upon which he kindly suggested that he might be able to help her out with that. "Of course, I wanted to see it," she noted, "because Lincoln greatly valued his Uncle and once revealingly said, 'Uncle Mord had run off with all the talents of the family." A call was made and another kind man with key in hand met her at Uncle Mord's house, where he first cleared the cobwebs from the door, unlocked it and gave her a rare, private tour. A quick one, of course, as there was not much of good old Uncle Mord's house to begin with.

In Indiana, she had a similar experience when she visited Sarah Lincoln Grigsby's gravesite, Lincoln's beloved older sister, at the Lincoln State Park across the street from the Abraham Lincoln Boyhood Home. "The woman at the entrance kiosk asked if I had visited Colonel William Jones house. I told her I had not, while refusing to betray or confess my ignorance of Colonel Jones to begin with. She urged me to talk to the park director, who upon my request, immediately radioed a ranger to ask him to take me to see the house. He unlocked it and gave me another private tour. Much to my amazement, I learned that Colonel Jones had employed Lincoln as a young man and that

Lincoln had stayed with the Colonel the night after he gave a campaign speech in the area for Henry Clay, the Whig presidential candidate, in 1844."

Finally, in Springfield, she noted that the docent who gave her the Lincoln home tour also generously spent time afterward giving her a personal tour of the neighborhood, explaining more about Lincoln's neighbors and his relationship to them. "When I finally reached the Lincoln tomb," Karen concluded, "I felt as if I had lost a dear old friend of mine and, after I returned to my car, I just wept. But I had saved New Salem for the very end, where I was able to find Lincoln alive, young and vibrant again."

She traveled with Lincoln and considered the places and spaces, the fields and forests, the flowers and fauna, the rustic wood and crude furnishings in ancient cabins, as well as the softer trappings of Springfield where his boys were born and loved and where he absorbed the blows from Mary, practiced law, delivered unforgettable speeches, excelled at politics and was laid to rest. As to that tomb where Karen wept, don't we all do the same, whether overtly and openly or deep within, we just do, responding as if it all just happened a moment ago.

But history is not about the dead, but rather about the dead's contribution to the living, as we keep them alive in soul, heart and mind. And it is upon us still --- the living to pay their hopes and dreams forward.

On her intimate journey, Karen made more than a mere physical connection but a deeply spiritual one, for Lincoln's life was of grace and as grace given is a forever commodity, it was most assuredly showered upon her.

The truth is that history, however distant and removed, can loom loud, vibrant, immediate and pressing to both the author of and the reader of that history

David Sullivan of Newmarket, New Hampshire, a Math teacher for the better part of his life, came to Lincoln later in life. He explained that he had always had the urge to visit Gettysburg, but that the pace of life and circumstance precluded. That was until some 14 to 15 years ago when he finally seized the opportunity to visit Gettysburg with a group from Exeter Academy. His first exploration of the Civil War, moved him so that he made a most impulsive decision to sign up for the Gettysburg College Civil War Institute the following summer. Just 5 days at Gettysburg College in the hand of great historians, it entailed daily lectures and seminars, battlefield tours, book signings, discussions, and, 5 days of eating, sleeping, drinking and talking about the Civil War only.

"The decision to attend the Institute profoundly changed my life," he wrote. So taken was he that he would attend again the next summer when focus was to be on Abraham Lincoln "I thought it would be wise to read at least one book about Lincoln by then," he wrote, "so I wouldn't be the dumbest kid in the schoolyard! Mind you, I had never read a book about Lincoln up to that point in my life. A math teacher for most of my life, I had never been a big reader due to reading challenges that I faced throughout my life."

Back home in New Hampshire after the Exeter trip, he learned that Doris Kearns Goodwin was to have a book signing for her latest book, *Team of Rivals, The Political Genius of Abraham Lincoln* nearby. He attended a lecture she gave and bought her 754-page book! It took him some time but he was happy to complete it just in time for the CWI Conference!

Never much of a reader, he has since read far more than 100 books about Lincoln, hundreds of Lincoln periodicals and newsletters from any number of Abraham Lincoln associations that he belongs to and dozens of books about the Battle of Gettysburg and the Civil War. "I've now been to Gettysburg often," he proudly reports, "either attending the Civil War Institute Conference or the National Lincoln Forum. I have visited every National Historic site in the country related to Abraham Lincoln and have had the great opportunity and pleasure to meet many of the well-known Lincoln luminaries from Ken Burns, famed film producer to Tony Kushner, the screen writer of the movie, *Lincoln*. The study of Abraham Lincoln has become my life's passion. I am forever hooked."

. *David Wiegers*, an accomplished photographer, is a life-long resident of Lincoln's Illinois who became a true Lincoln buff in the 8th Grade. He was first introduced to the Civil War at a very young age, when his grandparents carted him off to visit the site of the Battle of Lexington in Missouri. Also remembered as the Battle of the Hemp Bales, the Missouri State Guard bested Union forces there in a 3-day affair in September of 1861, further contributing to early southern bravado and rendering it all the more difficult for Lincoln and the Union to hold onto that precious border state. For divided, it was, as both the Union and Confederacy had been successfully recruiting in the Lafayette County region where the battle was fought.

His grandparents also took him to visit the Confederate Veteran's Home in Higginsville, Missouri where he first learned, to his surprise, that his grandmother had an ancestor who fought for the Confederacy. Brother against brother, indeed.

He first forged his abiding interest in Abraham Lincoln when his parents packed him and his 5 brothers and sisters into the back of the family's Ford Country Squire station wagon for what was an obligatory trip to visit their state's capitol, Lincoln's own Springfield. There "where his children were born and where one lied buried" and where he too would come home to rest. The growing interest in Lincoln that followed was supported by his favorite teachers, history teachers especially who nurtured his interest. "I could have well have become a history teacher myself or even an anthropologist, were it not for the fact that I had a Dad whose voice never stopped ringing in my ear, i.e. 'there is no money in it, there is no money in it."

Coupling his long time love of photography with his now determination to photograph and document the entire body of Lincoln sculptures and monuments, he is on a relentless mission to photograph and research all of the Lincoln monuments that he can reach. "Although I always appreciated the artistry of French's remarkable Lincoln at the Lincoln Memorial, my current obsession with Lincoln's sculpted image came much later in life," he wrote. "Growing up in Central Illinois, one could not ignore the ever present shadow of Lincoln. Decatur, Illinois where I lived for 35 years, for instance, was also the site of Lincoln's first Illinois home and there are several statues of Lincoln in Decatur alone, including one in Lincoln Square, one in front of the Macon County Court House and a very large piece on the campus of Millikin University."

Barefoot and wearing a hickory shirt and a straw hat, it is believed that Lincoln gave his first political speech right there in the heart of Decatur at the age of 20. He was urged by neighbors, who might have been aware of his burgeoning story-telling prowess, to respond to two candidates for the state legislature. Even then, his humility and courtesy were on ready display as he treated both prior speakers kindly and focused upon internal improvements and the growth of what was destined to become the great state of Illinois.

He began this effort to photograph and record the history of Lincoln monuments in 2005, when he photographed a large statue on the campus of Carthage College in Kenosha, Wisconsin. "It intrigued me so," he added, "but in trying to find out something about its history, I discovered that there was little to no information available. Repeatedly, I would encounter the same void elsewhere."

The working title of his book is *A Life Worth Remembering – The Monumental Life and Legacy of Abraham Lincoln.* Through his kindness, the moving artistry of his photography is on vivid display in these pages.

It all began for *Michaela Wieties*, a student from Racine, Wisconsin and winner of one of the National Lincoln Forum's 2016 scholarships to the Symposium, when her family went on a trip to visit family in Springfield, Illinois when she was very young. "We visited the recently opened Abraham Lincoln Presidential Library and Museum and I was captivated by the story the museum told," she wrote. "I had never really learned much about him before that visit, but I was eager to learn more. I had just met my new best friend and his name was Abraham Lincoln."

Several years later, they also took a trip to Washington D.C. and she was excited to see all of the monuments, but it was the Lincoln Memorial that just blew her away. "I was overwhelmed by it and by the respect it commanded," she added. "It was amazing." Ever since, she has been driven by a desire to learn everything she can about him; and as to her first book, it was *Who Was Abraham Lincoln* by Janet B. Pascal.

She collects Lincoln memorabilia, dolls, bobble heads and books. She pushed for more family trips to Gettysburg which she loved and when her parents tired of taking her to Springfield, she got her grandparents to take her instead. She continues to avidly read books and watch documentaries and in a world where her friends plead for cars on their sixteenth birthday, her only wish was to be a Civil War reenactor. Her Mom lovingly fulfilled it by sewing a complete reenactment dress with all the accoutrements. She shadowed the curator at the Civil War Museum in Kenosha, Wisconsin and she has participated in museum workshops and seminars on everything from 'Christmas with the Lincoln family' to the 'Iron Brigade' to the 'Civil War and Hollywood' to the 'Portrayal of Lincoln in Movies' to 'Women on the Homefront' to the 'Mourning Customs of the 1860s' to 'Teaching the Civil War' and more. She believes that Lincoln's political platform, activities, and leadership have so much to teach us today. She also believes that he speaks to us still, to us, to our lives, to our nation.

Paula Hopewell who is settled in Brookfield, Connecticut today, was a proud Kentuckian by birth. For 20 years, she lived on the south side of the Ohio River and just a few miles from Cincinnati, never far from the Mason-Dixon Line.

"As a school girl, in the second or third grade," she wrote, "I can well recall my teacher pointing out to us that the Presidents of both the Union and the Confederacy had been born in our state – Abraham Lincoln and Jefferson Davis. We sang My *Old Kentucky Home, Yankee Doodle*, the *Battle Hymn of the Republic* and *Dixie* with equal gusto and pride, accepting all of these as part of our heritage."

When she was 10 or 11 years old, her family visited Lincoln's birthplace in Hodgenville, along with *My Old Kentucky Home* in Bardstown and other Kentucky landmarks. A saver, she still has vintage postcards from those visits.

"In the 8th grade," she continued, "our teacher, Sister William, read Uncle Tom's Cabin out loud to us, one chapter per day. I remember her emphasis on the role that the Ohio River played in the book and in our country's history; our Kentucky had been a slave state, and the book's characters, Eliza and her child, would be free once they reached the Ohio side of the river," she explained. "After my move to Connecticut, I learned that Harriet Beecher Stowe had lived in Cincinnati before the War and her experiences there surely inspired the landmark novel. Perhaps Sister William told us that, but I had forgotten."

A point of human interest, as Paula noted that on a visit home not long ago, she enjoyed a reunion with Sister William at Saint Walburg's Monastery in Kentucky. She described it as sweet, while I note that it suggests just how kind and caring Paula is, in so remembering a source of light in her life.

She left Kentucky in 1984, making a series of moves to Minnesota, North Carolina, and finally, in 1997, to Connecticut. It was in the Northeast, she noted, where her Kentucky roots first became a topic of conversation, leading her to consider and often defend the impact that her home state had on her. The summer that she turned 50, in 2002, she asked her sister, Beth to join her on a Kentucky highlights tour. "My sights to see wish list included the Maker's Mark Distillery in Loretto, My Old Kentucky Home, and Lincoln's Birthplace shrine," she wrote. "While at the birthplace, we learned of the Lincoln boyhood home nearby at Knob Creek, where I began to realize that I was getting hooked on Lincoln. Beth insists I was hooked before we ever started the trip, but this is my story, so I get to tell it."

By 2006, as a major part of her life was unraveling, she took another trip back to another way stop in her life, Minnesota. Another major component in her personal "Road to Lincoln," however, was that she took Doris Goodwin's *Team of Rivals* with her. And with her and with her and so much so that the book was treated as a close personal friend.

"I'm not very clear on exactly what happened next," continued Paula, "as those years were tumultuous for me, but I do know that our son was in Georgetown Law School as Lincoln's 200th birthday approached, in 2009. Our visits to D.C. made it possible for me to visit two extremely impressive exhibits, the Lincoln exhibit at the Smithsonian's National Museum of American History *"Abraham Lincoln, An Extraordinary Life"* and *"In Lincoln's Hand, His Original Manuscripts"* at the Library of Congress." Finally and fully, this pulled her into the 'all out – no holds barred' study of Lincoln and his world. There was to be no turning back.

"Back home in Connecticut around the time of the 200th Birthday celebration, I was close enough to New York City to take advantage of many exhibits and events that fueled my interest in Lincoln, as my nest was emptying and I had time for this new avocation." Particularly strong in her memory were exhibits at the New York Historical Society, especially the one about *Slavery in New York* and a reading of the *Abraham and Mary Lincoln Love Letters* one year, at the Metropolitan Museum of Art.

As detailed as any portal of entry story that I received, I was taken by Paula's progression and think that its' depth may have been inspired by a few emails that were traded when we first connected, where we considered our Lincoln lives in a spiritual context.

She then highlighted a January, 2010 seminar on the *Emancipation Proclamation* held at the New York Historical Society where she met Harold Holzer, Frank Williams and George Buss, who all encouraged her to join the Lincoln Forum. All four of them, interestingly and gratefully, are among *Unfading Light's* stalwart collaborators. Now how's that for a spiritual connection.

Early in 2011, when her hometown of Brookfield participated in a series of Sesquicentennial events along with neighboring towns, 'Lincoln crazy' as she was, she was asked if she would be willing to give a talk on Lincoln, when the president of the local Historical Society suggested that she was their 'expert.' "I had never done any public speaking and I feared that I was out of my league, but I agreed to do so. It was July 14, 2011 and I have been at it ever since." She has never stopped doing so.

"I don't know exactly when I decided to have a relationship with him," Paula concluded, "but I obviously do, as my home is full of Lincoln inspiration, in the form of quotes, sculptures, books, a bowl, glass bottles and such. I even have two Lincoln dolls, from my daughter, one of which talks. What would Lincoln think of all this fuss? I think he'd be rather amused."

Paula, I rather think that he'd be most grateful. In each presentation you give, you teach and you turn a light on. You inspire. You remind. You prod Lincoln forward.

The equation is simple, the more people you reach and teach, the more people will emulate historical figures who simply give a damn about people. And the more Lincoln, the more Bobby, the more Martin, the more service above self and the closer we get to putting their visions back into play.

CAREER

Kathryn Harris was the president of the Abraham Lincoln Association of Springfield, Illinois, when we first touched base, what is the organization in the heart and epicenter of The Land of Lincoln, his hometown. While she remembers reading about and liking Lincoln as a child, the true interest of one who leads one of the most respected Lincoln Associations in the land came later in life and was ever magnified by her job. Her response to Question 1 was short, sweet and perfect.

"My initial attraction to Lincoln did not come as a result of having read something by or about him as a child or even as a young adult. My attraction began to grow when I became the Reference and Technical Supervisor at the Illinois State Historical Library (ISHL) in 1990. With my promotion to Director of this Library in 1996, my interest grew, mostly due to Thomas Schwartz, PhD, who was at the time, the Curator of the Henry Horner Lincoln Collection at the ISHL. In other words, my interest in Lincoln perfectly dovetailed with my professional career as a Librarian."

JOINING LINCOLN FORUMS AND ASSOCIATIONS

My friends, *Henry Ballone*, the treasurer and photographer of the National Lincoln Forum and *Joe Truglio*, the president of the Philip Kearny Civil War

Roundtable in Wayne, New Jersey just happen to be a tandem duo. They go to the same meetings, share the same sentiments, meet at the same diners and both live for their families and their belonging to Abraham Lincoln. Joe, who actually, and positively reviewed my book, *What Must needs Come – a Legacy of Gettysburg* for the *Civil War News* before I first met him, describes himself as a lifelong student of the War Between the States. Lincoln was to pre-occupy later.

"When you study the Civil War, it's only natural to be drawn to Lincoln, so the more I advanced, the more intrigued I became by Lincoln and the more I wanted to know about him," wrote Joe. "He just pulls you in." Accordingly, he joined the Lincoln Group of New York and began seriously studying Lincoln. He also joined the National Lincoln Forum and has become a regular at the Annual Symposium. He noted that what Lincoln did to fight the war, while loosely holding peace democrats, supremacists, abolitionists, racists, nationalists and more together and while also holding divided political coalitions and a divided government together were byproducts of pure genius.

Henry stands completely alone in that his response to the 'why Lincoln' question was truly unique. In fact, it fairly fascinated.

Before I share it, understand that he is a most active member of the Robert E. Lee Civil War Roundtable in Edison/Woodbridge, NJ, the Philip Kearny Civil War Roundtable in Wayne, NJ, the Lincoln Group of New York and, of course, the National Lincoln Forum. Bearing that in mind, he wrote, "My great interest in Lincoln is tied to the fact that I enjoy the company and the comradery of those who are invested in him. I go to Lincoln because I like his people. I like the spirit and the atmosphere of the meetings, I like the speakers, the historians, the excitement, the interchange, the belonging itself." Now his email address begins with 'civilwarnut' and he is, via sheer osmosis, an expert, but it is the people involved who matter most to him, while the knowledge gained is but a bonus.

When I first reached out to Bill or *Billy Grandstaff*, he was recuperating from surgery, but he was kind enough to advise me that he looked forward to responding just as soon as he could. He's just another Lincoln light in the world, who I have never met personally, who I really like. For like my friend, Henry Ballone above, I like Lincoln people as well. In truth, how can I not, given the all of this. They did not lead me to Lincoln, but they sure as hell and wonderfully reaffirm why I am here in the first place.

Billy Grandstaff, aka, cwbilly1865, tells you quite a bit about just who he is and that which he celebrates. Spiritually that is. He hails from Romeo, Michigan, a small town with inviting hiking trails and nature preserves on the urban fringe of Detroit, Michigan. He, like Henry and Joe above, is a joiner who is active in the National Lincoln Forum and his local Civil War Roundtables.

"The more I study President Lincoln, the more I feel the loneliness that surrounded the man," he wrote.

Interestingly, Billy didn't actually answer the question: he just passed 'Go,' ignored my 'What or When' and went straight to 'Why.'

LINCOLN THE DEBATER

George Buss does what he does best at the National Lincoln Forum Symposium in Gettysburg each November and then again, just days later, at the Gettysburg National Cemetery on '*Remembrance Day*' in that Adams County, Pennsylvania crossroads town where that most epic and meaningful of battles was fought.

Acclaimed impersonator that he is, he delivers the *Gettysburg Address.*

Aware of George Buss' story, I rather think that his unique relationship to Lincoln was simply destined to be. He grew up in Freeport, Illinois and attended Taylor Park Elementary School, which was adjacent to Taylor Park itself, the site of Leonard Crunele's *Lincoln the Debater*, which was dedicated there on August 27, 1929. Senator George Norris, the acclaimed United States Senator from Nebraska keynoted before an audience that included more than 100 people who had actually attended the August 27, 1858 debate. Interestingly, Norris' theme was much like ours, as he too contended that, "The spirit of Lincoln still lives" ever "emblematic as it was of human freedom."

Crunele's Lincoln, 12 feet tall, stands upon a base of rough-hewn red granite. With hands behind his back, Lincoln is presented as strong, wise and confident, just as he had been that day 71 years earlier as he performed in what is widely held to be the most important of those historic 1858 debates, not far from Taylor Park in what is today's downtown Freeport. It was there that Abraham Lincoln asked Douglas, "*Can the people of a United States territory, in any lawful way, against the wishes of any citizen of the United States, exclude slavery from its limits prior to the formation of a state constitution*"? Douglas fatefully responded, "*In my opinion, the people of a territory can by lawful means exclude slavery from their limits prior to the formation of the state constitution.*" And there it was, what was heralded to be Douglas' Freeport Doctrine, the one that so angered the south that it would, two years later, split the Democratic Party in two.

And while Lincoln would be denied a seat in the United States Senate for the second straight time, who there that day at Freeport could ever have imagined that Douglas' response to that fair question would make Abraham Lincoln the president of the United States two short years later.

In his youth, it was to that park and to that statue that George and his fellow 5th graders would go to eat their lunches when the weather permitted.

"You could find a place to sit on the granite boulder to eat, rather than on the grass," he wrote, "and fortunately for me, my legs were long enough that I could use his right shoe as my seat for lunch." At the time, he and his classmates knew nothing of its significance and, in fact, it wouldn't be until High School before he discovered a paragraph, in the pre-civil war section of his history text, entitled "Lincoln and Douglas at Freeport" before those once innocent lunch gatherings began to take on greater significance and deeper meaning. Just to think, it hit him, "*Something big actually did happen in Freeport.*"

Still later, he would take a '*Pre Civil War America*' course with a Doctor Rosenbaum at Ball State University. "On a day, I distinctly remember, Doctor Rosenbaum wrote this on the blackboard: Fugitive Slave Act - Kansas Nebraska - Dred Scott and the Lincoln Douglas Debates in that order," wrote George. "I was then surprised to hear him announce to the class that I was from Freeport and would I be able to share the significance of the Freeport Debate with the class. Fortunately for me, I had paid attention in school, had read the plaque on the granite stone marking the debate site and had even been given a copy of and read Freeport's Lincoln. I was still somewhat stunned, but able to respond and articulate respectably."

George Buss grew tall, grew a beard and had a body structure that was much like Lincoln's, leading co-workers, classmates and friends to start calling him Abe. He later returned to Freeport to teach, at a time when active citizens were committed to making the debate site more than a city parking lot. A script and play focusing upon Lincoln and Freeport was written by a Richard Soukup, one that George performed in and one that in 1994, drew the attention of C-Span, which filmed this Soukup-Buss production in Freeport and Jonesboro.

"My life was suddenly and forever changed," added George. "I had become Abraham Lincoln. I look upon it as my journey 'From Freeport to Gettysburg' and oh what a journey it has been."

KEN BURNS CIVIL WAR

What a blessing it was to connect with *Matthew Lakemacher*, a grade school history teacher and a proud member of today's 'Resistance' from Round Lake Beach, Illinois. In summers, he tours historical sites around the country and his personality and enthusiasm are such that his classes, without doubt, just have to be lively affairs.

"I've always considered myself to be a student of history," he wrote. "My earliest memory of the origins of that passion is from Middle School, when the students and teachers put on a Renaissance Faire and I got to dress up and play the part of a knight. For a while, my milieu was the Middle Ages, and undoubtedly, this was linked to my love of J.R.R. Tolkien and "The Lord of the Rings." But more importantly, I was drawn to the story, the mythology, and the epic spiritual battle between good and evil."

He then, in describing his great love of history, referred to the words of Tolkien's faithful Samwise Gamgee:

It's like in the great stories, Mr. Frodo. The ones that really mattered. Full of darkness and danger they were. And sometimes you didn't want to know the end. Because how could the end be happy? How could the world go back to the way it was when so much bad had happened? But in the end, it's only a passing thing, this shadow. Even darkness must pass. A new day will come. And when the sun shines it will shine out the clearer. Those were the stories that stayed with you. That meant something, even if you were too small to understand why. But I think, Mr. Frodo, I do understand. I know now. Folk in those stories had lots of chances of turning back, only they didn't. They kept going, because they were holding on to something . . . That there's some good in this world." And it's worth fighting for.

And then, the living history began pouring out of him:

It seems inevitable then that my focus of study would inexorably be drawn to the American Iliad, the Civil War, and its patron saint, Abraham Lincoln. While watching the Ken Burns Civil War series on PBS, I realized that the land of my sojourn had a mythology of its own and it was on a trip to Springfield, Illinois that I first connected with the Liturgy of Lincoln. I visited all the standard sites: his home, his law office, and his tomb (the fabulous museum and library had not yet opened, but I have attended numerous seminars and events there since). The one place that stuck with me, that gave me those 'sense of place' chills that I still feel to this day when visiting places like Gettysburg or the Lincoln Cottage in Washington, D.C., was the Old State Capitol Building. Standing in the House chamber, on planks of wood where Lincoln stood and worked and became the man who would free the slaves and save the Union, I could hear his House Divided Speech still echoing through time. I could see him giving the first draft of what would become his famous Peoria Speech in 1854, throwing his hat back into the political ring after a brief sabbatical, drawn back in over the evils of slavery and the Kansas-Nebraska Act. And, I could see his body lying in state before making that final journey to Oak Ridge and immortality.

As for Lincoln books, he explained that his shelves groan under the weight of them, but the ones that he continually comes back to for inspiration and insight are Allen Guelzo's Abraham Lincoln: Redeemer President, Gabor Boritt's The Gettysburg Gospel and Harold Holzer's Lincoln at Cooper Union: The Speech that Made Abraham Lincoln President." Also fascinated by those formative years that shaped the man he later became, he also is indebted to the work of Michael Burlingame and Douglas Wilson. But Richard

Carwardine's knowledge of nineteenth century evangelicalism and its intersection with Lincoln also had much to do with shaping his thinking.

"I will always treasure the week I spent in Oxford, thanks to the Gilder
Lehrman Institute," he wrote, "attending Professor Cawardine's lectures and
talking Lincoln and life in his parlor and over pints at his local, the Bear Inn."

Thank you, Matt Lakemacher.

DAD AND THE OLD ILLINOIS STATE HOUSE

Anne Moseley was up until recently, the Director and Curator of the Lincoln
Heritage Center Museum at Lincoln College in Lincoln, Illinois, having only
recently accepted a position at the University of Illinois. Anne's father, Den-
nis Suttles, was, in 1990, hired by a Dr. Cullom Davis, the editor of the
Lincoln Legal Papers as a research associate, charged with searching for
Lincoln legal documents throughout the counties he traversed while riding
the 8th Judicial Circuit. He worked out of the historic Old State Capitol in
Springfield.

"Every time I visited my father at work, I would hear new stories about
Mr. Lincoln and his life in Illinois," wrote Anne. "All of these stories led me
to Lincoln, but the very first story I heard may have been enough to do the
trick. It was told by Dr. Wayne Temple whose wife, Sandy was a site inter-
preter at the Old State Capitol and she just happened to be giving a tour in the
Secretary of State's office one fine day, where she discovered that an item in
that room that was a component of the tour had disappeared."

Well it just so happened that Anne, all of 6-years old, had been in there
earlier and taken it. So, the short of a long story was that she was in trouble,
upon which Doctor Temple took Anne into his office to share a tale about
Lincoln's son.

Well familiar, it's the one about Tad's doll, Jack, who was getting into all
sorts of trouble. So much so, that his execution had been ordered, which Tad
knew would require him to be buried in the White House Gardens, destroying the landscape, upsetting the gardener and resulting in the gardener com-
plaining to the president. So Tad and his father met and the president asked
Tad just what kind of trouble Jack had been in and Tad responded, "Jack has
not been attending to his picketing duties and has fallen asleep at his post, for
which he will be executed." President Lincoln gave it a lot of thought before
telling Tad, "Well that seems like a high price to pay and I believe I will
pardon Jack but just this once. He needs to take great care in the future." He
then proceeded to write a pardon for Jack. Thinking this had solved the
problem, it was not long lasting for the very next day, as Jack made another
mistake, it led to his demise and execution. His father was given no addition-

al opportunity to intervene, as Tad took direct action. Lincoln's Generals might be tamed or subdued by his Dad's inclination to pardon but not Tad.

"As a young girl, this wonderful story peaked my interest in the Lincolns," wrote Anne. "This one story about President Lincoln's relationship with his boy made him real to me. He was a father, spending time with his boys and not just the Great Emancipator I later learned about in school."

Just a children's story about a doll named Jack, one that touched her forever and that she still takes to work with her every day.

JUST ANOTHER ABANDONED HOUSE

Joan Chaconas just happened to pass by a boarded up, vacant, old house in Clinton, Maryland. Struck by it, it just seemed to reek of history and story. For the record, Joan insists that she has always found it difficult to pass by a vacant house without exploring it. But this place and this time, her innate curiosity indeed paid off. She investigated and way led onto way and in 1975, 45 years ago, it was brought back to life as a museum, where she serves as History Specialist.

She just happened to stumble upon the Surratt's family home, tavern and hostelry and what also once served as both post office and polling place. Built by John and Mary Surratt in 1852, Mary upon the loss of her husband and the later loss of her slaves (Maryland constitutionally banned slavery in 1864), became financially strapped, rented the house out and moved to the infamous Row House on H Street in Washington D.C. and the rest is history.

The Surratt House Museum today boasts of a new Visitor's Center, Research Center and Library. "We have come a long way and have much to offer," Joan wrote, "but I personally cannot escape the fact that I first embraced Lincoln through the portal of his death. It is, however, a part of the study that also fascinates and continues to be advanced."

"At the time," Joan continued, "I was unaware of the intricate details surrounding the assassination or about the people behind it, but over time, I have come to know a great deal about Lincoln's life and contributions as well as his death. What I find most fascinating about Lincoln's story—is that it is compelling drama. It has everything—hardship, perseverance, stubbornness, glory, brilliance, comedy, love, hate, pathos, war, sadness and tragedy."

This home also long served as a safe house on the Confederate underground, which flourished in southern Maryland and it was the first stop Booth and Herold made upon fleeing Washington.

Given my pet-peeve about flagrant injustices, I am compelled to suggest that whatever may or may not have been regarding Mary Surratt's alleged role in the conspiracy, there was no evidence to support the same and the

Military Tribunal surely and sadly railroaded her. It is a wonder that Stanton didn't look to convict everyone in her H Street neighborhood.

ALL IN THE FAMILY

"When I was seventeen, I asked my nearest relatives to share what they knew of our family," wrote *Marilyn Krowl Rexilius*. "I was interested in their memories and any documents or tales that would help me take a journey back in time. Among the discoveries that wowed upon my own intense search was that I was the second cousin of Abraham Lincoln four-times removed. I became the family historian and have devoted much of the last 59 years to turning over the rocks in an effort to learn more about the fascinating people with whom I share a blood-line."

She did not look for her relation and belonging to Lincoln. But it was there and it was detailed and true.

Her, 4x Great-grandmother, Hannah Lincoln was the younger sister (as was her twin sister Lydia) of the Abraham Lincoln who was born on May 13, 1744 in Berks County, Pennsylvania and who was later killed in his field while frightened sons Mordecai, Josiah, and nine-year old Thomas witnessed the tragedy that day in May of 1786 in rural Jefferson County, Kentucky. Hannah and her husband John Harrison, whose family was traced back to the Jamestown Colony stayed in the Valley, but all of their children left to begin new lives in Ohio in the early 1800s.

Originally from Pennsylvania, this one branch of The Lincoln Family moved with nine children. The parents were John and Rebecca Flowers Morris Lincoln. They had traveled a long distance from Berks County to the Valley of the Shenandoah with its meandering river, when John, the patriarch was in his 50s. He was known locally throughout Augusta and Rockingham Counties as *Virginia John* Lincoln. Included in the group of Lincoln children was his wife Rebecca's son, Jonathan from her first marriage. He was a prosperous farmer in the Shenandoah Valley, which lay in the shadow of the Massanutten Mountain Range, overlooking breathtakingly beautiful, fertile rolling hills.

Abraham Lincoln, the eldest child of John and Rebecca had been known as Captain Lincoln, given his service to his locally organized militia unit in the Revolutionary War. Even though he had inherited land and was on his way to becoming a gentleman farmer, he had been infected by the then popular malady called the 'itch to go west.' Abraham and wife Bathsheba then went to Kentucky with Abraham's cousin who was a member of the Boone clan.

As it happened, Marilyn joined the Shenandoah, Augusta and Rocking-ham Historical Societies in Virginia in order to better mine information that might be hiding in the nooks and crannies of archives and records. As many of Abraham Lincoln's cousins lived in the Valley there during the Civil War, she also was interested in scoping out their feelings regarding their famous cousin. A few locally published books revealed some useful information about the Lincolns who had stayed in the Harrisonburg/Linville Creek area.

These members of the family were in the lofty Planter Class and they owned many slaves. Jacob Lincoln, Abraham Senior's brother apparently had more slaves than any of his neighbors and Jacob himself built a plantation on the Valley Pike Road (Route 11) with an elaborate white house, a house she noted that still stands and was for sale at the time she wrote.

"A young Congressman Lincoln from Illinois was, in touch, by letter with a family member in the Valley during his time in office," noted Marilyn. "Apparently, he had not been told very much of the story of his ancestors. Since he lived in poverty as a child. It makes me wonder if he was ever told that he had come from an influential and privileged family (as it happened, of course, he did get wind of this). This family back in Virginia, however, was certainly well aware of him and his connections and they hated him for his actions during his term as President, as those decisions affected their lives and human property'"

While home is in Everett, Washington, Marilyn is among the small group that gathers once a year to honor President Lincoln and those ancestors of his buried in that well-groomed cemetery just a few miles north of Harrisonburg Virginia. The cemetery is under an old but healthy tree that provides shade and it overlooks a patchwork quilt of rolling hills with a panorama of the Shenandoah Valley as a backdrop. John Lincoln (Virginia John) and his wife Rebecca Flowers are buried in this small family plot with other Lincoln family members. John and Rebecca were Abe's great-grandparents who came to Virginia from New Jersey/Pennsylvania with their nine children. Their eldest child, Abraham, was Abe's grandfather and namesake.

Apparently, after Virginia seceded from the Union, President Lincoln' s two first cousins, who still lived in the Valley, were vocal about their hatred for him. Yet when Sheridan's soldiers showed up to burn Abigail Lincoln Coffman's barn, she pleaded with them to spare her barn and livestock because of her ties to our Lincoln. "*I think she missed the irony of requesting a familial favor while denouncing him,*" suggested Marilyn.

Darla Moe is an engaging and gentle woman who hails from Sacramento, California today and who with her husband, David, crosses the country to attend the Symposium in Gettysburg each November. I have traded many an email with her and she has generously forwarded files of information to me.

Information received includes detailed charts and long lists of names clearly attesting to the validity of familial connections to General Grant, President Franklin Delano Roosevelt and others. There also and most importantly are news articles about the deaths of her Grand Army of the Republic

GAR veteran grandfathers, death certificates that attest to disease and maladies first contracted while serving the Union and even muster and discharge records. She has more than done her homework.

Understand, her long reach into the past is not about her, but rather about honoring all of them and celebrating their stories and contributions. As to her road to Lincoln, the path is direct and certain. Family led her to the Civil war, which then took her directly to him.

Philosophical fool that I am, Darla's loving witness to her ancestors was compelling but it also reminded me that we are but one human family. We are. We know this. Our science recognizes this. We are now billions and we have since the dawn of time insisted upon putting up walls and lines that separate, but we are all cousins, however many times removed, who the hell knows. Yes, Mr. President, you and all those you want to deport and the refugees you won't let in and the Muslims and the Mexicans you can't stand and the leaders of Black Lives Matter are all related.

Darla's Great Grandfathers, Alonzo Spencer, Josiah Walker and Philo Burtch all hailed from the upstate New York (Rome and Albany areas) where Darla herself was raised. They were all Lincoln Men and if you trust the data, at least 2 and maybe all 3 voted for him in 1864. We know that they served in engagements like Cedar Creek, Cold Harbor, Petersburg and that one went to the infamous Libby Prison and that they all served for long and survived the war. Survival didn't mean that they didn't pay a great price. They did.

"Finally and most importantly for me," Darla noted, "I learned that Great Grandfather Spencer had died from disease contracted during the late rebellion, upon which, I just began to cry. It seemed to me that the War of the Rebellion was suddenly very, very recent. I guess I felt that the Doctor who had filled out Great Grandfather Alonzo Spencer's death certificate in 1890 must have felt that the war was only yesterday as well, even though 25 years had passed. I felt like crying for every person who had to live through the nightmare of it."

Darla, ever inspired by the fact that her ancestors, ordinary farmers from small villages in upstate New York, who helped to keep our country from fracturing, were Lincoln Men, has devoted the better part of a lifetime to discovering just why.

Lincoln cried for them all as well. It is why he strolled the halls of the White House in his robe in the dead of his sleepless nights; it is why the migraines, why the deep-set lines in his face, why the great sadness and mist in his eyes.

JUST A GOLD POCKET WATCH

Paul Mellen's innocent purchase of an old gold pocket watch led him to join The National Lincoln Forum and to begin to explore the depths of Abraham Lincoln.

An eBay sale, the 18kt gold pocket watch had been owned a by Civil War Paymaster, Major Jonathan Ladd. "Naturally, I was interested in who Major Ladd was," wrote Mellen,"and I was shocked to learn that he was there at Lincoln's deathbed at the Peterson House on April 15, 1865 at 7:22 a.m. Major Ladd actually timed Lincoln's death for the Doctor with the very pocket watch that is now in my possession. Upon discovering this, I clearly knew I was going to begin to have a relationship with President Lincoln."

He went on to discover that colleagues of Ladd's also had been watching the show at Ford's Theatre when Lincoln was shot. Included among them were William T. Kent who assisted Dr. Leale by using his pocket-knife to cut open Lincoln's clothing for examination, Newton Frerre, who also assisted Dr. Leale and is remembered for having kept Lincoln's bloody shirt collar as a souvenir and Major Joseph Potter who escorted Mary Lincoln, Clara Harris and Major Rathbone out of Ford's Theatre.

As to Major Ladd and his life, his family, his story, Paul has work to do. His detour to Lincoln just could delay that investigation.

REMEMBERING BIG

I am going long, for which I apologize in advance.

I wish it was a laugh out loud barn-burner or a tale that powerfully moves the soul and sets the spirit soaring. Oh, there is a knock down-drag out blizzard, but no adventure, no danger, no inspiration, not even any comic relief.

An inconsequential children's story, all it does is pinpoint the source of my 60-year belonging to Abraham Lincoln.

March 12, 1950, it was my 10th birthday and the mighty sum of $4 was burning a hole in my pockets, as I trudged through a raging blizzard which, from a young boy's perspective, was delightfully pummeling us for a second day. My brother, Bob, saint that he was, joined me on this mission to bring home some marvelous toy that my four brothers and two sisters might also enjoy. Trained to share long before we took our first steps, we did not have to be musketeers to live in the light of 'All for one and one for all.'

The Toy Store on the corner of Passaic Avenue and Main Street in Hackensack, New Jersey did not satisfy, so we painstakingly trudged on in our rattling and squeaky boots, some 5-blocks further north on Main Street to Packard's, the store of stores, a converted mammoth, old 4-story industrial building. Wonderful and cavernous, its wide wood-plank floors were coated with a daily sprinkling of fresh, inviting sawdust.

Long before the advent of the shopping mall, it offered a one-stop shop where everything, from groceries to furniture to wall paper to toys to clothing, etc. was sold. Attracting folks from all over northeastern New Jersey and New York City, the entrance alone included a travel agency and a barbershop to the right and a restaurant and a liquor store to the left and, once through the doors, a pharmacy, a bakery and yes, the bookstore that gave me pause.

There, ever so surprisingly, I faced a sudden quandary, whether to bear left up the escalator, the predetermined path, or to pause in the Bookstore, which had just called out my name. While the greatest of toy stores lied two floors above.

I know, I know, F.A.O. Schwartz in New York City is supposed to be as good as it gets, but Packard's Toy Store in the 50's and 60's was just as, if not more, magical. It boasted of rare gems from faraway lands including Germany, Italy, Russia, India, England and anything found in the Sears or Montgomery Ward catalogues. To go see Santa at the North Pole there, you literally boarded a Christmas train which wound through snow covered hills and fields of candy canes. If that sounds like an exaggeration, remember children who are condemned to become adults do not lie, they just remember big.

That said, Santa did hang out over the mountain at the entrance to a North Pole that existed for the children only. Upon exiting the train, Santa loudly "Ho, Ho, Hoed," welcomed all and filled the hands of each child with a Christmas coloring book, a small box of Crayola crayons and a box of rock candy. It was ever so much more than a candy cane at Packard's and like the Animal Crackers, the candy came with the string handle that intrigued.

Yet, for what were still unknown reasons, books and I had already begun to enjoy relationship.

So no matter my good intentions and my brother's understandable prodding, I never got to the fourth floor, the intended destination. The bookstore lured me in. They have had their way with me ever since and I mourn the loss of bookstore after bookstore today, as they are daily being taken out by the brave new world of the Amazons and crushing technology.

I, of course, digress for what matters is that I found two treasures. The attractive placement of two 'Young Americans' biographies, upright and in the center of a small round table, that could not be missed, they just reeled me in. There looking upon the face of President Abraham Lincoln on one and that of General Robert E. Lee on the other, I settled and pondered. Only a $1.19 each, the price was right and I selfishly weighed the additional personal costs of dishing both the great toy and my duty to the precept of 'one for all.'

I decided to pay both of those costs.

Bob and I intrepidly made our way back into the blizzard and while I felt good about my purchase, Bob was, to say the least, puzzled, dismayed and put out by my failure to stay on mission. Two books, after all, were not what he had bargained for, when he agreed to accompany me through this snow of snows.

The knee, thigh and waist high deep drifts and the strong northeastern wind that whipped and slashed waves of snow across our faces made the going tough. So on our way home to 138 Poplar Avenue, I called an audible and told Bob that we ought to stop at Jack's Candy Store on the corner of Poplar and Main and only blocks from home, where I could get him a cup of hot chocolate. Even more importantly, I used my substantial change to buy sodas and two 5-cent candy bars for all 6 of my siblings in an attempt to assuage my guilt and save face. Strange to think that transformative portals to forgiveness were once found in packages as small as O'Henry and Mounds bars, but while venial and not mortal, I had no doubt sinned.

While drawn to history at school, little did I know then of the power, wonder and inspiration that was soon to explode within me. I was to discover something that would grab hold of me and never let go.

A holiday because of the snow, it was so spectacular that it held out the promise of a second and even third day of freedom from school. A magical day, there was everything from my favorite chocolate cake with the cherries, to the traditional gathering with my brothers and sisters, to the igloos we built in our yard (and I do mean real igloos), to the snowball fight with the Montesanos, another family of 7, the Bednashes and the Mustos on our block, to the sleigh riding on Borg's Hill, where sweet Mrs. Borg, as ever, welcomed all the children of Hackensack with hot chocolate and warm cookies.

The memorialization of the day, however, was not rooted in such grand events, but rather in the gifts that I had so spontaneously and inadvertently chosen, gifts that, up close and personal, forever invited me into the worlds of Lincoln and Lee.

Excited about my purchase, I found myself sneaking out of bed that night after the house had gone silent, in the certain knowledge that the morning would bring no call to the classroom or responsibility. And there in the upstairs hallway, dimly lit by a fifteen-watt bulb, I curled up on the floor with my warm Native American (or then 'Indian') blanket and got lost in the lives of two men who were on different sides in different roles in what Winston Churchill called *"The least avoidable conflict in the history of the world."*

There amidst the warmth and security of 138 Poplar Avenue on a snowy night with my head and shoulders braced up against one wall in the upstairs hall and my feet pressed against the base of the other, my intimate relationship with two men who knew much of sacrifice and duty and honor began. That they were on opposite sides also taught me a great deal about living paradoxes and remembering that, no matter the inevitable revelations of the truth and the perilous onslaught of reason, stories can still be complicated things.

I remember neither the titles and nor do I have any idea who the authors were, but they were likely written with young teens in mind and with plenty of colorful renderings. All I know is that they were enough and while Lincoln steadily ascended and absolutely became, as it were, my ideal, there was still enough of Lee in me to write *What Must Needs Come – A Legacy of Gettysburg,* which focused upon him and that which drove his thinking (mind, heart and soul) on that most fateful day, the third day at Gettysburg, the day that the tide most assuredly turned for our Lincoln.

In my search for History, I also have dived deep into the lives and legacies of Thomas Paine, Thomas Jefferson, Henry David Thoreau, quite a number of Civil War Generals, Secretary William Seward, both Teddy and FDR, Harry Truman, John Kennedy, Malcolm X, Bobby Kennedy and a host of *'coulda-woulda-shoulda'* been' presidents.

But the greatest and sustaining passion, the longest dive, the one study and belonging to that has never skipped a beat or ever slowed is this one that I have long enjoyed with Abraham Lincoln.

I celebrate my Maggie, my family, my faith, my students and the lingering hope that the singular greatness and light of Lincoln might once again help us put the brakes on yet another, dark collision course with the abyss.

Figure 1.1.   In the city where I was born and where I was first mesmerized by Lincoln, he solemnly and contemplatively sits, in what he himself described as the 'Very Garden of Gethsemane,' preparing to bear the mighty burdens. *Source:* Lincoln the Mystic, Jersey City, NJ - by James Earle Fraser 1930. Photographed by Dave Wiegers.

Chapter Two

The Ever Fixed Mark

In Shakespeare's Sonnet 116, he immortalized these extraordinary words, among those rare handfuls to be heralded forever:

> Love is not love
> Which alters when it alteration finds,
> Or bends with the remover to remove.
> O no! It is an ever-fixed mark
> That looks on tempests and is never shaken;
> It is the star to every wand'ring bark,

I appropriated the term *fixed mark* as the object of the second question posed to my acolytes of Lincoln, as we are interested in the trait, the value, the quality, the attribute that resounded in Lincoln to which each of us have been drawn, that something about him that forged our belongings to him.

Explicit or implicit, celebrated or closely held, these fixed marks determine why we write, teach, study, ponder and devote so much of our lives to our 16th president. After all, why this reverence?

The reservoir of qualities and attributes is, of course, as wide and deep as one can imagine; and while I anticipated that most would tap the more familiar like honesty, humility, compassion, kindness, courage, I was wildly surprised with just how wide, diverse and intriguing the responses were.

One in our attachment and belonging, our ports of entry are so very different.

We never stop chasing Lincoln and exploring his great faith in America's promise, its institutions, its people and so too, in posterity and in us. It is the same faith that saw us through our darkest moments, fashioned our dreams deferred and inspired our calls to action and willingness to sacrifice for one another and the land we love.

155 years and monumental change notwithstanding, Lincoln and saving the soul of America are ever joined at the hip. This is a simple truth.

In considering his 'ever fixed mark,' *Jack C. Waugh* noted that Karl Marx, an admirer of Lincoln, once said of him that he was "One of the rare men who ever succeeded in becoming great, without ceasing to be good." While a profound testament that powerfully speaks for itself, Waugh went further and explained that "Lincoln's humanity, humility, rudimentary and unchanging goodness only and ever expanded during the Civil War." This personal advance, this reaching higher still despite the chaos and horror of it all. This despite the devastating toll, the incredible loss, the monumental suffering, the burden he bore.

Remarkably, the harsher and more ominous it all became, the gentler and stronger and more spiritual he became. The more he was tested, the higher he reached, ever stronger in mind, heart and spirit. In a climate where most would descend, he rather and only ascended.

Such as this, Waugh insisted, is what always drew him to Lincoln, a man who never ceased to advance and to grow better still.

The proof of what he lived is etched into the burrows, pockmarks and crevices that found a home in Lincoln's beautifully, haunting face, what our Frank Williams described as a *"forlorn and pine cone"* face, one that bore living witness to the cost of freedom for all. In it, the sleepless nights, the mourning, the migraines, the souls of the 'all too many' who fell, the relentless cries of agony and the profound personal sacrifice of people everywhere.

"Long ago," Waugh continued, "a student once asked, what one word best described Lincoln? I blurted out, 'kindness,' for the kindness that defined him played a large role in making him great and certainly rendered him an example for all."

In this reflection, Waugh fairly and so very movingly considered Lincoln's greatness and goodness, his humanity and his humility and, ultimately, his kindness, which may well have been the driver of it all.

"*A minore ad maius*," from the lesser to the greater, I thought, for Lincoln never ceased growing and piling on layer after layer. Greatness is never static. It evolves and expands.

The word I personally pluck from a veritable sea of prospective 'fixed marks' is one that I have long held tight to. In light of this effort, reevaluation of it was in order and labyrinths of thought later, 'magnanimity' it remains. Born on the wings of his humility and compassion, it is that great and rare quality that enabled him to humble himself as he raised others up and to ever and always keep his eye on the prize, the issue or goal at hand. He would never sacrifice the end game or goal, in any way, shape or form, to political consideration or personal vindication or need or popularity or pocketbook.

Abraham Lincoln and selflessness were a tandem duo and, pure and simple, if he was anything, he was selfless. To have been magnanimous always is to put self and self-consideration forever on the back burner, which is largely something human beings simply don't do.

Certainly, something that is impossible for presidents and yet here, the anomaly.

Examine anyone else in American political history and I assure you that you will come to discover that as great as so many of them were, Lincoln alone meets the extraordinary test of having so completely sacrificed and bled out for others over the course of his life. Tried by the relentless fire and fury of war and politics, he managed to hold tight to a guiding principle and standard that quite literally sets him apart from the rest. Yes ambitious and determined to leave a mark that would give meaning to his having lived, but selflessly so. Deeply political, he wanted to win and "be esteemed by his fellows," but never at any cost or price.

In the race for the United States Senate in 1855/1856, he had 44 votes on the 1st ballot to Lyman Trumbull's 5 which together would have given him the victory. But when the Democrats switched to their popular Governor, Lincoln feared the worse and in the end what were once his 44 all voted for Trumbull, securing victory for an Anti-Nebraska man. What ultimately mattered was sending an anti-Kansas-Nebraska Act/no extension of slavery into the territories man to the United States Senate and not wearing the laurel wreath himself.

That is what it is to be magnanimous.

Consider his selection of Edwin Stanton to be his Secretary of War, the same Edwin Stanton who treated him so outrageously when they met on behalf of defendant, John Henry Mandy, who was being sued for patent infringement by Cyrus McCormick in the famous Reaper Case in 1854 in Cincinnati. Lincoln arrived, having fully prepared, with his arguments and brief in tow, unaware that he had been replaced by the big guns from Washington, led by Stanton who treated him like a 'holier than thou' bully does. Stanton precluded him from playing any role whatsoever in the case and would not even permit him to sit with his fellow lawyers in the courtroom. He ostracized him socially as well, as Lincoln was never invited to dine with the legal team of which he was a part.

In private, Stanton went so far as to refer to him as a *Backwoods Gorilla*.

Nonetheless, Lincoln stayed to hear the case and to see the "great" lawyers in action, to go to school if you will (when in truth his Brief was as strong as those of the Big Guns). So never carrying a grudge or personal vendetta, he plucked Stanton, whose ability he had seen in action, out of the ranks of lesser War Department officials and elevated him to the top. This is mind boggling to 'we lesser mortals' and is truly magnanimous to a fault.

Then consider General George McClellan as well, who as Commander of the Army of the Potomac, slighted Lincoln again and again, so much so as to retire to bed while Lincoln was waiting in his foyer. This without so much as a beep from his Commander in Chief for so long as he retained faith in his ability to command.

While there are 45 collaborators, there will, as Jack C. Waugh alone has already established, be far more than 45 responses to this query. Simply put, our good collaborators refused to play by my 'What is that one characteristic or trait' ask, likely because it made no sense to them. It wasn't, after all, one mere attribute that drew them to Lincoln, but many and this narrowing down to one or even two or three proved understandably difficult, if not impossible, for those who had ever viewed Lincoln through a wide angle lens and never a narrow or limited one.

Lincoln after all is a wide-angle lens study and fascination.

These were the rough-cut results.

At the very top of our hit parade were *Perseverance* and/or *Determination* which was referenced by fully 9 of our collaborators. Right on the heels of it were *Compassion* and *Empathy* which were hailed by 8. *Wisdom* and the *Capacity for Growth* and/or *Humility* were flagged by 6, *Strength of Character* by 4 and *Kindness* by 3. Two collaborators then pointed to his *Sense of Humor* and/or his *Story Telling Ability*, to the depths of his *Vision*, to what was defined as his *Personal and Spiritual Complexity*, to his *Leadership* and *Loyalty* and finally and interestingly to either his *Sadness* or to the combination of *Logic and Sadness*, which historian, Richard Brookhiser, maintained to be an extremely rare and instructive combination.

Among those coming in with but one vote each were *Honesty, Humanity, Faith*, the *Ability to Inspire, Righteousness*, the *Courage to Defy the Passions of His Time* and, wait for it, the flip side of the same or rather his *Appreciation of his Time*, his *Unwillingness to Vilify an Enemy*, his *Refusal to be Defined by his Past*, his insatiable *Love of Learning*, his *Forgiveness, Political Insight*, simply being a *Self-Made* man, *his sense of Belonging, Hope*, even his *Refusal* to either give in or to give up and finally, and last but not least, my own *Magnanimity* to which I hold tight.

Were I to have gone long and wide like most, magnanimity would have been followed by the compassion and empathy combo and then by humility.

The fact that but 1 of 45 looked to 'Honest Abe's' honesty as their 'ever fixed mark' is a point of great interest to me now, especially in light of the fact that the anti- Lincoln counterpart serving in that sacred office today is a consummate liar (daily growing and approaching 18,000 lies told), devoid of any interest in the truth. Given the egregious level of dishonesty today, one wonders if a light might again begin to be shed upon the extraordinary grace that can ultimately be showered upon a people when their leader is simply honest and open with them, as Lincoln was and as one would hope all presidents ought to be.

While I have boxed and categorized all responses in order to paint a picture of the whole, so very many responses were multi-dimensional as to either defy classification or to muddy the waters of any effort of mine to do so.

Michelle Krowl wrote, "Lincoln conquered so many obstacles in life, yet retained an essential humanity and decentness about him under the most trying circumstances. Through it all, he still retained his essential nature as a man who sympathized with the plight of others and acted on that empathy, while finding delight and release in humor."

In but two sentences, she focused on no less than 5 clearly identifiable *fixed marks*, humanity, decency, compassion, empathy and humor. And hey, humor alone is, at once, a tool, a refuge, a resource, a weapon and more.

"As president," she continued, "he shouldered burdens that would have crushed many men. He carried the weight of trying to keep the union together, of prosecuting an unpopular war, negotiating his policies with Congress, suffering the death of a beloved son and responding to the emotional needs of his wife, all the while knowing that his decisions on many fronts had life or death consequences and that the abilities of subordinates to carry them out were, certainly in the early years, questionable at best."

Yet Lincoln met these forces and the myriad crises that demanded his attention head on, the all of which led Krowl to the observation that "On a basic level I am inspired to try to understand how Abraham Lincoln managed to be Abraham Lincoln."

On a more specific level, she then added that she was inspired by Lincoln's ability to consistently value the cause at the expense of self. "He was an ambitious man to be sure," she added, "but one who knew when larger principles or goals were at stake and ever acted to promote the cause rather than himself."

The text of Lincoln's August 23, 1864 *Blind Memorandum* was noted as a case in point. Written, as detailed in Chapter 1 at a low point, when chances for re-election seemed unlikely, Lincoln vowed, upon defeat, to work with the Democratic President-Elect to save the Union before March 4, 1865, because the survival of the country and the freedom of the slaves came first. That and neither victory nor re-election nor personal vindication nor affirmation nor satisfaction nor ego.

"At times," concluded Krowl, "when I am at risk of behaving in a petty manner or looking out for myself, I remind myself of Lincoln, get perspective and consider the greater good. While I cannot say that I heed my better angels in all instances, they do prevail more often than not in these 'What would Abraham Lincoln do' moments."

To sum it all up, Krowl opened the door to the *fixed marks* of faith, humility, determination, decency, perseverance, compassion, empathy, humor, and above all else, I believe, to the capacity to inspire and pay forward both a vision and a dream. A Motherload of fixed marks indeed.

Frank Williams wrote, "Lincoln's character," as Winston Churchill observed, "is the one from which all others flow." Lincoln's political courage, self–effacement, humor and empathy" were also identified by him.

He strongly asserted that Lincoln's trust in his own judgment, what was *"a logically learned behavior,"* contributed strongly to his greatness. Like anyone, no matter how great, he made his share of mistakes, but the key, Williams maintained, is that they were never born of self-doubt. Then too, as has already been argued and will be often repeated by others, he rarely, if ever, made the same mistake twice.

Churchill managed to brilliantly endear himself to *'we Lovers of Lincoln'* with the above quote. For he celebrates just how great was Lincoln's capacity to sustain and nurture a free people, lessons that were certainly not lost on Churchill, who like Lincoln, would fight with reckless abandon to nurture and sustain a free people himself.

Then too, if character is courage, which we might freely assume, what volumes are yet to be written, exploring the character, courage and spiritual bond between Lincoln and Churchill.

Here again, there are no less than five "fixed marks," all wrapped up in notions about character, which Churchill insists have their roots in Lincoln. Oh, Character, thy name is Lincoln. So said one of the most formidable heroes of the 20th Century.

This notion of Lincoln as resource and-or source, via which to develop and enhance character, fairly fascinates and is notably what drives the very theme of this work.

Steven Raymond added, "What most inspires me about Lincoln, even more than his eloquence, is the mind behind it. I think Lincoln, more than any national leader since, had a capacity to see things beyond the horizon, to understand what they meant, and to spell them out in terms everyone else could understand. His explanation of the meaning of the Civil War in the Gettysburg Address is a classic example."

Yes, that vision thing and-or depth and-or insight and-or understanding thing. Oh, what it is to see the jumping off point or the prime mover, but then again and also, to see all of the parts of the whole and all of the forces that will be set in motion. Both the big picture and the prospective end game or results. Yes, to have envisioned the all of that at one and the same time, for that is just what Raymond asserts.

Lincoln, in fact, did view everything through a clear lens that demanded that he and his administration do their duty and do their best in the ultimate faith "that right makes might" and that they be willing to do that duty unto the end. But the times, the price paid, the exacting standards, the duty itself and all of the rest had been chosen by neither Lincoln nor his peers. The crisis, the improbable challenge of a bitter Civil War, the ponderous weight of centuries of slavery and all that it brought to bear had rather been chosen for them.

What Lincoln first brought to it all was his faith in the right, his faith in honor and justice, along with his trademark humility, compassion and empathy. In *the Cooper Union Address* that so stunned the eastern Republican elite, his rousing, "Let us have faith that right makes might" were mere words –just words- and yet they became the very ground upon which Lincoln stood, the active force, the sinew and soul, the abiding spirit and living tissue of his presidency. All of the policies and activity that he set in motion and all of the improbable and lasting contributions that he was to make were byproducts of that same rich faith.

For he would have his administration, "Do its duty to the last."

Raymond here speaks to Lincoln's genius, vision, inspirational writing ability, commitment, dedication, faith and more.

Going forward, there will be many, like Waugh, Krowl, Williams and Raymond above for whom the 'fixed mark' is a bright constellation, but also some straight shooters like me who, ever appreciative of the bright constellation and/or veritable sea of characteristic wonders, dare to hold one up above all others.

Interestingly, *Douglas Egerton* definitively tells us that his *fixed mark* is Lincoln's "endless capacity for growth."

He refers, at the outset, to the promise that Lincoln made to Frederick Douglass when they first met and said, "I think it cannot be shown that when I have ever taken a position, I have ever retreated from it." Later on, there also is Douglass' own affirmation of this, when others worried so that Lincoln might renege on his promise to issue his Emancipation proclamation on January 1, 1863, Douglass calmly reminded them, "If Lincoln has taught us one thing, it is to rely upon his word."

And so it was.

As to the ideal, the fixed moral point, the mission, etc., Lincoln was strong and firm, but he was forever growing, learning, adapting and experimenting in order to advance the mission or objective, which ultimately culminated in preserving the Union, eliminating slavery and setting the table to raise up all in the race of life. The final pieces of his vision, of course, went unfulfilled in that death was all too sudden and soon.

What interests Egerton is that Lincoln had that rare ability to keep his eyes focused upon the prize, the mission and the end game, while taking risks on course corrections and new ideas. Yes, he made mistakes, but he did not make the same mistake twice. This assertion will, by the way, be the one most often repeated and affirmed going forward.

Neither pride, nor politics nor personal considerations nor even the vagaries of public opinion ever stood in his way, although he sometimes had to wait for public opinion to come round. Timing mattered and strategy was applied, but he refused to ever let those in the wrong stand in the way of his doing what was right and even that, which in the offing, may have taken a toll on both him and the popularity of his administration.

He remained, in the midst of a perilous crisis, wise enough to know and appreciate the great strength and capacity that his still United States of America was blessed with. As such, he relied upon the hope that tides do turn and that the darkness of his "What will the people say" cry, upon receiving the news from Chancellorsville on May 6, 1863, would, in the not too distant future, give way to the game changing and blessed news of July 4, 1863.

In just two months, darkness gave way to the brightest of sunshines.

For when the siren songs of victory at Gettysburg and Vicksburg came across the wires and into the Telegraph Office at the War Department where Lincoln, ever anxious for news from the front, waited, it rendered total and ultimate victory inevitable. The tide in both the western and eastern theatres of the war had forever turned. The Mississippi was now in Union control and Lee's Army of Northern Virginia, the Confederacy's strike force and sledge-hammer, lost its very ability to go on the offensive.

Just two months earlier, the news was foreboding and dark. But General Thomas J. *Stonewall* Jackson died and General Ulysses S. Grant proved relentless and tides turned and while hundreds of thousands would tragically die in the final two years of battle, the South had no military hope of prevailing, so long, that is, as the North had Lincoln and that commitment to do his duty to the last.

"While reminding my students of Lincoln's capacity for growth," wrote Egerton, "I also point out that one of the curious ironies of the war years is that no politician enjoyed a resume as lengthy and strong as that of James Buchanan. Having been a Congressman, Senator, Minister to both England and Russia and Secretary of State, he had the most impressive resume since that of Thomas Jefferson. Sure, he faced an unprecedented crisis in the face of southern secession, but lacking any semblance of Lincoln's hope and faith, he was doomed to stumble forward from crisis to crisis, "leaving modern scholars to view his presidency as a dismal failure."

In contrast, Lincoln lacked both the resume and the standing, boasting of a good run in service to the Illinois State Legislature and but one stint in the Congress of the United States, where his *Spot Resolutions* and battle with President Polk over the making of the War with Mexico angered most of the folks back home and endeared him only to Henry David Thoreau, Wendell Phillips and the abolitionists.

There he set himself apart, among the outcasts and the dreamers.

But while arguably ill-prepared for the impossible task that awaited him, one that he had already suggested to be "Greater than that which confronted Washington," he was, given his sense of duty and obligation, his deep understanding of the issues in play, his oath and sacred vow to "preserve, protect and defend," his courage, his faith in himself and what Egerton looks upon as his "wisdom and his brilliance," simply predisposed to succeed. He would relentlessly pursue, adapt and even study, which, for instance, included reading everything on military tactics and field command that he could get his hands on.

Oh yes, ever in a state of becoming more, he would grow and weigh and measure others as well and extract the very best from all.

> As a scholar of Reconstruction, one of the questions I get the most often is about what the course of post-1865 American history might have been, had Lincoln not gone to the theater on that fateful Good Friday to watch Our American Cousin. Obviously, we will never know. But when one considers Lincoln's infinite capacity for growth, historians can make educated guesses as to what would have been his course of action in dealing with the defeated South.
>
> I believe that we can unequivocally say that he would never have accepted the rising tide of southern resistance and vigilantism as did Andrew Johnson. Again, as Lincoln promised Frederick Douglass during their first meeting: "I think it cannot be shown that when I have taken a position, I have ever retreated from it."

We can only surmise, but it is my belief that as a postwar president, Lincoln's star would have shone even more brightly. He would have had no tolerance for the hatred and subjugation and he would, at least, have taken some of the sting out of what was to become the evil, un-American and despicable world of 'Jim Crow.' This sad, still reverberating, component of our history would certainly have been impacted for the better. To what degree, we are, of course, left to take our best educated guesses, and yet, the longer Lincoln served, the better the situation would likely have become.

"I think, for me, the 'fixed mark' has been Lincoln's ability to express himself, to communicate the foundational values of liberal democracy and to make them seem worth fighting for," wrote *Harold Holzer,* our most prolific and relentless of Lincoln historians. Pointed, direct and typical of him.

Neither a defined truth, trait, word, clause, but rather a moving declarative sentence that bears witness to his ability to express, synthesize, educate, elevate and inspire. Holzer's *fixed mark* is seen as an active, living and moving verb with an object that forever remains at the epicenter of our American experiment. What Lincoln communicated fashioned a belonging to his constituents that resonates throughout the entire course of our history and continues to speak loudly to those today who resist a leadership that has dared throw his moral compass away.

Explaining further, he wrote:

> In the book I co-edited with the late Governor Mario Cuomo, *Lincoln on Democracy*, these values and these resonant expressions, boiled down to free-

dom, self-determination, equality and opportunity. Of course, I have been
motivated, in my research and my writing through the years not only by my
admiration for Lincoln's core and unchanging beliefs, but by the mobility, for
want of a better word, of the means he used to communicate them – both
verbally and pictorially. In other words, I am still attacking the complex problem of Lincoln's relationship to his constituencies through words and images.
And I think that his abilities there transcend fixed values and demonstrate an
enormous flexibility and understanding of modern politics. Understanding
them still keeps me occupied.

That Lincoln was a master practitioner of the art of politics and, given the
limits of his age and time, a master communicator and an artist with both
words and ideas, is a given. What Holzer here contends, however, while not a
given, intrigues and fascinates as the thought of going higher and going
beyond the limits of 'fixed marks' certainly should. Rendering compassion
or kindness or humility and the like as life forces capable of evoking both
political and practical responses ups the ante' of our study of Lincoln. It is no
small thing to turn the constructs of character and the words and images
evoked by it into agents or tools of political and/or governmental exchange
and communication.

It's all extraordinary and I look forward to where Holzer goes with it. To
transcend anything is no small thing and yet to look upon Lincoln as an
instrument of transcendence is spot on.

I just love *Edna Greene Medford's* response.

She affirmed that what most impressed her about Lincoln was his ability
to forgive and his abject unwillingness to vilify an enemy. What fascinates is
that he, to our knowledge, never saw those Confederates who he looked to
subdue as evil and that it was in his nature to treat those with whom he was
embattled with a measure of respect and understanding. This despite all the
madness and suffering inflicted by them. However misguided and wrong,
they ultimately remained his and they belonged to the United States of America that he would keep.

"His *Second Inaugural Address* says it all," wrote Medford and indeed it
does, as solemn and prayerful and generous and spiritual an inaugural as any
that has ever or will ever be penned. "Here is a man," she continued, "who
could have offered a scathing indictment of southern guilt for the war. Instead, he placed the blame on the entire nation, and argued for "malice
toward none" and "charity for all."

Beyond this, she also was impressed with his continued willingness to
alter course when warranted. Were he not a man of faith and courage, it is
unlikely that he would have been able to course-correct as he did. "He had
very definite ideas about what he wanted," Medford contends, "but was
willing to change direction if one plan did not work and he was pragmatic,
which is not a bad thing to be in the middle of a war."

Having begun with forgiveness, she added an unwillingness to vilify and then courage. Still to come were his practicality and pragmatism and now and finally, she wrapped it up with his rare ability to overcome personal and societal sensibilities in order to do the right thing. "It would have been easy for him to give in to the racial fears and prejudices of the age," she concluded, "but for the cause of Union, he pressed to end slavery."

She put me in mind of the recent demand for the removal of Confederate monuments, a contemporary vilification. At a glance, it was, to great degree, completely understandable and maybe even warranted. For sure, they did rise, in the first place, because zealots wanted to keep fighting the war in the only manner that remained open to them. In effect, the monuments rose up in celebration of a continued defiance during the brutal and vile Jim Crow era, when life for African Americans had barely improved. If at all, that is - and the sons and daughters of the Confederacy intended to keep it that way.

Still, one can debate to what degree they were playing either offense or defense.

The trap I have fallen into is in having come to know some of these Confederate Deities up-close and personal, which leads to the fledgling hope that some consideration be given to the depths of their individual stories and places in history. But the operative principle is that association with the Confederacy, in and of itself, demands condemnation and removal. Period. End of story and in a perfect world, that would indeed make sense, but there has never been a perfect world.

The overarching contention of those who would tear them all down suggests that they were all without souls. Sure, a Nathan Bedford Forrest and those like him who so violently hated deserve to be torn asunder (and so too, selected founding fathers, Andrew Jackson, Woodrow Wilson and others whose racism was red hot and furious), but there are a considerable number of Confederate leaders who, however misguided and flawed, were complicated men living in a most complicated time. Some of them were neither without souls nor even, dare I suggest, some 'fixed marks' of their own.

Having discovered with great interest, for instance, that General Thomas J. Stonewall Jackson's ancestors agree that memorials to him ought to be destroyed, I would respectfully ask if they know how fiercely he believed in the equality of all before God, or that he purchased 3 slaves, at their own request, to keep them from being sold into the horrific Deep South, or that he opened a school for slaves in violation of the law, or that his slaves were generally nothing more than his friends. Nothing extreme or inhumane was asked of them and they were free to engage in personal pursuits. His best friend in life, beyond his beloved wife, Anna, may well have been Jim Lewis, a slave and cook, who rode with him by choice and would gladly have taken the bullet for him as the dusk and darkness descended upon the Wilderness on that fateful May 3 1863 evening. Indeed, Jackson loved Jim Lewis, African American, one of the pall bearers at his funeral.

Trusting that what comes will be for the best, I will raise no protest but that doesn't mean that I won't mourn the loss of some monuments, here and there, that I may, once upon a time, have communed with. Thomas A. Stonewall Jackson's among them.

As ever, I guess that I just stand with Lincoln who forgave in the moment in 1865, Lincoln who would have nothing to do with running them down or arrests or trials or executions or further bloodshed. Yes, I stand with Lincoln who would not, as Edna Greene Medford reminds us, "vilify an enemy."

But then too, Lincoln couldn't possibly have foreseen the mountains of marble, bronze and stone that were to be devoted to honoring, memorializing and celebrating the Lost Cause, what in essence, became a celebration of those who fought to preserve slavery and a witness to the red-hot and searing bigotry of those who despicably and long called grown men, "Boy."

Of all the *fixed mark* responses received, *Richard Brookhiser's* was, far and away, the briefest. He wrote only, "Logic and sadness. The combination is not common."

Rather than support his statement, he just dropped it on me and allowed it to speak for itself, which naturally drove me to pause and dwell long and hard upon it. In its very brevity, lied the silent supposition that those who know Lincoln would understand; and with that supposition, the attendant measure of respect for the reader.

His fixed mark was "Logic and Sadness," what was to me, at first blush, a wholly unanticipated response.

I was fascinated by it, by the thought that Brookhiser's belonging to and great study of Abraham Lincoln was driven by these two forces: by the sadness that seemed to just ooze or drip from both the term and Lincoln himself, the sadness that often morphed into brooding melancholy, deep depression and the 'suicide watches' of his friends in New Salem and Springfield. And then by the logic or reason with which he engaged the all of his life's work. For of course, this was Lincoln. Sadness was his constant companion and so too the search for meaning and understanding and purpose that it drove. After all, there just had to be meaning and so the application of reason and logic, the tools via which to extract some sense out of it all.

His response to the early loss of his mother, his sister and his Anne Rutledge and the doubt, the mourning, the emptiness, the suffering and the darkness culminated to great degree for him, I believe, in an eventual denial of self or selflessness. The vagaries of life and chance and fate indeed wildly wielded its swift sword in his youth, seriously wounding but not breaking him. He would question the cosmos and life and he would begin his lifelong shadow-boxing match with an elusive but ever present God. He also would write his brooding poetry, which I just happen to like and despite what the critics say, I'll take it over the critically acclaimed *Love Song of J Alfred Prufrock* every time. Then in sadness, he turned to logic and reason, to a lifelong search for knowledge, to the attendant search for that which was immutable and true, to the search for that which was constant, from the Law to Euclidean Geometry and the preciseness of surveying, to the stuff that made sense, and so too, to that which he ought to aspire to do and be in the face of the all of it.

His ultimate response was to serve and to inevitably deny himself, to first, as he suggested in his initial campaign speech in New Salem on March 9, 1832, leave a mark of noble note on behalf of his fellow citizens and to later go so far as to "Restore the Union," to save "The Last Best Hope of Earth," to "Free the Slaves" and to dream of and strive to "Raise up all in the race of life."

There was a logic to all he did, to his efforts to apply science to politics, to his deferring to Lyman Trumbull in the 1855 U.S. Senate race, to his being everyone's second choice at the 1860 convention, to bringing all of his rivals into his cabinet, to pulling disparate and diverse people and factions together and to, so often, holding them together against a present will, to extending such incredible tolerance to Mary and to those who both thought and acted differently than he, to his tactical utilization of humor and story and to ever so much more.

I am here put in mind of our friends, David Hirsch and Dan Van Haften, who in their *Abraham Lincoln and the Structure of Reason* rather brilliantly argue that Lincoln's reckoning with reason went so far as to his applying geometric formula and proofs to the manner in which he structured and wrote some of the greatest speeches in the English tongue.

Yes, out of sadness and despair, he fashioned his life's mission, naturally honed the extraordinary humility, compassion, empathy and magnanimity that drove him and, certainly and most importantly, effected a leadership that left a legacy that is among the greatest in history.

And yes again, out of logic, the relentless pursuit of knowledge—the exceptional communicative skills—the precision and inspirational force of his writing—the making of politics, a science—his brilliance and his vision

The more I consider Brookhiser's *fixed mark,* the more taken I am by the way his mind works.

Todd Brewster responded clearly and affirmatively, "That's easy. It's his humility."

Brewster's *fixed mark*, in fact, gives life to my own, as there can be no magnanimity where there is no humility.

Given his ever humble Lincoln and Lincoln was as humble as anyone of the 45 who have had the privilege of holding the office of the presidency of the United States of America, Brewster noted that this didn't stop his enemies from viewing him as a tyrant, a self-aggrandizing and self-righteous tyrant. But what surprises Brewster are the encounters he still suffers with some who look upon Lincoln that way today.

Blind to his person, to his words and to his accomplishments, they look upon him as the author of our national ills. In all likelihood, it is my opinion that looking upon Lincoln with such disfavor can only be a byproduct of either latent, overt or deep seeded racism, given the fact that he freed the slaves, celebrated the performance of the more than 180,000 once slaves who fought for his Union, fought in the trenches to pass the 13th amendment and suggested that they be given the franchise in his *Last Public Address* in response to a serenade on April 11, 1865. Brewster further asserts:

> Call me naïve, but I am taken aback by this. Except for the occasional provoc-
> ative voice on the Right or the Left, I was used to the near unanimous popular
> opinion of Lincoln as a political, moral and even spiritual giant. But I find
> there to be a new boldness to such assertions, one that actually foreshadowed
> the shocking and divisive rhetoric of Donald Trump. These hecklers today
> mean to be more than provocative. They are reasserting the racial and political
> dividing lines that have gripped America in some of its darkest days.

Brewster again reiterated that Lincoln, despite the compassion and empathy that defined him, truly was a polarizing figure in his own time. That he won the Presidency alone led the southern states to secede; and he freely asserted that it was the "fire in the rear" that often proved to be even more vexing to him than the mighty armies of the Confederacy. The exacting bill to be paid for the neglect of dazed and troubled founding fathers, the well-intentioned authors of the band-aide compromises of 1820 and 1850 and some 80 plus years of vacillation had already been forwarded to the house on the corner of 8th and Jackson in Springfield, Illinois before Lincoln even boarded the train for Washington.

The cost of the reckoning on slavery shocked everyone as the conflagra-tion, the horror and the madness, the 630,000 souls lost and their widows and their orphans were all wholly unanticipated and shocking.

There at the center of it all stood Lincoln and his tortured soul. Brewster concluded with this impassioned observation.

> I am puzzled that someone who so carefully took the measure of each side in
> every decision he made, who expressed himself so often, and so genuinely, in
> a self-deprecating way (or what was a humble way), whose respect for the rule
> of law and for the moral standing of the nation often overrode his personal
> wishes, and who repeatedly spoke to being humbled by God (to the degree he
> believed in God) and to the difficulty, the impossibility, of any man to com-
> pute God's purpose, that this man could ever be seen as using instruments of
> violence to impose his mortal will on others.

We have often heard it said that "To be great is to be misunderstood" and as a teacher of history, I have often encountered the very disconnect to which Brewster refers, a dissonance and, in all honesty, an ignorance that startles. It startles not because an individual has been misinformed or is in need of being educated on some matter, but rather because it comes with this accusatory air of authority and the nigh on palpable maliciousness to which Brewster refers. At first blush, it seems aimed at severing us from our goodness and our belonging to our so very diverse brothers and sisters, but also, I fear, to severing us from our national soul, from those advances in our past that rendered being an American something special.

Sadly, this is darkly manifested and celebrated, and dangerously so in the Trump era.

Lincoln was great and he need not be misunderstood for his life was a straight arrow and he was indeed humble to a fault.

So when Brewster hears a misguided student suggest that "Abraham Lincoln oversaw the greatest mass execution of Native Americans in our history" or "Lincoln was definitely a racist" or "Freeing the slaves was nothing more than a political calculation" or—and indeed I tremble in even writing this—that Donald Trump (forgive me) is a greater President than Lincoln or Washington," it is then when I realize anew that great attention, relentless attention, must be paid to our "Getting Right with Lincoln" now.

Rabbi Jonathan Sarna's fixed mark, like Brewster's and mine, was referenced by him and him alone, the old shibboleth that Lincoln was indeed *"the same on the inside as the outside."* No hypocrisy. No prevarication. No deception. No phony. He came as advertised and with him, what you saw was just what you got.

He was as close to flagging the "Honest Abe" mantra as his 'fixed mark' as one could be and yet he looks to the proof of that quality rather than the quality itself. For the devil is in the detail and in the deep recesses and in the dark corners and in the private moments. Now typically, the devil is unmasked by the historians and the historical auditors who dive down deep with their magnifying glasses in tow to dig up the darker 'factoids' in a life that diminish. But there was no devilish 'there—there' with Lincoln, who always comes out true. In fact, the deeper one dives into him, the greater the clarity.

Honest and true with the public, with the people he personally touched and with himself, he was right with all.

Sarna points out that *"The ancient rabbis especially praised those who were the same on the inside as on the outside"* and that his having read the private letters of Lincoln, in fact, verified the fact that the one squeezing the pen and committing words to paper was, in fact, the same as the one standing on the stump or facing the crowd or fashioning policy.

"You shall cover the wood with pure gold from the inside and from the outside*" (*Exodus 25:11), that is the wood that would comprise the Holy Ark of the Covenant where the sacred tablets of the Ten Commandments were to be housed. Nothing could be clearer as even the Ark itself is the same on the inside as on the outside.

I also was surprised to learn that the Hebrew word for face (the outside) is *"paneem"* which is so very nearly identical to the Hebrew word for interior (the inside) which is *"pineem."* There, this perfect marriage of inside and outside and the balance and symmetry in both the physical and spiritual realms. As such, both Hebrew scripture and language strongly suggest, as does Rabbi Sarna, that the face we present must be a reflection of what lies hidden within.

Ahh, the eyes and the mind of the artist.

When I first read *Wendy Allen's fixed mark* response, my mind inexplicably turned to a never to be forgotten scene in Thornton Wilder's haunting classic, *Our Town*, the one where Emily Webb so movingly confronts the fact that we human beings fail to appreciate the wonder that is locked inside each and every moment, the "Goodbye to clocks ticking and Mama's sunflowers—Oh earth you're far too beautiful" moment. The moment she asks the Stage Manager if anyone ever fully realizes the wonder of life as they live it and he responds, "No. Saints and poets maybe, they do some."

Lacking any direct correlation, my mind drifted a bit on the wings of those 'Saints and Poets' for there by the side of the poets are the artists who see and appreciate what most of us miss. Our eyes may be open, but we do not see. Simply put, I surround myself with images and paintings of Lincoln whose face has ever inspired and yet I miss, oh so clearly miss, what Wendy sees.

Oh yes, the artist's eyes, the artist's soul. Wendy explained:

> Lincoln had a beautiful face. I love the daguerreotypes of him, especially the impeccably reproduced prints that show every fractal flaw (what I learned were, in effect, recurring and often random and chaotic geometric patterns). The old portraits of Lincoln—the ones we admire today—are modest and rarely glamorized. Even in his most authoritative poses, he wears only a long black coat, a simple white shirt, and a twisted, uneven tie. On a good day, he might have combed his hair.
>
> Signature shadows define him. The length of the shadow under his nose betrays its substantial size. The dark sockets of his eyes sink beneath strong brows. Lines are carved into his forehead. Unusually high cheekbones cast downward slashes that accentuate his sunken face. The creases between his eyebrows are so deep, so permanent, one would swear he had been born with them. And then, there is his glorious mouth. There is barely an upper lip, except for the royal 'M' shape in the center. And his crazy bottom lip dips and sways, as if its designer did not have a chance to finish it.

The men and women who painted, sculpted, and photographed Lincoln during his lifetime would have known him personally. They would have spent time with him. Each would have been affected by his presence. Some would have liked him, and some perhaps not. All must have worked self-consciously, knowing that Lincoln himself would be evaluating the results.

I have no such encumbrances or distractions. I can love Lincoln from a distance. I can paint him as I would a landscape, without fear of his reaction. I cherish that freedom.

"Lincoln's face is universally familiar. He is instantly recognizable, even from just a sliver of his brow. And yet, there is still so much to interpret and discover. That is why I assign numbers to my paintings instead of naming them. I want viewers to interpret and discover Lincoln—to feel him—on their own terms, without further suggestion or interference from me. My hope is that, by transforming the black-and-white and sepia images of the past, I can keep Lincoln within our grasp. I want people to see him as a modern figure, still powerful and relevant and with much to teach us.

I am lifted up by Wendy Allen, by her sight and insight, her desire to keep Lincoln within our grasp, her determination to sustain his power and his relevance and by her 'to paint is to teach' artistic philosophy.

Rich Thompson, who like Wendy Allen, brings Lincoln alive for us through his unique and compelling art, wrote "A lot is written about Lincoln and his honesty which I truly appreciate, yet for me, Lincoln was the very personification of perseverance," rendering it alone his *fixed mark*.

For Lincoln was tenacious and he mightily persevered and he was absolutely committed and he did what he certainly believed to be the right thing to do. Commitment is always born out of the belief that a cause is just and true, out of what can only be moral imperatives, out of righteousness, honor and goodness. It is always the justice of the cause that gives way to the commitment that then gives way to the perseverance and tenacity needed to sustain and fulfill.

Against all odds, he would save the Union and give voice to the sacred dictum that everyone, everywhere ought to be free.

For embattled he would be and not just with the Confederate armies and their leaders in Richmond, but also with Radical Republicans and Congressmen and Senators across town and with members of his own Cabinet and with newspaper editors and political power brokers and spies and traitors and draft resisters in his rear and with Peace Democrats and with those nagging racist sentiments and nativist philosophies and foreign powers that considered taking advantage of the trouble afoot.

Lincoln rather bound his country to the spirit of sacred and untested ideals, one of which was that slavery was pure evil. "That he was able to pull the country together against all odds fascinates me always," wrote Thompson. "No matter the opposition, no matter the nature of the seemingly impossible challenges, he kept going forward with a constant perseverance and faith that those untested ideals would prevail."

While I here argued that commitment is born of righteousness, goodness and honor – of moral imperatives, I must throw out the disclaimer that it also can be born of selfishness, evil, greed and the dark supposition that one is superior to another, without which there would never have been a Civil War and without which all of human history would have been so very different.

It is what distorts and clouds our vision and our path even today.

Steve Koppelman focused upon the "Gentle firmness of Lincoln's will" which was buttressed by his political genius.

Koppelman wrote, "The political Lincoln to me has always been the most fascinating. I don't think the average person realized what a skilled and gifted politician Lincoln was. The fact that the United States stayed together as the indivisible entity that it is, becoming the greatest and most powerful country in the world, allowing us to achieve greatness domestically and in two world wars, is directly due to his vision, strength of character, and ultimately his political acumen."

Saving the nation and assuring that it live was, as Lincoln himself so movingly suggested, what he also saw as the pathway to saving the rest of the world, by demonstrating that "representative government could prevail and grow in prosperity as no nation before it had ever done."

Asserting this, Koppelman added, "He knew then, as I believe today, that this country truly is the '*Last best hope of earth.*' The depiction that I have always had, and what I believe shows greatness in a political leader (and is much needed today) is what Ulysses S. Grant once said about him: "It was that gentle firmness in carrying out his own will, without apparent force or friction that formed the basis of his character."

There is no question about this, as it was Lincoln's "gentle firmness" that brought and kept disparate political factions together to sustain the war effort and to keep the Union and to end the abomination of slavery. It took that same "gentle firmness" to keep the disparate members of his great cabinet together.

My *fixed mark,* suggested *George Buss*, Gettysburg's own Lincoln today is "personal and it came to me when I heard Senator Paul Simon say, 'It is every American's duty to get right with Lincoln.' Impersonating him was one thing, but Simon made me realize that I had a corresponding duty to get him right, to know him intimately and to perfect my presentation and representation of him."

Buss began by doing a Lincoln-Douglas debate gig with a friend. He had the height and the hair and the interest and he just kind of stumbled into it with limited knowledge and understanding. "*Then Paul Simon (*United States Senator-Illinois*)* woke me up," said Buss, "and I realized that I needed to grow into Lincoln. Requests to do Lincoln in family settings, in war settings and requests to do his great speeches were coming in and it was one thing to utter his words, but quite another to be him."

So he went to work and he began by attending the Painter Lectures in Springfield and then, while working on a C-Span Lincoln-Douglas project, he had the good fortune to meet Harold Holzer who invited him to attend the Lincoln Forum. "I have been to them all," said Buss, "and I have made it a point to read and reread every Lincoln book that has been published in the last 30 years. I have them all and almost all are inscribed by the authors."

To be an acclaimed impersonator requires knowing much more than the words. The voice has to be right and so too the pace, the gait, the inflection, the mindset, the mood, Where he was, what he was and how he was in the moment all matter. "So yes," Buss concluded, "I have gotten right with Lincoln and I work constantly on my mission to perfect my representation of this greatest of men. I am blessed and honored to be doing so."

I have such great respect for each and every one of my collaborators and *Matthew Lakemacher* is one of the gems. To say that he is wildly enthusiastic about the study and teaching of history is an understatement. For he is truly on fire for it.

On fire for the conscience of our history, the morality of our history.

"The "fixed mark" for me, the quality that I find most important and instructive about Abraham Lincoln is something that is shunned by most politicians today and that is the ability to change," he wrote. "What today we call flip-flopping and what the media or partisan pundits are quick to label as wishy-washy or politically expedient, I think Lincoln understood to be honest and mature. I am drawn to Lincoln the skeptic and Lincoln the scoffer because I've been there in my own spiritual journey. Sometimes doubt is the only intellectually honest position one can take and there is no genuine faith to be had without it."

Not for nothing but I argued the same thing earlier, i.e. my Father James Carroll's, "It is only in the doubting that I find my belief." I believe that Lincoln, in his own shadow-boxing with life and with God and with the great issues that plagued his time, lived right in the heart of this vortex, always somewhere between the darkness and the dawn. Matt continued:

> So I am there with Lincoln in the late 1830s when he openly ridiculed the Christian faith and perhaps wrote a little book on infidelity. I'm there with him in 1846 when he had to publicly answer questions about his religious beliefs and lack of church membership as a qualification for Congress. But Lincoln changed. Lincoln matured. I'm also there with him when he wrote his *Meditations on the Divine Will* in 1862. I'm there with him when he wrote arguably the greatest sermon of the nineteenth century in his *Second Inaugural Address* and became one of the greatest theologians in United States History, alongside Jonathan Edwards and Reinhold Niebuhr.

I too am there with Matt and his bearing witness to this 'greatest of sermons,' what was a most remarkable testament of faith. In God and in Divine Providence, to be sure, but even more so in his country, his time and, above all, in us.

> Lincoln also changed with regards to his views on race. Although it's been fashionable for some (I'm looking at you Lerone Bennett and Thomas Di Lorenzo) to immediately label Lincoln a racist from the perspective of contemporary politics and for others to simply excuse some of his earlier statements (such as those in his debates with Stephen A. Douglas) as just being the political maneuvering of a deft politician, my study of Abraham Lincoln has led me to conclude that neither view is correct.
> He was a product of his place and time, growing up in a slave state and being part of the white diaspora that migrated into southern Ohio, Indiana, and Illinois to get away from the slaves as much as the slavery. He was no abolitionist but in the end, he wrote the Emancipation Proclamation and laid the groundwork for the 13th Amendment. For most of his adult life, he probably did not believe in the equality of the races (few abolitionists did for that matter), but he invited Frederick Douglass to be an honored guest at the White House (entering through the front door!) and in the final speech of his life, he became the first president to suggest giving some black males the right to vote. John Wilkes Booth was in the crowd for that speech and the rest is history.

To his conclusion, I would but add that it also was Douglass who he took such delight in seeing at the reception at the White House following his Second Inauguration. *"Here comes my friend, Douglass"*! He was most interested in Douglass' reaction to his Address and, of course, when he got to him and asked the question, Douglass replied, *"It was a sacred effort. Mr. President."*

In but a few meetings, they had grown close and they knew the heart of each other which is why Douglass, upon initially being stopped by guards at the door of the White House that evening and told that none of his kind could enter, retorted, *"No such order could have emanated from President Lincoln."* Douglass pressed, got word to Lincoln and, of course, Lincoln quickly intervened. Speaking in his hometown of Rochester at City Hall in the wake of the news of Lincoln's death, Douglass suggested there was consolation in that white and black shared a grief that rendered them "more than countrymen but kin." (Kendrick, *Lincoln and Douglass' Last Encounter*).

As to her *fixed mark, Karen Hawbecker* fires off 5 of them in her first sentence and soon ventures off into a spiritual reflection that points to a sixth that may be the most important of all to her. And so, equanimity it is.

> My study of Lincoln is motivated by the myriad stories that illustrate the astounding nature of his forbearance, his abiding compassion for others, his incisive sense of humor, and his overarching complexity, but his ability to

choose not to take offense and to forgive others astounds me. I think of Stanton's early treatment of him and of McClellan's insulting behavior toward him. His equanimity in the face of that type of treatment is part of what draws me to him. His abilities and capacities seemed to have been broader, deeper, and more insightful. And I think that's an understatement as I write it. He seemed truly to have been someone who was born to fulfill a significant role and emphatically did so.

I am a member of the Church of Jesus Christ of Latter-day Saints and among my religious beliefs is one in a pre-existence—that is, that we all existed in spirit before we came to experience life on earth in mortal bodies. In that premortal life, I believe we prepare to play certain roles and to fulfill certain responsibilities on earth. We therefore come to earth with what I look upon as 'software loaded,' packaged with talents, strengths, and pre-dispositions that we can use to bless the lives of others here on earth and to carry out particular purposes.

Based on that religious construct, I feel quite certain that Abraham Lincoln must have agreed to play the significant role he did in saving the Union and being instrumental in bringing slavery to an end in this country and that he came to earth with great capacities to fulfill that role. Lincoln made statements during his life that show he believed he had a purpose to fulfill and fretted that he would not leave his mark as he must. It was that belief that fueled his ambition and pushed him toward his destiny. It is partly because of my belief that he fulfilled a significant responsibility that he agreed to before this life that I hold him in such high regard and that fuels my abiding interest in him.

As for me, while my faith and belief construct are different, I agree with Hawbecker in that we are all wired, albeit differently, to prospectively do great good on earth. We are all challenged to ascend and as Lincoln would have us do – to be of good and of grace on this earth. Some accept the challenge and a few, like Lincoln, sacrifice all and go above and beyond to make their forever difference.

But sadly, far too many simply do not. Their eyes never fully open. The spirit never fully awakes. Victims of ego, selfishness and indifference, they fail to embrace the fullness of life.

Karen's Lincoln was the polar opposite of this, for he knew nothing, nothing whatsoever of ego, selfishness or indifference and the gifts God gave him were paid forward every single day of his life.

However troubled, difficult and dark, abundant and blessed were his days.

Paula Hopewell focuses upon two *fixed marks, kindness and compassion* in a clear and short witness to the life Lincoln lived. She wrote:

> He knew suffering from an early age, his own and that of others. As he grew up, he suffered the losses of a baby brother and, tragically, his mother, whom he helped to bury. He was not yet 21 when his only sister, Sarah and her baby died in childbirth."

Though he was not a religious man per se, he studied the Bible and used its lessons and language, in his life and in his writing.

He grew up on the frontier, in the border regions of Kentucky and southern Indiana. He was heavily influenced by Kentuckians throughout his life, some of whom came from slaveholding families. These include his wife, Mary Ann Todd and his best friend, Joshua Speed.

He developed an ability to work with people of diverse backgrounds and opinions.

When he was a boy, he shot a wild turkey and the story goes that he was so upset by the experience that he refused to hunt large game again.

He was gentle. Two of my favorite examples of this are his condolence letter to Fanny McCullough and the letter he wrote to Grace Bedell, the little girl from New York who convinced him to grow a beard.

He was a loving, indulgent father to his sons. He, along with Mary, was absolutely grief stricken when their darling child, Willie, died in the White House in 1862. (And Eddie before him).

I love Lincoln's *Second Inaugural Address*, and I am unfailingly moved by its language and sentiment. I have dubbed this speech our *'national prayer of reconciliation.'*

Lincoln's emotional depth is reflected in the last portraits of him, taken early in 1865. I am struck by those eyes, by the resignation and surrender, by the toll the War took on him, the personal responsibility he felt and the struggle he endured.

In relating her response exactly as it was presented to me, there is a snapshot of key components of his life that she obliquely relates, leaving it to you to tie the same into her celebration of his kindness and compassion. Suffice it to say, these two qualities, both intrinsically and extrinsically, reverberate in the same and, without doubt, in every nook and cranny or crevice of Lincoln's life's service.

Anne Moseley jumps right on the *"perseverance"* bandwagon, but not before first discussing the amount of study that the life and legacy of Lincoln demands and that it is, in fact, the study of his character that interests her the most, in that he remains one of our most exceptional role models.

She noted that her once museum last highlighted certain core character traits of Lincoln or what were Honesty, Empathy, Intellect, Perseverance, Leadership, and Vision, while also explaining that these were but some of the vast character traits and that they would showcase from year to year.

We, like Moseley's Museum, are here examining Lincoln and reflecting upon his legacy through the portal of character and Anne gets down to the nitty gritty in stating "I believe that my favorite character trait of Lincoln's is perseverance."

Lincoln, she suggested, demonstrated how great was his perseverance as early as 1833, when the Sangamon County surveyor offered Lincoln a position as Deputy Surveyor, a job that he was utterly unprepared to do. But rather than refuse, he would read whatever he could get his hands on about it and go to work. She quoted William O. Stoddard:

> *That was enough for the man of iron perseverance. He took the book on surveying and went out into the country to board with [schoolmaster] Mentor Graham. In six weeks he was ready to report to Mr. Calhoun for service. They had been weeks of precisely such unflinching mental toil as he had for so long a time trained himself to endure.*

As president while others lost faith, Lincoln stayed the course, persevering through much criticism about his leadership. Robert Wilson, a friend and political ally of Lincoln's, appropriately and pointedly noted that *"He realized that the labor of administering the affairs of the Nation would be arduous, and severe, and that he had made up his mind, that he could, and would do it."*

Throughout the Civil War, Lincoln stayed the course, refusing to abandon his principles or take the easier route. In 1862, he wrote to his secretary of state, William Seward, *"I expect to maintain this contest until successful, or till I die, or am conquered, or my term expires, or Congress or the country forsakes me."*

What Lincoln faced might have discouraged a lesser person, but with steely resolve, he stayed the course.

As to his perseverance, the fact is that Lincoln simply didn't quit on anything or anybody. Most of us do because life beats us back and we come to believe that we just can't win them all. We pick our spots and do the best we can. But he didn't give up and he, in fact, demonstrated this quality long before 1833, given his insatiable appetite to learn and to get his hands on yet another book to read. That's what he did – that's how he was wired - he read more, studied harder, prepared more diligently and positioned himself to do whatever life demanded. Thank you, Anne.

Bob Willard wrote, "The total package, I guess, is the complete answer, but to zero in on just one quality, it must be his sense of self. He was humble while at the same time undoubtedly aware of his major gifts that would be a source of so much pride in other folks. He also had a sense of responsibility in using these gifts, i.e. in wanting to do something worthwhile that would allow him to be remembered."

Short and sweet and there you have Willard's *fixed mark*. He knew himself, he knew his worth and he would give it away in sacrifice to save a nation, end more than 300 years of bondage for oh so many and leave a legacy that would change the world.

Indeed, a legacy that would change you and me, those I love and all Americans and prospective Americans, which is, after all, why we write, almost desperately longing to pay Lincoln forward because it simply matters so damn much.

"And this above all to thy own self be true," said Polonius. We know that Lincoln read those words and that he was certainly true to them. Polonius may not have been worthy of such words but Lincoln was.

Darla Moe of California, again like so many, points to any number of *fixed marks* but his spirituality and *"firmness for the right"* appear to be at the top of her list, even though she writes of his wisdom, thoughtfulness, intelligence and sensibility first.

She interestingly refers to the latter as a comfort to the student of history.

The more we read about his actions and decisions, the more we marvel at his ability to wade through complex problems and come to resolutions that may not have been perfect, but were certainly effective and that enabled him to keep moving forward and always towards that greater goal of a unified and resolute nation, free from the curse of slavery.

The salient point is that unlike today when the latest news story dictates what direction the president might move in that day, devoid of either Lincoln's sensibility or thoughtfulness or reason, Lincoln's *"firmness for the right"* is a revelation and a hope that the day will again come when genuine principle drives the public agenda and discourse. As to this, she readily admits to suffering from a "Father Abraham" syndrome.

As to the question of spirituality, she wrote:

"For all of the discussion about President Lincoln either not belonging to a religion or not believing in God at all, I, to the contrary, rather think that we have never had a president who was more grounded in the belief that a power beyond our own was guiding us and would continue to do so. I find an overarching sense of spirituality in nearly everything the man wrote or spoke about in public or in private that is known to us."

A man of faith myself, who but refers to himself as a student of history and not a scholar either, it has long been my feeling that Lincoln was wrapped in grace and that grace literally poured out of him. I look at that face, at the paintings of Wendy Allen and Rich Thompson, at the photographs of Dave Wiegers, at the *Night Walker* who stands before the West Virginia Statehouse or at the wise and gentle soul who sits upon the throne in his Memorial, at the many images of him upon my walls and I see the great grace of God, a grace that is still palpable to me.

The simple truth is that God never had a more faithful servant. And like Darla, I find it in his words, as no other president so mastered the fervent use of scripture.

It is faith that enables one to believe in that which is better to come. Lincoln believed and dreamed because he had faith in our capacity – in "we the people" to do God's work - which as President Kennedy observed, *"must truly be our own."*

And so we pray that we, as a nation, may once again go towards the light, the light that Lincoln so faithfully extended to us even now. For we must cast off the madness and vileness of a leader, who in the face of a grave crisis born of racist cops who so wantonly and freely executed George Floyd in plain view of all for the sin of being black, threw fire on the flames in relying upon the ancient whims and words of a callous segregationist, "When the looting begins, the shooting begins." Dear God, save us all from Donald Trump.

For *Dave Walker*, the *fixed mark* is his *drive*. "It really started when reading about Lincoln's early life, especially the years of losing a mother and only sister and gaining a step-mother, as well as his New Salem days," wrote Walker. "Lincoln was driven even then and I love that quality about him." *Yes, driven to get his hand on another book, to keep reading, to keep gaining knowledge, to ascend towards a better life, to be of help to neighbors and friends and to make a mark for himself in this world.*

Walker observes that he so appreciates Lincoln's drive because he has been wired the same way. "Lincoln came from nothing," he continued, "and each situation confronted in his life prepared him to be better—to be a better lawyer, a better representative, a better father, a better man and eventually, a better President. He never took offense and although he lacked a proper education, he became self-taught. That took that thing called drive. Starting with those Blab Schools and on to Mentor Graham in New Salem, he was always diligent in his studies and in my opinion, those six years in New Salem were his College education."

One might add that the all of this took a modicum of courage as well. Courage and diligence are, in fact, the alter egos of drive. If you want it, you damn well have to work for it and as to this, our Lincoln was all in, the poster child and inspiration for motivational speakers for all time. It is a confounding marvel just to think that he could quote the Bible, chapter and verse or that he could refer to any line in a Shakespearean tragedy or that he could pluck a line out of any Robert Burns poem or for that matter, any of the Romantics. Or to imagine that he had 'drive' enough to master Euclidean Geometry on his own.

"He made mistakes," continued Walker, "but he learned from them and never made the same mistake twice. A driven man, he set goals, he set out to achieve them and he never looked back. When he left the prairie and the farm, he left them forever."

For *David Sullivan* whose responses appear to be framed in a spiritual context, the fixed mark is '*a goodness that gives way to good works*,' moral efforts—to an active compassion, an empathy and a faith that ultimately enlightens and ascends.

"As a boy, I had two heroes in my life, my Father and Hopalong Cassidy," he wrote. "My father told me to 'Live in the present moment and follow your passion' and to never stop learning, and not for knowledge alone, but for the enjoyment of realizing the magnitude of life. Most of all, my father was a man of high moral principles who possessed an inherent compassion towards others."

He does not overtly tie his Dad to Lincoln. He sees no need to do so, as the connection is so very clear. *Res Ipse Loquitor*, the thing speaks for itself. I love his Dad. How can you not love his Dad and, not for nothing, but I too must admit that I am old enough to have enjoyed and appreciated 'Good-old Hopalong Cassidy' as well.

"Abraham Lincoln also was a man of high moral principle who possessed an inherent compassion towards others. When asked about his religion he said, *"When I do good, I feel good, when I do bad, I feel bad, and that's my religion.* Everything I have read up to this point in my quest to learn more about Abraham Lincoln comes back to this simple but profound quote."

He continued, "Whether it was pardoning a soldier from the death penalty for falling asleep at his post or pardoning hundreds of convicted Dakota Indians about to experience the same fate, or visiting hundreds if not thousands of both Union and Confederate soldiers in hospitals throughout the Civil War, Abraham Lincoln practiced what he preached. His compassion towards others and his good works drove and defined him. Ever moved by Lincoln's acts of mercy, the line that always loudly resonates with me is, '*If the Almighty gives a man a cowardly pair of legs, how can he help their running away with him.*'"

Schuyler Colfax, the then Speaker of the House in his *Reminiscences of Abraham Lincoln by Distinguished Men of His Time* (p 342–343) related the incident of an Old Man's appeal to Lincoln upon behalf of his son who was to be shot by a firing squad upon orders of General Butler. The same Butler who had only the day before sent a telegram to the President begging him not to interfere anymore with cases of military justice, accusing him of destroying all military discipline.

At first hesitating, Lincoln was reported to have exclaimed, *"By jingo, Butler or no Butler, Here goes"*! Scribbling a quick note to him, he showed it to Old Man. It read, *"Job Smith is not to be shot until further orders from me"* and signed Abraham Lincoln. Disappointed that it was not a pardon, the tearstained father expressed his misgivings only to hear a smiling Lincoln say, *"Well my old friend, I see you are not very well acquainted with me. If your son never looks on death till further orders come from me to shoot him, he will live to be a great deal older than Methuselah."*

And then, there is his *"When you have got an elephant by the hind legs and he is trying to run away, it is best to let him run."* There had been too much blood and Lincoln wanted no more. He wanted nothing of vengeance or punishment or judiciary proceedings or vindictiveness. He wanted to live what he had already preached in his Second Inaugural. *"With charity for all, with malice toward none,"* he would bind up the nation's wounds indeed.

The Sullivan *fixed marks* of goodness, morality, kindness and faith fashioned the compassion and empathy that so defined Lincoln, who would, in that spirit, go forward to breathe new life into a nation now truly dedicated to the old proposition that "All men are created equal" and that government must look to afford opportunity for all.

David Wiegers relates but one trait or characteristic only and a universal one at that. Interestingly, not the adverb or the adjective, but rather the subject itself, Humanity. That word and the blank canvass of the artist.

And while it takes reading between Dave's few lines and it is never directly asserted, what I drew from his thoughts is that we Americans look to find ourselves or to see ourselves in Lincoln and if that is not possible, to at least extract pieces of him for ourselves. Just as the painter or the sculptor "takes his blank canvas or his lump of clay to shape Lincoln in his or her image, we all do much the same," he suggests. In doing this, even in thinking or imagining or wondering about this, we also mysteriously shape and define ourselves.

Of Lincoln, of America, of you and me.

In his first line, Wiegers self-deprecatingly alludes to his own life's frustration and suggests "I am not particularly artistic." Having seen his work as a photographer, let me just offer a Dickensian retort of "balderdash, poppycock and humbug" and move on, for an artist, he is.

"There is something about Lincoln's face that draws me to it," he explains. "I appreciate how each artist who attempts to give us their Lincoln brings so very much of himself or herself to the task. Each sees Lincoln differently even though they are using the same source materials, the same life masks and the same photographs. So I view Lincoln, like they do, as a blank canvas, via which his humanity invites us in."

Extract what we will, the point is that there is no end to the good and the rich bounty that is there to be extracted from Lincoln in the first place.

Somewhat understandably, *Joan Chaconas* of the Surratt House Museum in Maryland, is drawn to his murder, the murder of an extraordinary and so very good man and she refers to the same, to his death and the nation's great loss as her *fixed mark*. While obviously neither a value nor a characteristic, she rather looks upon loss as just that.

A despair and tragedy that remarkably, Joan insists, remains palpable and not just to her, but to all who revere the promise of America.

"I cannot go to Ford's Theatre without being moved and taken by what happened there," she wrote. "It still brings tears to my eyes. Can you imagine that? Still, as odd as that may sound. Still! I live with the great man who was gone too soon, with the kind and gentle man who was broken by the loss of

Eddie and Willie and his wife's inability to cope and by the chaos at Ford's Theatre on that tragic, 1865 Good Friday."

The night that John Wilkes Booth called his band of conspirators into action, it was only Lewis Powell who attempted to fulfill his charge along with the leader of their band. As Powell wildly and madly attacked everyone in Secretary of State Seward's household, David Herold who was holding the horses outside the Seward House on Lafayette Square, bolted. As for the blundering, George Atzerodt, he never got beyond the bar at the Kirkwood House where he was to take out the Vice President. John Surratt was long gone and on his way to Canada where Holy Mother the Church would give him sanctuary and Mary Surratt, certainly never proven guilty, would take the extra hit for the perpetrators of the vengeance.

One that we have never quite reconciled ourselves to, leaving loss, Lincoln's loss and that of other martyrs, at the heart of the American Experience.

In a brief statement, *Mel Maurer* of the Cleveland Civil War Roundtable wrote, "My *fixed mark* is character itself. He remained true to himself and his principles, despite facing the kind of challenges that would have made most bend to the will of others. And he faced rather extraordinary challenges, the kind that are known to only few in history. So, I think of him, as many do when trying to make decisions of my own: "What would Lincoln do, I ask"?

Mike Movius of the Puget Sound Civil War Roundtable, like Maurer above, suggests another telling and 'one of a kind' *fixed mark* . One word only and with both thanks and apologies to the *Lord of the Rings* , it is "one word to rule them all" or to comprise them all. He wrote, "I am drawn to his complexity."

"Certainly the image of the self-made man is attractive," he continued, "but I am taken by his ability to be both the one who keeps them laughing while also the one who is the most thoughtful or the one who goes deepest. While dealing with a trying marriage and great loss, he maintained the single-mindedness to save the Union and to liberate a people who had been in bondage for some 300 years."

He noted that Lincoln also was self-deprecating and filled with doubt, yet ever confident of his abilities and sure of his goals. The consummate politician, he was honest to a fault yet wise enough to rely upon the ever shifting tides of public opinion.

In short, what you saw was what you got, but beneath it all, there was an infinite array of moving parts, and among them, some that were in conflict with each other or shall we say --- complex.

For *Rebecca Morris*, the *fixed mark* was his resolve. Like Movius' complexity, her response is brief, pointed and sure.

"I appreciate his resolve in the face of all the difficulties he had to deal with," she wrote, "Generals who wouldn't fight, a cabinet that often disagreed with his vision, a tragic family life. A lesser man would have buckled after four plus years of carnage and defeat but his resolve never wavered. Whatever it took to bring the Union back together was all that mattered to him and setbacks were simply obstacles to be overcome and never a reason to give up."

Oh yes, loss was Lincoln's steady companion. There was his Mom and Sarah and Anne Rutledge and her love. There was Eddie and Willie and Colonel Edward Baker, his son's namesake and United States Senator, who died in one of war's earliest engagements at Ball's Bluff. There was his first race for the Legislature and the 1856 and 1858 failures to reach the United States Senate and his Sangamon River never got dredged and his "Spot Resolutions" attacking President Polk and his War with Mexico resulted only in the loss of the support and the affection of those he served. He may have won more court cases than he lost, but loss and the Circuit he rode were constant companions and there were the debacles of first and second Bull Run and the Peninsula Campaign and its Seven Days and the Wilderness and Fredericksburg and dozens more. There was the loss of peace, of sleep, of joy, of lingering innocence and of what remained of youth and vigor. There was the loss of the 630,000 dead whom he carried upon his shoulders and the loss of any harmony in his home-life and ever so much more.

In the arms of all of the above, Rebecca, along with all of our other *'trumpeteers'* of perseverance and tenacity, would have us remember that he never quit, never stopped advancing, never stopped learning, never lost hope or faith, never stopped planning, executing and searching for the right Generals, never stopped fighting, thinking, writing, meeting, giving, the all of which today poignantly reminds us of both who we were and who we are and, above all, of what we ought to be.

Christopher Oakley was first taken by the fact that Lincoln was "deeply human, down to earth and open to all." He was approachable, touchable and he led with his heart. The mind would catch up, but the heart would lead. He then, in a pointed flurry, added humor, humility, wisdom and forgiveness.

"Where to begin? For me, Lincoln was a deeply human man who in many ways was well ahead of his time," he wrote. "*It was almost as if he was sent from the future to ensure that mankind progressed.* He was not without faults. He was not the saint that many want him to be, but he always seemed to be several steps ahead of everyone else and never lost sight of the grander picture. He had an intuition about the American people that few have ever possessed.

Honing in on Oakley's suggestion that Lincoln was "*several steps ahead*" or that he had "*an intuition about the American people*" or that he felt "*a calling to do all that he could*" is revealing, for these three capacities were providential and aspirational and of the sort that one might hope would be emulated in all presidencies. Sadly, they are nowhere in the equation today.

Forgive me, but Oakley touched that always raw nerve.

Dwelling upon his reflection that "It was almost as if Lincoln was sent from the future to ensure that mankind progressed," *I wonder, as I write, if he might not also be sent from the past in order to do the same for us today.*

That after all is our theme, our playbook, our hope.

Michaela Wieties looked to the *fixed marks* of 'strength' and 'compassion.'

"Firm in what he believed but compassionate in his actions," she wrote, "He led the charge to keep a nation together in a battle of brother against brother and laid the groundwork for a new nation to emerge on the other side of a colossal civil war with much work still to do, but also with the ability and determination to do it. His words, even now, fill hearts with hope.

A so very human, vulnerable, spiritual and touchable Lincoln, the icon who comes down from his pedestal and into the trenches with us.

"For me," she continued, "his humanity is borne out in his treatment of his soldiers both during and after the war. He understood the fear and uncertainty the soldiers felt about the imminent battles and he lived with pangs of guilt and remorse. He was compassionate and generous with his pardons, despite the fact that many of his advisors were not happy and did not agree with his actions. They felt it was a sign of weakness, while to him, it was rather about the inherent value of the lives of each and every one of the American people."

A boy who disappointed his father because he could not shoot a wild animal, a boy who would nurse wounded creatures back to health, his reverence for life and his compassion and empathy were part of the package that defined him, long before he boarded that train for Washington in 1861.

The art of brevity was a tool for a good number of our collaborators, as a brief sentence or the power of a single sentence or even one word often sufficed.

Lincoln was a self-made man," wrote *Dennis Perreault.* "Born into poverty, but blessed with an excellent, inquisitive mind; a gift for writing clearly, concisely, and accurately; an understanding of the great issues of his time; and the willingness to alter his position as he encountered new information and new experiences."

Billy Grandstaff – One word only, E*mpathy*. We know exactly what he means and we can all take it from there.

Eileen Patch – "His fixed mark was his Hope in our nation's fragile experiment, in equality and in of, by and for."

Mel Berger – It was Lincoln's Leadership in that he applied the same to the nation, the military and his "*Team of Rivals*."

Win Anderson – She rather uniquely identified his Refusal as her *fixed mark*. Specifically, "His refusal to give up on the *Declaration of Indepen-*

dence, our inheritance, our greatest gift, on *All men are created equal*. Period."

For my friend, *Henry Ballone*, it was two words only, Loyalty and Belonging.

For *Robert Brugler*, it was, *Play it again, Sam*, perseverance.

"One of the qualities that I most admire about Lincoln was his ability to overcome adversities in all stages of his life," he wrote. "He was able to persevere. He always learned from his mistakes and evolved and adapted.

Joe Truglio, like Brugler, went with Perseverance as well, along with "a sense of fair play, compromise and the ability to get to the crux of a problem and convey it to a mass audience."

Paul Mellen held up four inter-related *fixed marks*. "Lincoln," he wrote, "is the icon of integrity, commitment, endurance and freedom. Every American owes their freedom to our greatest President, Abraham Lincoln."

Al Azinger, of Illinois State University, in his few thoughtful sentences, held up both political insight and courage as his *fixed marks*.

He wrote, "I find information about his political insight and ability to flourish in the most difficult of times to be very intriguing. He also had the courage to appoint cabinet members and advisors from those he thought had the most to offer in spite of their own ambitions and political leanings."

There's something soothing in asking a probing question that asks people to identify the reasons why they devote themselves to "Getting right with Lincoln." Soothing, because there can be no wrong answer, but rather and only answers that elevate the thinking of others who share the same passion. Soothing, because it's nice to be able to agree with each and every response while continuing to hold tight to your own. Soothing, because the grip on your own begins to loosen. Soothing, because you cannot help but be affected by the insights of so many thoughtful and learned people, who in so many ways, come together to elevate a collective understanding of one who so devoted himself to elevating us all.

Soothing, because we all know just how much our America, his America, needs him and all of these fixed marks to be adopted and appropriated anew in this moment in time.

Character is everything, it is often said, and here, via the voices and hearts of a band of Lincoln enthusiasts, many character analyses of Lincoln have been shared and briefly explored.

All are enjoined by the fact that they sing their own songs of praise, and why not, for each and every varied and disparate *fixed mark* is just as true as the next.

But no one is perfect and while he comes awfully damn close, not even Abe Lincoln.

So fairness dictates closing this chapter with a brief review of what may be looked upon as failings, flaws and ways wherein character may well have, in the crucible of experience and growth, diminished rather than elevated.

* He was clearly far too lenient with his boys and he certainly neglected to discipline them. This to the dismay of his law partner, Billy Herndon, especially, but also and often to his White House staff and official visitors. On the plus side, he sure got the loving right.

* However deserving and it was indeed deserved, he mistreated and harshly embarrassed his wife, Mary, a time or two that we know of and he may for long have been less than emotionally honest with her. One expects love and belonging to be celebrated and not subdued or repressed as theirs was. Mary's temper, mood swings, bouts of depression and fury regularly, if not always, served to render home life intolerable, but Lincoln's long escapes on the circuit, avoidance and silent forbearance were not necessarily the antidote to their unresolved struggles.

Always, there is, no matter the limitations of our knowledge, the haunting warmth, devotion and tenderness of Anne Rutledge juxtaposed to the storm and the madness that was Mary. It has been near 100 years since William Barton wrote his 1927 romantic *The Women Lincoln Loved* and it is still "the same – the same old story."

"A matter of profound wonder," Lincoln called his marriage to Mary at the outset and indeed that is just what it remained.

* While he eliminated this practice upon being confronted 'up close and absurdly' with a near duel with broad swords with James Shields on Bloody Island of all places, he was prone, in the springtime of his political life, to sometimes fairly and sometimes unfairly and, every once in a while, even maliciously, assail political opponents in printed editorial broadsides in publications like the *Sangamo Journal*. Now, he'd never let go of his timely use of sarcasm, but he did indeed leave the vituperation behind.

* While no historian has yet to adequately solve the riddle of his relationship with his Dad, we well know that they were wired differently. He wouldn't hunt, he spent too much time with those "fool" books, his mind wandered and he, at least spiritually if not palpably, openly resented his father's very way of life. A cog in the wheel of a dysfunctional and troubled family, Abe looked upon having to suffer the beatings he took from a father who did not spare the rod and to whom he had to give his wages for the first 21 years of his life as a form of enslavement. But still, his slavery aside, there was grace and respect enough to devote a bonus year to his father as he established yet another farm in Macon County, Illinois.

What one wonders about and questions is that Lincoln never invited or arranged for him to meet his Grandchildren and never visited upon learning that his father was seriously ill and dying in 1851 because he was "doubtful that it would not be more painful than pleasant." Nor did he attend his father's funeral. Rationales or excuses, of course, have been suggested and he did sign the occasional, cryptic letter, "Affectionately," and he bailed him out financially a few times, but never reconciled himself to his father's lack of ambition, illiteracy and way of life.

We are left to wonder if our Lincoln ever stopped to think of the value of the things that were handed down—a keen sense of honesty, an aversion to the inhumanity of slavery and that precious 'gift of gab' or ability to spin a yarn and tell the kind of stories that kept them laughing.

* As to those stories, they could be racy and bawdy and often racist. While he was on the right path, he was, in oh so many ways, a product of his un-enlightened age, where few if any believed in the true equality of the races. While never wavering on the injustice and inhumanity and sin of slavery itself, still he, for the better part of his life, harbored notions of white superiority. The mantra of 'equality before the law but not before society or in all things' long defined the limits of his liberality. It wasn't until the White House years and Lincoln's encounters with Frederick Douglass, Elizabeth Keckley, Sojourner Truth, and especially with his 180,000 plus African American boys in blue where he saw the light and let go of any lingering prejudices, The above noted, he ever treated all with the outstretched hand of kindness personally.

In the end and finally, he embraced the notion that not only ought they to be finally and fully free, but also and maybe even more importantly, equal.

* Then too, while his position on slavery, as expressed in his *First Inaugural* was understandable in that he was a lawyer who understood the limits of Constitutional authority and the duties of a president who swore an oath and looked first to quell a seething rebellion, there is always the lingering question. . . . Was not, as Thoreau had already written, conscience, morality, justice and the right superior to the law? Certainly, he would brilliantly work to bring these disparate forces together to effect great change in years to come, but we, historical knit-pickers that we are, still dwell upon just where his head was when he wrote some of the more oppressive passages in that *First Inaugural.*

It is, I suppose, why we are a Lincoln-*Second Inaugural* people.

Still, I hear the *First's* stirring and moving closing and its "*Mystic chords of memory*" and "*Better angels of our nature*" and I am carried away.

Abraham Lincoln never entirely disappoints.

In retrospect, each of my six questionable flaws come with explanations aplenty and we are left with nothing that is entirely or finally damning. Others, of course, may have longer lists than mine, but this is all I offer, as I have no will or taste to ever view depression, melancholy and psychological mystery or proclivity as flaws. None among us have failed to swim in or, at least, test those waters and being human is no flaw. And neither will I vilify his final escape from the tentacles of the vile bigotry of his day. As to my six, beyond the madness of the politics of his day, they are all dressed in sadness and sorrow for that which was empty and/or missing in his life.

Then too, juxtaposed to our *fixed marks*, they are but blips on the radar screen. All in all, Lincoln astounds.

Figure 2.1. On the edge of a bench, that I passed by hundreds of times and sometimes sat, with arm gently outstretched, he invites all to sit with him awhile and chat and so we shall. *Source:* Seated Lincoln, Newark, NJ - by Gutzon Borglum 1911. Photographed by Dave Wiegers.

Chapter Three

Connecting and Conversing

What I am about to dive into is a joy to work with. It is one thing to disregard reality and drift off into the dream world where the imagination freely takes flight, but it is quite another to do so in concert with 45 other good souls who soar into the mystical clouds with you.

We are off to enjoy the conversations we would most have liked to have had with our Lincoln.

We know him well and have been there by his side when there was nothing more exciting for him than getting his hands on another book, or when he told the good people of Sangamon County of his desire to be of service and to be "esteemed by" them, or when he held firm, "like a chain of steel" for the Union and broke the chains of slavery. Yes, with him, in the laughter, the sadness and the ever up and doing of his days, where we cheer for, worry about and celebrate with.

Throughout it all, his relentless self-educating, his determining to 'leave a mark for good,' the high achievement, the carnage and the rising up of his "Last best hope of earth," we have been there. So we have words of sympathy and wisdom to offer and both questions to ask and concerns to share. Some are light and amusing while others, having to do with everything from politics to policy to public sentiment to the horror of the war to his faith and depression will be anything but.

There also are the even more profound matters of love and intimate loss.

Cognizant of the gifts that he passed down to us, we realize that we also have obligations and duties to satisfy, as it is incumbent upon us to mirror the light he shed and to do our part to "disenthrall ourselves and so save our nation" once again. Never, has it been more important to *Get right with Lincoln* and do as he would have us do to serve and enlighten.

Some of us go to him with historical baggage in tow, comprised of stuff that it will be well to lay down and release. As such, questions will be direct, pointed and aimed at filling the missing pieces in with answers. Others go to him in wonder and amazement, looking only to be with and listen. Then too and of course, we all go to him in a spirit of thanksgiving. How can we not?

We have all had our private and personal imaginings, but here, uniquely, we air and share and probe together.

On his pedestal or not, we go to him entirely undaunted, for he would be the last man to have ever considered himself special. A man with a limitless array of positive attributes, he was ever one to put people at ease and nothing he extended or released escaped the portal of his deep-seeded and irrepressible humility. Ever ambitious to matter and to serve, of course, but that didn't mean that he ever deemed himself worthy.

Henry Villard, a reporter for the German press ran into Lincoln late one evening at a rail station some 20 miles west of Springfield in the midst of the Lincoln Douglas Debates. A hard rain began to fall and they took refuge together in a railroad boxcar. They had time to kill and spoke, off the record, I assume, of all things political. (*The Atlantic* – Commemorative Civil War Issue/Recollections of Lincoln, November 2011)

Sharing his own doubts about his chances in the United States Senate race against Judge Douglas at that time, Lincoln, with a broad smile and laugh, proceeded to share his wife, Mary's electoral handicapping. "*Mary insists that I am going to be Senator and President of the United States, too. . . . Can you imagine. Just think of such a sucker like me as President.*" Villard pointedly noted that Lincoln concluded with "*a roar of laughter and with his arms around his knees, shaking all over with mirth at his wife's ambition.*"

In truth, he was the butt of so very many of his own jokes or self-deprecating remarks, as Villard, who was no fan of his cruder jokes, also attested to.

Not long after in 1859, he talked to Jesse Fell, the founder of Illinois State University (for which Lincoln handled all legal work) and a close, personal friend, about gathering material for a brief autobiographical campaign sketch. "*There is not much of it,*" said Lincoln, "*for the reason, I suppose, that there is not much of me.*"

On this question of greatness, permit me to share another line or two that I picked up from Burlingame (from *A. Lincoln, A Life, p. 361* and *An Oral History of Abraham Lincoln, John G. Nicolay's Interviews and Essays*, p. 87) relating one of the many times Lincoln spoke with a delegation of clergy in the White House. To the full delegation, he said, "*I am very sure that if I do not go away from here a wiser man, I shall go away a better man, for having learned here what a very poor sort of man I am.*"

Then later to one minister, he added, "'*I may not be a great man,* straightening up to his full height—*I know I am not a great man.*" He added that it was well that this was so in that it humbled him to go to God upon whom all must rely.

Lincoln led, neither with his right nor his left, but rather with a humility and kindness that put all comers at ease. No matter how busy or pressed or troubled, he "laid everyone down easy," including those rebels and their rebel leaders who sought to destroy him and his country. We go to him with the strength that comes from knowing that all things, big and small, serious or ridiculous, even painful and probing, will neither vex nor trouble him. He had already spent 4-long years in hell and astonishingly arose from it "*With malice toward none, with charity for all*" on his lips.

In his *The Lincoln Enigma*, Gabor Boritt wrote, "It is a cliché by now, yet still true, that history is a never-ending conversation between the past and the present, and among Lincoln scholars, the goal still is—some will call it anachronistic—to find the truth. So it is good that our cab stops and we are forced to get out and take stock."

In commenting upon a work of my own, *What Must Needs Come – A Legacy of Gettysburg*, Tracy Power expressed the same thinking as Boritt when he kindly wrote:

> The author's intensely personal musings on his and his family's history and on the grand and awful sweep and meaning of American history remind us that neither history nor historical fiction are anything like simple stories about what happened long ago, but rather continuous dialogues with the people who inhabited that past. I admire Rich's passion and creativity and his desire to share this story with everyone interested in examining some of the deeper truths of the Civil War.

Well, our cabs have pulled over and stopped, Gabor Boritt, as we join that "never-ending conversation between the past and the present," Tracy Power. In search of that truth and those deeper truths, with one extraordinary man who inhabited that past.

Our 45 Lincoln men and women, interestingly, voiced interest in what was precisely 45 distinct topics of conversation, upon a wide-ranging array of issues and events, a spot on 45. While most of these, 32 in fact, were owned by a single individual, 13 of them were widely shared.

Of those shared, 8 just wanted to listen, at least initially. They just wanted the stories and jokes, the tenor and tone of his voice, the force of his personality and even the soulfulness of his compassion. 4 of that 8 specifically preferred their conversation to be over dinner, where all would be relaxed and undisturbed. One wanted to be in the room with his Cabinet when he announced his intention to issue the Emancipation Proclamation on July 22, 1862 or aboard the River Queen at Hampton Roads on February 3, 1865 when he met with the Confederacy's peace delegation or simply in the crowd when he delivered his *Farewell* or *Gettysburg Address*. In the front of the crowd, of course, where neither a word nor an inflection would be lost.

Somewhat surprisingly, 6 wanted to speak with him about his writing, about his perfected craft. Where and how this master's ability to forge arguments so precise and cogent and moving and memorable? Where and how the poetry and music of his words? Of the 6, 3 were published historians, who while wordsmiths themselves, were in awe of his unique ability to say so very much in so few words.

There were 4 who wanted to address faith, spirituality and religion. Two prepared specific lists of subjects and questions that they hoped to cover and one, admittedly myself, who wanted to know, if in any way, he felt the presence of God or a force beyond himself as he wrote pieces as extraordinary as his early 1863 Thanksgiving Proclamation or his March 4, 1865 *Second Inaugural Address*. And not necessarily as he wrote the *Second Inaugural* but as he delivered it. For as Frederick Douglas said, it was indeed a "sacred effort."

There were another 6 who wanted to speak with him about the toll and burden of the war and 3, most interestingly, who wanted to bring him into time with us, so as to gather advice from him regarding healing our divided land today, which, of course, is why we write in the first place.

There were 2 interested in speaking with him about his grief and the death of Willie specifically, the suspension of the writ of habeas corpus, reconstruction, his melancholy, his pain and the issue of race. As to reconstruction, one also wanted to talk to him about what he might have done to better deal with the racial divide; and to take a bite out of the coming horror of Jim Crow and the advance of the Lost Cause mythology. As to the loss of Willie, one wanted to specifically ask whether or not Willie, whose loss was so deeply personal, somehow became another casualty of the war, leading him to look upon all of the other fallen boys in blue as his own sons as well.

Here, the 32 topics or prospective conversations that had but one author. Letting them fly, these conversations were to revolve around the following:

His devotion to the law—the source of *"With malice toward none, with charity for all"* - which version of the *Gettysburg Address* he used—what his vision for his country was immediately after the war—his relationship with his Dad—his Step Mom—consideration of the Jews generally and Isachar Zacharie in particular—Jack Armstrong—Anne Rutledge—his Mary or that *"matter of profound wonder"*—on painting his portrait and introducing him to what we have become—on all things family including those Virginia slave owning relatives—on his Army and the body count that grew beyond all imagining—on the Emancipation proclamation—on whether or not the essentials of winning the war and eradicating slavery were a single policy—on whether or not his daily "public baths" were a burden or a benefit—on his relationships with his Cabinet, his Generals, the soldiers, key politicians and close personal friends—about his family, children and daily life or what was the personal and not the political—on just 3 things that he might have done differently—on the genesis of "*As I would not be a slave, so I would not be a master*"—on surviving even Day 1 of the war, much less 4 long and horrendous years—on his Cabinet—on what it was about George McClellan that we don't know—on simply maintaining hope and faith—on what he would have said to both Generals Ulysses S. Grant and Robert E. Lee on the day of the Army of Northern Virginia's surrender—on his devotion to the United States Constitution—on the subject of equality versus hypocrisy—on the language at the conclusion of the Gettysburg Address—on Robert Chew, his charge and the lack of a response—on his understanding and insight of the American people and the American mind—on what he felt on April 4, 1865 as he entered Richmond and embraced the once slaves and on whether or not, he had goosebumps—and even on why he so interestingly brought Tad along with him.

As Richard Brookhiser so very kindly wrote me, not long ago, in commenting on an earlier piece, "There is a lot to chew on here." Indeed there is and we will chew on it all.

A rambling we will go.

THE WEIGHT OF THE WAR

Joe Truglio, Paul Mellen and *Robert Brugler* were all interested in speaking with Lincoln about how he managed to deal with the extreme pressures and horrific burdens of the war itself.

Joe Truglio piled on, as he wondered about the added burden of dealing with the death of his own sweet Willie, his son in the context of the tens of thousands of other fathers' sons.

Paul Mellen piled on with the 'brother versus brother,' via which they confronted one another in uncompromising horror and carnage."

Robert Brugler went so far as to outline a laundry list of attributes and dispositions that Lincoln held tight to and that helped him to sustain and inevitably prevail. Lincoln did, of course, make war rather than accept the dissolution of the Union, a position that remained objectionable to many. To Lincoln, secession was treason and he would fight, not to punish, but rather and only to preserve the Union and representative government. To him, it was an unassailable duty of his oath of office. He had no option and to that end, he would bear any burden and pay any price.

Here, Brugler's conversational list of Lincoln's qualitative resources and tools as a warring commander in chief—for justice, right and the good— reason and logic—knowledge and wisdom—humility, compassion and empathy—courage—eloquence—faith and spirit—understanding and forgiveness.

Given Brugler's desire to address the all of the above with Lincoln, he was destined to have a long and detailed conversation. For it is one thing to speak about that which transpires, yet quite another to speak about all that practically, mentally, reasonably, emotionally and spiritually drives you to fashion that which eventually transpires in the first place. The former is objective, tangible, direct and pointed, while the latter is incredibly complex, subjective and often elusive.

As to the burden of the war and its impact on Lincoln and how it is that we can try to begin to understand or measure it, I think first of the legacy of Mathew Brady and Alexander Gardner and their haunting pictures of him. The second factor I wonder about is his long history with depression and how it is that this did not consume him or keep him from attending to his unpleasant and weighty duties. Then my mind turns to Drew Gilpin Faust's seminal work, *This Nation of Suffering,* and the monumental loss and the weeping and wailing that rained down all over the land, his land, his people and their common tears. As to the fourth measuring rod, we consider the time he lost and the price he paid in the effort to simply find officers truly capable of leading soldiers and the toll this alone took. Then there is the extraordinary measure of this man who in forgiving all other entities, took it all upon himself. As Lincoln would have it, there would be none left but he to shoulder the weight of it all, the weight of *"The events that had controlled him."*

Eventually, he so movingly gives it all to God.

As to those photographs, they bear the images of one who arrived in Washington strong and virile, who grew old and broken in his years in the White House. They again reveal that hauntingly weary face. Each military campaign, each bitter battle with its exorbitant casualties and the death of each of the 630,000 fallen is etched in the coarse lines hollowed out and into his careworn face. On his face, the rivers and rivulets of red blood spilled on every sweet field of green or rye or peach or apple and into every meandering stream or raging river and on the steps of each white clapboard or stone church. On his face, the sacrificial offering of young boys of 15 and old men of 70 who fell with eyes wide open, quizzical and haunting.

Too soon, too soon for each and every one of them. Too soon for the boys in blue, too soon for those in gray, too soon for Lincoln, too soon for all the widows and orphans and mothers.

Lincoln's face, in a very real way, became the face of the war itself and of the wholly unanticipated price paid to set men free and to restore a Union that he deeply believed to be *"the last best hope of mankind."* To mark the haunting progression, see Gardner's November 8, 1863 image, Brady's January 8, 1864 and finally, Gardner's February 5, 1865.

Then, as to his lifelong battle with depression, one wonders, can't help but wonder, how it is that he exhibited an irrepressible and deeply rooted strength in coping with the equally irrepressible burden of the war. He inspired, he moved, he recreated, he rendered all that came to pass sacrificial, solemn, even sacred.

Throughout his life, the melancholy, the hypo, the depression was part and parcel of life and so too the suicide watches. We know this well, as Billy Herndon, his friend of 18 years, reminds us, "*His melancholy dripped from him as he walked.*" What astounds is that he prevailed despite it or that he subdued it in order to give all to duty.

He did so, I believe, as Joshua Wolf Shenk observes in his *Lincoln's Melancholy: How Depression Challenged a President and Fueled His Greatness* by holding tight to his sense of humor and by perfecting his commitment to quietly reflecting before making critical decisions. Reflection became an art form to him. Oh yes, he agonized and mourned as he paced the dark corridors of the White House in the dead of night but, more than anything else, he dwelled upon the latest reports and circumstances and ideas presented to him, the all of which he would ultimately take in and spit out anew with a course of action. Sure migraines, insomnia and the ever resonating currents of despair, but more than anything else, the application of his certain reason to the business at hand, the work at hand, his Union, freedom, a new nation.

I believe, truly believe, that he was only able to save our nation, free the slaves and commit us to our new birth of freedom because he had the night, when he'd pace the halls of the White House forever puzzling his puzzler, ever applying reason to the dangers at hand. In Schenk's illuminating work, he captures Lincoln in a moment of triumph at the 1860 Republican Convention where "*the roof was literally cheered off the building for him*" and where grown men so celebrated that they threw their hats and canes into the air for him. You would think that he would have been ecstatic. And yet as the crowd dispersed and the hall emptied, William Bross, the Lieutenant Governor of Illinois found Lincoln sitting alone with his head bent in sorrow and his hands pressed to his face. He told Bross, as Shenk sadly tells us, "*I am not very well.*"

There, the classic image of Lincoln's profound melancholy. Oh so many friends and colleagues of Lincoln's attest to this, but I submit that Lincoln, as he prepared for the presidency and throughout his presidency, fought another battle within, to keep that demon who roamed within him back home in Springfield and out of his White House.

He could no longer walk in the shadowlands. There was no time for standing still. He had finally "*crossed Fox River.*"

As to Drew Gilpin Faust's, the former president of Harvard University's *This Nation of Suffering*, note that there are thousands of books that dive into this arena, but this is the only one that dives deep into the heart of this horrific morass and stays right there. The loss, suffering and mourning touched literally every household and were it not your family, it was your neighbor's or friends at church.

The death rate during the Civil War was six times the rate that it was during World War II and were it to have been fought today, more than 6.5 million would have died. And that's not even factoring in the 50,000 civilian deaths during the Civil War that James McPherson estimates. Again, no one saw this coming. They went in blind and they came out of it dead, lame, broken and disheartened. Throughout it all, there was Lincoln in the Telegraph Office desperately waiting for the latest news from the front. Hoping against hope! The Commander in Chief, upon whom the death of each soldier and each tear came crashing down. There in the Telegraph Office, Lincoln, the first to be stunned, the first to bow his head, the first to say, 'How long, oh Lord'!

In Faust's book, she movingly refers to the Confederate poet, Sidney Lanier who wrote, "*How does God have the heart to allow it*"? A question that we still ask today, a question that we have never stopped asking. How did God have the heart to allow it? Lanier reminds me of Walt Whitman's resounding testimony, celebrating Lincoln upon having merely survived Bull Run, that one day, that oh so bitter day that he withstood and that "*sealed his greatness forever.*" Yet that was but the first of what would be hundreds of days like that and he remarkably withstood them all, increasingly looking to God and inevitably committing the blood, slaughter and devastation to sacrifice, atonement and mercy in his *Second Inaugural Address*.

Out of utter misery, the hope of a new nation that these many years later is still torn. Red states, blue states and the same old great divide, where racism and bigotry, the sore and malignant vestiges of the Civil War haunt us still. Sadly, the misery that was the Civil War still festers and it has come roaring back with renewed fervor and vigor today. And so, our plea, "*We must go to Lincoln. We must get right with Lincoln*" and the fleeting grace that was ours when he walked through Richmond on that hot April 9, 1865 and all—all—for one brief moment in time, were free to be the sons and daughters of a nation, awash with the blessings of new found freedom. Exultant in that freedom and possibility and hope.

As to the burden Lincoln bore in finding Generals capable of leading men and in giving him victories, this may have been inevitable and certainly understandable. They were all, after all, on "on the job training."

All the political commissions aside, even his West Pointers were wholly unprepared. All they studied at West Point was mathematics and engineering. They had only one minor class in military strategy. And hell, there had never quite been a war like this before. Consider that the largest army ever taken into battle by the United States before the Civil War was 14,000 men and that

General McDowell would have 30,000 in his command at Bull Run. Consider that General McClellan would then, in short order, have more than 100,000 in his command.

Then consider that this was to be a new kind of war, where the Von Clausewitz *"center of gravity"* that must be annihilated was not ground or territory or a particular city or state or river or hill as in the past, but rather the armies in the field. Lincoln who understood this early on had a difficult time convincing his Generals of it.

He grew increasingly frustrated with men like Generals Don Carlos Buell and William Rosecrans and frustrated with George McClellan's abject lack of aggressiveness. As to the Army of the Potomac, McClellan was arrogant, narcissistic and disrespectful to Lincoln who remarkably took no personal offense. The issue for Lincoln was that McClellan had the "slows." Notably, Lincoln famously asked him what could "possibly have tired his horses out" when McClellan dared to blame his lack of movement upon their condition.

Outside of General Ulysses S. Grant's performance in the West, there was little to encourage Lincoln early on. In the Confederate Army of Northern Virginia, McClellan saw monsters, illusions, numbers and power that did not exist. When he finally took a roundabout shot with his Peninsula Campaign, he was dramatically driven back when 'Bobby Lee' took command and drove him off the peninsula during the "7 Days Battles." Lincoln did have the purported victory at Antietam that gave way to the illusion upon which to hang his *Emancipation Proclamation*, but even McClellan's possession of those famous cigars, Lee's orders and superior numbers earned him but a draw on that bloodiest and most bitter of all days.

With McClellan finally in the rear view mirror, General-in-Chief Henry Halleck and Secretary of War Edwin Stanton kept parading men to the command of the Army of the Potomac who were woefully inadequate, men like John Pope, Ambrose Burnside, and Joseph Hooker, all of whom failed. Hooker outrageously opined, upon assuming command that the nation might need a "dictator" to rescue it. Lincoln famously responded that *"He would risk the dictator"* if he would only *"Go forward and give us victories."* But after the disaster at Chancellorsville and Lincoln's cry of *"What will the people say – what will the people say,"* Hooker was replaced by a lackluster George Meade just days before Gettysburg, where Meade got very lucky in giving field command to the ever more capable Winfield Hancock.

Lincoln interestingly erred here in that command had first been offered to General John Reynolds, commander of the Army of the Potomac's 1st Corps and arguably that army's best, but Reynolds would only consent were there to be no interference from Washington. Ironically, Reynolds would have done well with Lincoln as it was Halleck who he knew and wanted nothing to do with. Sadly, he was to die only a couple of days later as he rushed to Gettysburg to support and relieve his friend, General John Buford whose dismounted cavalry forced the issue west of Gettysburg, in order to hold the heights east of Gettysburg. "How goes it John," he yelled. *"There's the devil to pay,"* responded Buford from the cupola above the Lutheran Theological Seminary. Turning, Reynolds yelled to his men, *"Forward men, for God's sake, forward,"* as that devil, in the form of a sniper's bullet, struck him in the head, killing him instantly.

Saved by Gettysburg, the High Tide of the Confederacy, the dramatic reversal of fortunes and still Meade failed as the opportunity for him to destroy General Robert E. Lee's army long presented itself. The Potomac's flooded waters boxed his Army of Northern Virginia in for more than a week, leaving them exposed and vulnerable. Lincoln wrote his famous (never to be sent) scathing letter to Meade, crying, understandably crying, about the gravity of so great a lost opportunity.

Out west, Grant had been busy taking forts and cities and rivers and green fields and mountaintops in Tennessee, while crushing and destroying armies in the process. Complete control of the mighty Mississippi River was the prize at Vicksburg but so too were the near 30,000 prisoners removed from a Confederate command that was already bleeding men. Grant took Forts Henry and Donelson and then Shiloh and Vicksburg and the seemingly impregnable Lookout Mountain in Chattanooga.

Once upon a time, the jealous old guard in the Union command complained to Lincoln that Grant was a drunkard and ought to be removed from command. The complaint led Lincoln to famously joke about sending a case of whatever it was that he was drinking to all his commanders. After years of costly bobbing and weaving, on March 10, 1864, Lincoln promoted Grant to the rank of Lieutenant General and gave him command of all Union armies. Responsible to Lincoln alone, he would commit good men whom he well knew, men like Generals William Tecumseh Sherman and George Thomas, the Rock of Chickamaugua to tame Tennessee and Georgia and Philip Sheridan, his own Cavalry commander who would tame General Jubal Early in the Shenandoah campaign and cut the Confederacy off from its bread basket.

As for Grant himself, he would go after the Confederacy's *"center of gravity,"* one Robert E. Lee and his Army of Northern Virginia. Zealous and fierce, he would be relentless. No longer was the quality of command, a burden for Lincoln to stress over, although the rising body counts indeed were.

What price victory? What price an end?

When the fighting was done, one might reasonably assume that the great price had been paid. Lincoln affirmed this in his incredible March 4, 1865 *Second Inaugural Address.* The people, the country, redeemed and cleansed, *"with malice toward none and charity for all,"* could freely go forward *"to bind up the nation's wounds and to care for him who shall have borne the battle and his widow and his orphan."*

The blood spilled for freedom, for goodness and grace, was sacrificial, redemptive and even holy in Lincoln's hands.

"As Christ died to make men holy, let us die to make men free," heralded Julia Ward Howe in her *Battle Hymn of the Republic.* "Oh be swift, my soul to answer, be jubilant my feet"! Be jubilant, can you imagine that?

Be jubilant. Really?

That all were free, sure, but that was a brief and fleeting dream as Jim Crow and dark racism corrupted. That the guns had been silenced, of course, that a nation was reclaimed, certainly, but it was oh so difficult to be jubilant in 1865.

With the spirit of God resting upon his trembling shoulders, Lincoln forgave all and upheld all, for mercy is the wellspring of compassion and forgiveness and charity is the wellspring of kindness.

He wanted to shoulder it because '*He made the war.'* And shoulder it, he did.

But with broken hearts and broken bodies and broken homes, all were left and destined to pick up the pieces of lives interrupted, lives devastated, lives in shambles. They were the living embers of a sacrifice so great, a sacrifice beyond comprehension and they would sadly and soon come to discover that even the freedom fought for wasn't free.

All of this and there in the background of it all, Lincoln's extraordinary admonition, *"I claim not to have controlled events, but confess plainly that events have controlled me."* Ultimately, it wasn't on him either as he laid it on a biblical source and a just God in his *Second Inaugural.*

What must needs comes. That was it, simply that. *What must needs come!*

PUBLIC OPINION BATHS

Unlike presidents today, Abraham Lincoln's office was never closed to the public. For long, our presidents have been entirely insulated and removed from the people and while the people constitutionally remain the master, it has been a long time since the people were welcome to knock on the president's door and lay their burdens down. The walls and the barriers and the Secret Service and the metal detectors and the phalanx of security personnel so separate the people from their president today that we no longer even think in terms of "we the people" above all. We forget that when Harry Truman carried his "grips" from the White House to Union Station on the day Dwight David Eisenhower took the oath of office in 1952, he said, when asked how he felt, *"Great, this is the day I got my promotion."*

In America, the people rule but I fear we have largely forgotten this. There can be no doubt that President Trump has forgotten this, as people are but puppets to be manipulated.

When Lincoln was in the White House, the average American did have to suffer the inconvenience of waiting on line, but they were entirely free to just stroll into the White House, get in the cue and wait their turn to talk to their president. Interestingly, they didn't even have to knock on the front door as the White House was not the military fortress that it is today.

I often think of the Henry David Thoreau sentiment that for every advance you make, you leave something else behind forever. We have paid a price for growing bigger, faster, technologically sophisticated, ever more boastful and 'holier than thou.'

We have paid a price for our far more sophisticated weaponry, for our violent history of assassination and threat and, of course, for our world on edge and the madness of contemporary international relations—not to mention Covid-19 distancing and isolation and life interrupted,

This is what *Billy Grandstaff* would like to talk to Lincoln about, both as to the impact it had on him and as to what it means today for a president to have no direct contact with the people. For sadly, in 2020, it is all smoke and mirrors, as we have a president who refuses to answer even the legitimate questions of a free press that he deems the "enemy of the people." He performs, puts on shows at staged rallies and spews vitriol, hatred and lies via twitter. It's all a one way street. He talks, rages, invents, but he does not listen to the cries of his own. There is no dialogue, no give and take. The presidency in 2020 is a grand production, an all too real 'reality show' wherein the free, open and unfiltered voice of "we the people" is but a sounding gong.

Bill wrote, "We understand that even though politicians need to be thick skinned, they are still insulated from the general public. Imagine waking up daily to the thought of being surrounded by needy people, walking into your home and demanding your time to solve their problems. As a truly humane man, Lincoln felt the desire to try to respond and react as best as he could."

While I trust that it was not always honored, the rough schedule for Lincoln was, by today's standards, absolutely absurd. It was fully 4 hours, from 10:00 a.m. to 2:00 p.m. on Monday, Wednesday and Friday, with a break on Tuesday and Thursday when it was a mere two hours from 10:00 a.m. thru Noon. Can you imagine?

Can you even imagine?

Of course, we know that he broke for meetings with cabinet members, members of Congress, officers and soldiers, other officials, Willie and Tad and sometimes even a raging Mary.

The war, the army, the carnage, the loss, the slavery issue, foreign relations, fiscal issues, Indian relations, opportunity-economics-railroads, political-cabinet- congressional machinations, the endless writing alone. It was all so demanding, harsh, emotionally taxing and suffocating and yet he devoted hours to "*What can I do for you*," to their problems back home, to their requests for jobs or pardons or the desperate need to get their sons or husbands home, to their opinions about the war, the Union, slavery, to their requests for action on slavery, to their prayers and hopes, to their ideas, inventions, land use issues, sales pitches ---ad infinitum.

His small staff would plead with him to lessen the load and he would argue that "*They ask for so little*" and "*If I can help, that's the least I can do for them.*" What's miraculous about the all of this is that he damn well tried and often did what they asked of him.

He followed through, got back to them and damn well cared.

Unlike today, he did his own writing and produced thick volumes of it for historians to peruse and ponder and he devoted long hours to listening to and addressing the longings and tears of ordinary citizens. So it is not that he managed a great war, won that war, saved the Union and freed the slaves that is the wonder of his presidency. It is rather that he achieved the all of this and more under the circumstances here illuminated.

Here's a brief addendum. It's the tale of one who was so distraught that he didn't even wait for the daily public baths, one who rather woke Lincoln up in the dead of night at the Soldier's Home.

A Lieutenant Colonel William Scott sought to retrieve the body of his wife who had tragically died on August 13, 1862 when two steamboats, the George Peabody and the West Point collided on the Potomac in southern territory (120 died). Despondent, he came to the Soldier's Home, a few miles outside Washington where Lincoln's family spent the summers. As it was somewhere between 2:00 to 2:30 a.m., Lincoln uncharacteristically said something along the lines of, "*Am I to have no rest? Is there no time or spot when or where I may escape this relentless demand*"? He blew him off, but the next morning, the president of the United States knocked on his door at the Willard Hotel, put his arm over his shoulders, apologized for being a brute, and acted to do all he could.

This is no tall tale, just a vivid reflection of how improbably generous this rare leader of men was. (Jim Blake, Chairman of the Fifth Regiment New Hampshire Volunteer reenactors, *President Lincoln's Cottage Blog*, January 10, 2010).

WHAT HE MIGHT HAVE SAID TO LEE

Jim McGrath, who simply reveres history, was very brief and pointed. What he would be most interested in speaking with Lincoln about was simply this. He wrote, "We know the advice that Lincoln gave General Grant in anticipation of the meeting at Appomattox, as to "*letting them down easy* which Grant was likely, of a mind, to do anyway. What I would like to know is what he might have wanted to say to General Lee."

Truly, we have no idea, but we are free to imagine.

For here, we have the man who he offered command of all Union forces to at the outset, a man who gave him nightmares for four years and contributed more than any other Confederate commander to his migraines and inability to sleep, a man, who was on both the wrong side of the war and the wrong side of history, and yet one who he, no doubt, respected.

In fact, the one thing we do know is that Lee was on Lincoln's mind the week he died, when in the presence of his secretaries, he openly wondered and worried about how Lee must feel. This was our Lincoln, after all, who rewrote the book on compassion and empathy, our Lincoln who commiserated with those who walked in dark places, sad and depressed, our Lincoln who wondered, and dare I say, even worried about Lee in the wake of the surrender.

I wonder if he heard Lee's voice, his *"Those boys in blue never feel like the enemy."*

And I imagine that he might have told him that his valiant command would be treated honorably and given the fairest of terms. He would have communed with him and acknowledged how difficult a time it must be for him. He would have shared his sense of loss and said that, in the end, there were no victors.

He would, with words, do exactly what General Joshua Lawrence Chamberlain and the Army of the Potomac did on the field when the Army of Northern Virginia bowed low to lay their weapons and battle flags down. Together, they demonstrated absolute respect and honored the fallen.

MELANCHOLY AND RESPONSIBILITY

Todd Brewster, author of *Lincoln's Gamble*, responded that he was "More interested in just listening to him than talking to him." Yes, "just to be with him and to hear him tell a joke or tell a story or give a speech." But this overarching interest in just being there was then followed by a pointed and particular interest in speaking with him about the '*pain and the lifelong melancholy*' that relentlessly plagued him, about the shadowlands where he so often wandered.

Brewster began by referring to William Herndon's observations about Lincoln's melancholy, suggesting that it didn't have so much to do with his own personal pain and sorrow but rather and more so with the rest of the world that he inhabited. He took upon himself the weight of the world. He took responsibility and lived as if he truly was his brother's and his sister's keeper. Herndon, again and in fact, insisted that this was Lincoln's own peculiar brand of melancholy. "A melancholy that dripped from him as he walked"!

As to the last line above, Brewster asserts that it is one of the descriptions of Lincoln that he most appreciates.

This thought led Brewster to reflect upon the *Episcopal Prayer Book's Confession of Sin.* "*The Plea for Forgiveness*, which has to do both with what we have done but also with what we have left undone. There is, in this, a collective responsibility for the iniquities of the world and I think it is similar to what Lincoln felt and felt quite keenly."

"This idea that Lincoln was someone who believed that we share our sins can be read alongside his notion of "union," added Brewster. "Lincoln saw Americans as a single people because the nation was founded upon a collective belief in 'one sacred' concept, which I believe to be that of universal liberty. As long as slavery was tolerated, this identification with liberty was a fraud and because this was a "union," not a faction, it was a fraud for the abolitionists as much as it was for the slaveholders. We live together, we stand together, we fall together."

Just as Abraham Lincoln did, we might add.

Brewster went further, "Decades ago, a famous orchestra conductor told me that if he had an opportunity to be in the presence of Mozart, he would not be as interested in talking to him as he would be in observing him. In fact, the conductor said, he would be fascinated to simply watch Mozart conduct a rehearsal. I feel much the same way about Lincoln. I would like to watch him in a cabinet meeting, in a playful moment with one of his children, in a court room during his early days as a lawyer. And if I were to engage him in one thing and one thing only, I would like to hear him discuss the meaning of one of his favorite poems, perhaps something by one of the so-called Graveyard Poets, William Cowper or Thomas Gray, that he loved so much. "

As for me, I often note that Lincoln never took anything personally. It was never about him. It was always bigger than him. Brewster so reminds us of this, because his comments clearly reinforce the notion that Lincoln lived in communion with others. Not my pain but yours, not mine but ours.

This reminds me of the one law in *Leviticus* that has always spoken loudly to me—"*Do not stand idly by!*" Oh what power lies in such an empathetic and compelling charge or call or cry"—"*Do not stand idly by!*" Lincoln, who was intimate with the Bible, was hard wired to heed this call.

The iniquities and sins of his nation were, accordingly, his and they weighed down upon him, as they did upon all who lived in the light. Lincoln chose to accept this, to shoulder the weight, to bear the burden, to set so great a sacrifice in motion and to induce atonement and healing. To live in Lincoln's light is to recognize that all of us, in our own day and time, are likewise called to shoulder the iniquities and sins of our country and community in our day. All are called. Indeed, that is if we still believe in the meaning of "We the people."

In his day, Lincoln broke through the pall, the melancholy, the madness, the darkness that had long settled over both him and the land he loved. The truth is that he had to lay even the melancholy and darkness within down as president in order to give his all to address and attend to his Union, Democracy, Slavery and Freedom.

FAITH, EMANCIPATION, AND THE RIVER QUEEN

Rabbi Jonathan Sarna, Paula Hopewell and *Matt Lakemacher* joined hands together in turning our dial to the question of faith. Lincoln, his shadow boxing with God and the evolution and advance of his thinking about spirituality is a fascination.

Rabbi Sarna focuses specifically upon his friendship with Jews and his standing up for the Jewish people, while Lakemacher and Hopewell dive deep into his beliefs, his spirituality and the words that he spoke, faithfully, to elevate and lift the American people and to give them hope.

Sarna writes, "If I could speak to him, I would ask him more about his relationship with Jews, and especially with Isachar Zacharie, the Jewish chiropodist, with whom he spent so much time in the White House." Having already explored this, the key takeaways were and remain the fact that Lincoln, unlike the masses, had nary a prejudiced bone in his body. Then too, he was as intimate with the Old Testament and the Talmud as he was with the New Testament and the doctrines of Christianity.

Matt Lakemacher was all over the place, but his oars certainly dipped deeper into questions of faith. As to it, he wrote, "I'd like to be there with Lincoln to discuss 'the better angels of our nature,' to expound upon the idea that 'the Almighty has his own purposes' or that 'the judgments of the Lord are true and righteous altogether.' I'd like to be there to discuss his *Meditations on the Divine Will* or to consider grief with Lincoln in the Bardo, after the death of Willy and the carnage of the Civil War. "*The will of God prevails,' even if God's purpose is different from our purposes*" and his ways beyond our understanding. Like Job, sometimes we just have to accept that he is God despite our circumstances and like Elijah we have to listen for that still small voice. Those are the words and the moments and the conversations that I'd like to share with Father Abraham.

Like my friend, Matt, I often think about his "*Better angels of our nature,*" wonder where they are and pray for their resurgence. Every day, I wonder just how long, we, like Job, stripped of all that we revere and hold dear about our America, can continue to survive in the belly of the beast. Every day, I have my 'why God' moments of despair, my 'how can this have come to pass' moments. Like Lincoln, I acknowledge that "*The Almighty has his own purposes,*" and that "*The judgements of the Lord are true and right-*

eous altogether" and that *"The will of God prevails"* and like Lincoln, I know there is oh so much beyond my comprehension and understanding.

But wrong cannot be right and dishonor cannot be honor and injustice cannot be justice and hatred cannot be love and indignity cannot be dignity and I want to scream, "Why God" and like Christ on the cross, I want to cry out, "Why have you forsaken us!"

But then, I am everyday reminded, again and again reminded, that the all of what we today endure is the construct of our own sordid politics, of the evil of a Supreme Court decision that dares to say that "money is speech," of the Democratic party's insistence upon giving us a candidate in 2016 who so very many people did not trust and upon the Trump inspired rising of the dark underbelly of American racism, bigotry and ignorance. We, the American people and not God, did all of this. We allowed the all of this. In our righteousness and our ignorance, we let the darkness in.

Finally, I am reminded, most assuredly and inevitably reminded of President Kennedy's, *"On this earth, God's work must truly be our own."*

Lincoln was a lot better at giving God his due and at letting God off the hook for his awful war and the horrific carnage and the death of the 630,000 that "must needs come." It was not of God, it was of men, he said in his *Second Inaugural* and the war was, in the end, the so very costly sacrificial atonement for the great sin of slavery. God is just, Lincoln maintained, and the price paid was in keeping 'with the blood spilled with the lash.'

Providence would be satisfied.

Lincoln, who for so long doubted, richly affirmed God as president, a God who looked upon a bigger picture with different purposes than man could possibly discern.

As our president today bows to dictators, abhorrently betrays our allies and friends, walks away from our treaties and vows, ignores the suffering of the poor as the rich grow richer, criminalizes the innocents who somehow still believe America to be the refuge for the "tempest tossed," steals their children from them and tells brave women of color in Congress to return to their countries of origin, we bow our heads. Our souls cry out for deliverance. And we, like Lincoln, shadow box with God whose purposes in the all of this, we cannot see.

And there we are again slapping ourselves in the face and reminding ourselves just as we did the day before that this is on us. On, We the People!

While Lincoln reminds us that God's purposes are not ours to understand in the first place, what is a profound expression of unbridled faith.

Lincoln, our sad Lincoln, in grappling with what was beyond the pale, was able to compartmentalize and to understand and to cut God some slack. Out of monumental suffering, he forged a new beginning, a re-consecrated nation and the hope that America just might be made worthy of the great grace of God.

As to our travails today, we do not know. We cannot know, but we hope and I, like Matt and millions of others daily worry, ponder, object, stand up, pray and try to cut God the same slack that Lincoln did. It is, after all and again, as Lincoln ever reminds us, ours to reckon with and to give to God and to providence. It is on us!

I was not at all surprised that *Paula Hopewell* went to faith, for when she first communicated with me, she did so from a rich faith-based perspective.

She wrote, "I would like to know more about Lincoln's thoughts on religion and spirituality. I would like to ask him the following: what were his earliest memories of what his parents taught him? What did he disagree with and why? Did he discuss his questions and doubts with his parents, especially his mother? His stepmother? Did he have any friends to talk to about this? Did he try to understand on his own"?

Continuing, she wrote, "What parts of his religious upbringing did he agree with? Did he have memories of going to church? Did he miss anything about attending church? Did his religious doubts cause him problems socially? Did he keep his doubts to himself?

What Lincoln might offer Paula in response would certainly be a revelation, in that so much debate surrounds our Lincoln and just what he did or did not believe. What fascinates is that ironically and maybe even ridiculously, most religious sects once did their level best to claim Lincoln for their own over the years. Born into an old Baptist sect that believed in pre-destination and determinism and a bit of brimstone, hellfire and damnation, in the belief that God had pre-ordained what would come to pass for all, there is no question but that Lincoln long carried fatalistic baggage.

Even as a young boy, I'm certain that he'd have no tolerance for the 'you have no skin in the game, pre-destination nonsense.

What we know is that melancholy and depression taxed his mind and spirit. It is there to be found in his brooding poetry and his doctrines of necessity and reason. I love the tales of a so very young Lincoln standing on the tree stumps, mimicking and making fun of the latest minister's sermon, as legend goes that he well remembered them all, whether worthy of remembrance or not.

Two Presbyterian churches would later be connected to him in both Springfield and Washington. They too were old school, Calvinistic enclaves as well. But he came to both of these out of grief over the death of his two sons, Eddie and Willie, and not out of faithful belonging. He came because two ministers won his trust and his friendship and he had faith in them, if not their doctrine.

But throughout his life, Lincoln got along extremely well with men of the cloth, enjoying their company and freely and often conversing with them. Carl Sandburg, Allen Guelzo via his *Abraham Lincoln: Redeemer President* and Richard Cawardine are among the many historians who pointedly bear witness to this and to the fact that he celebrated and heralded Christian concepts and values and worked with Christian ideas while never declaring himself a Christian. So too do a cast of characters in his life, including William Stoddard, a White House aide, the ever present Noah Brooks and Ward Hill Lamon, friend, protector and one of his earliest biographers. Again, our *Lincoln the Enigma*, who as Herndon quipped, "*kept half of himself secret, away from the general public, and then kept half of what was left even from his closest friends.*"

What a great, revealing and telling Herndon observation that is.

He got on well with and apparently long discussed the scriptures with ministerial friends like Dr. John Allen, devout Presbyterian and physician in New Salem, the Reverend John Hogan, a fellow legislator and the Reverends James Lemen, Jr. and Hoyes Miner in Vandalia and Springfield. He later grew particularly close to Presbyterian ministers, Dr. James Smith of Springfield and Dr. Phineas Gurley of Washington D.C. upon the deaths of Eddie and Willy respectively. In order to claim him for Christianity, a myth went viral after his death that having died on Good Friday, he was that Easter to have officially become a member of Washington's New York Avenue Presbyterian Church. There was, however, simply no evidence whatsoever to support such a claim.

It was the Reverend Lemen, I believe, who effusively detailed their conversations about the Holy Scriptures and Lincoln's reported presence at his services, while suggesting that Lincoln was like "that philosophical apostle, Thomas" who struggled with doubt, but not unlike thousands of Christians." Again reminding me of my aforementioned reference to Father James Carroll's "*It is only in the doubting that I find my belief.*"

As did Lincoln, I believe.

In the White House years, one can make the argument that he met with ministerial alliances and ministers almost as often as he did with politicians. One can also argue that he gathered strength and renewed hope from them. Being with was never considered to be a waste of time to him. And of course, there's his famous 1846 *Handbill* in response to the Reverend Peter Cartwright's charges of infidelity and the later fact that he was deeply concerned about and worked to assure that chaplains were everywhere available to his soldiers.

As to Cartwright, his opponent in that 1846 congressional campaign, Lincoln had the moxie to stop by one of the good Reverend's Revival meetings, not long before the August election. Noticing Lincoln, when it came time to call all the sinners forward to repent and accept the Lord Jesus, Cartwright called him out, inviting him to come forward. When Lincoln politely declined, Cartwright shouted something along the lines of, "Well then, Mr. Lincoln, where are you going"? Without skipping a beat, he loudly replied, "*Why Mr. Cartwright, I am going to Congress.*"

Can't help but love that.

Lincoln also seemed to have a profound connection to the Quaker community and their pacifism, a conundrum that he freely addressed with them and one that did not stand in the way of their forging a special bond. This was manifested in meetings with official delegations as well as with some special women. There is first the extraordinary response from Elizabeth Comstock upon his request for whatever "encouragement" they might afford. Here, her response:

> *Abram, we believe we have a message from the Lord for thee,* she wrote. *He has laid a great burden upon thee, and thou canst not bear it alone. It is too much for thee. He says, be of good courage and I will be with thee. I will not leave thee nor forsake thee. Thou shalt prevail, only be of good courage. Cast all thy burdens upon Him. He is the great burden-bearer. Nothing is too hard for HIM. The destiny of this great nation is upon HIM. Do not try to carry it thyself. Look to HIM. He will guide thee. He will give thee wisdom and thou shalt prevail. May it not be that GOD has raised thee up, like Moses, to be the great emancipator of HIS people? To establish the nation united and free? As HE said to Joshua, only be strong and of good courage.*

Lincoln indeed prayed with them and Elizabeth Comstock thoughtfully recalled that "His countenance was so changed that he looked as though he had the victory." (*Lincoln and the Quakers*, Bassuk p. 16)

Eliza P. Gurney, the wonderful Eliza P. Gurney, the one who visited Lincoln who may well have had as great an impact upon him as any other visitor or suitor, the Quaker with the rich and beautiful soul who so moved Lincoln. First, there was her visit, along with 3 others, to the White House on October 26 1862, where they prayed, meditated and gave their hopes to God.

Then, there was her resounding letter. The "*I believe the prayers of many thousands whose hearts thou hast gladdened by thy praiseworthy and successful effort 'to burst the bands of wickedness, and let the oppressed go free' that the Almighty may strengthen thee to accomplish all these blessed purposes*" letter of August 8, 1863.

Followed by his moving "*fiery trial*" and "*I am but a humble instrument in the hands of our heavenly father*" and "*If I had my way—if my will prevailed, we cannot help but believe that he who made the world still governs it*" letter of September 4, 1864. "*The purposes of the Almighty are perfect and must prevail,*" Lincoln affirmed.

On this question of faith, there is ever so much more and there is the fact, as Richard Carwardine emphasized in his *Lincoln: Profiles in Power* that it was the religious leaders that went to bat with their faithful for him in advocating for his just and necessary war as well as his re-election. Hundreds of ministers proselytized for their "rail splitter" and his war and his cause. From altars and at camp meetings, they did this.

The faith community was on a mission to reelect Abraham Lincoln, member or not, who they all somehow saw as one of their own.

So this is it: He never belonged to any sect or declared himself a Christian, but he was conversant in all and, as familiar with or more familiar with the scriptures than any ordained minister was. He looked to the faith community and they most certainly looked to him. He bonded with all, spoke the language of all, freely and willingly prayed and came to be revered by all.

"Be perfect, as your Father in Heaven is perfect." proclaimed Jesus or so it is written in the *Gospel of Saint Matthew*. A tall order indeed and while he may have fallen short, as all do, Lincoln, at least, aspired to be and do his level best.

His brother and sister's keeper, he lived the life of a man of faith.

Had he not believed and had he not devoted himself to service and sacrifice, by the way, there could never have been the beauty or the power or the wonder of his *Second Inaugural*.

In the end, while I share Paula's curiosity and would love to hear Lincoln's response to her questions, it is ultimately of no consequence. For it is not what he believed that matters. It is rather how he lived and while he was not a practicing Christian, he lived like the most faithful of Christians, the most faithful of Jews, the most faithful of all who look to the Divine to guide and secure.

Matt Lakemacher added this:

> *I have often visualized jumping in my Historical Time Machine, as Gerry Prokopowicz likes to call it on "Civil War Talk Radio," and deciding what one event or moment I would most like to witness for myself. I usually land on the first reading of the Emancipation Proclamation, and I am seated with the cabinet at that table in the famous Francis Carpenter engraving.* The Gettysburg Address *would be a must see, if for no other reason to see the crowd's reaction to what must have been an underwhelming speech at the time (I'll arrive right after Edward Everett is done speaking though, thank you very much). Or, I wouldn't mind sitting in with Sherman, Grant, and Porter aboard the River Queen as we talk winning the peace with the Commander in Chief, in my favorite Lincoln painting, by George Healy. For me, though, I'd prefer a private conversation with Lincoln where we could talk about spiritual things, about his religious beliefs, his struggle with doubt, and his ultimate faith in God.*

While quite a few of our collaborators longed to be with Lincoln at Gettysburg, I believe Matt alone places himself in the Cabinet Room on July 22, 1862 when Lincoln announces his intention to issue the proclamation and on the River Queen by Hampton Roads on February 3, 1865, where Lincoln, having successfully secured his 13th Amendment eradicating slavery in the United States, finally meets with the Southern Peace Delegation, the one that he assured Congress was not in Washington in order to first win the vote on the 13th Amendment and the glorious abolition of slavery.

In simply being a fly on the wall, although Matt would much rather appear as is, on that July 22, 1862 morning when Lincoln met with his cabinet at the White House, Matt could go a long way in setting a historical record straight. There is no question as to the fact that Lincoln shocked them, that his mind on issuing the *Emancipation Proclamation* was fixed and that, while he wanted them to speak freely from their hearts as to their position, he would entertain recommendations on content and wording alone. As to substance and objective, he would not be moved.

He had long worked on it in the quiet of the Telegraph Office in the War Department while waiting for the next loaded telegram from the front.

While we know that Edward Bates, as Attorney General, had likely already provided Lincoln with basic, although less than definitive legal cover, Bates alone may have been fully aware, if not that day, that it was coming soon. So too, those two with him, when he leaked news in a carriage ride. Matt might be able to tell us just how strong Stanton and Seward were in their endorsements—and just how different what Chase actually said was as opposed to what he wanted the world to believe he said—and just how strong Montgomery Blair was in his opposition, as he believed it would cause them to lose the Fall elections—and just what it was that the quiet ones, Gideon Welles and Caleb Smith, may have contributed.

Of course, we know that Lincoln agreed with Seward as to the question of timing. That is Seward's, "*It could be seen as our last shriek on the retreat*" and that it was better to tie it to a moment of strength or victory. As such, it was announced later after the dubious victory at Antietam, rather than upon the heels of what then would have been McClellan's disastrous Peninsula Campaign.

As to the famous and celebrated Francis Bicknell Carpenter painting, I am sure Matt will attest to the fact that they never posed for the portrait and that, in keeping with the informality of Lincoln's cabinet meetings, were more than likely sprawled out all over the place, one prone on the couch, two with their feet upon the table and another rocking back and forth in his chair.

What I believe he'll take from it is the seriousness and solemnity of it all, the strength and emotion in Lincoln's voice that history cannot affirm but that we are somehow certain of, as he roles the dice and dares to risk, while defining just what his constitutional war powers were. Rendering the slaves in those states in rebellion against the United States "thenceforward, and forever free" was monumental. And while the *Emancipation Proclamation* may have been deliberately devoid of Lincoln's ringing phrases and poetic usage and with all the "*enthusiasm,*" as it was said, "*of a bill of lading,*" the power of "thenceforward and forever," at least and oh so meaningfully, 'slam dunks' it home.

All his doubts notwithstanding, all his concerns as to just what impact this would have on the morale of his troops and upon the very ability to recruit, all the fears he had as to the impact on his understandably precious, slave-holding border-states and all his understandable concerns about prospective political fallout aside, he did this. It took courage to do this and courage he had, as he noted that he was absolutely determined and willing to grapple with whatever followed, be it Seward's contention that England and France might intervene out of concern for King Cotton or Blair's fear that Republicans would suffer electorally or the mighty litany of concerns that he himself had for so long weighed and measured.

The price of the war had grown far too great. Yes, the clarion call of Webster's "Our federal union, one and inseparable, now and forever" first, but it was time to make it about something more.

It was time to begin setting men free.

As to Hampton Roads aboard the River Queen on February 3, 1865, what an extraordinary gathering, one where the soon to be conquerors gathered with a delegation of the soon to be vanquished and where Matt interestingly places himself with Generals Grant & Sherman and Admiral Porter, the military commanders who had fashioned the inevitable.

Interestingly, there among the stars, he looks like he belongs, the absence of a uniform notwithstanding.

We all know that Lincoln, sly fox that he was, wisely kept this rather impressive delegation at bay, so as to prevent their presence from becoming a political excuse to forestall the vote on the 13th Amendment. Again, he earlier replied to the Congressional inquiry as to whether there was such a delegation, by circumspectly affirming that there was no such delegation in Washington. True, but only because he had them militarily and secretly sequestered elsewhere, ironically in the care of Ulysses S. Grant, the commander of all Union forces and the one who had relentlessly pursued, punished and inevitably decimated Bobby Lee's celebrated Army of Northern Virginia, who were then still, but not for long, under siege at Petersburg.

Movingly, when this delegation passed through the lines there, Confederate and Union soldiers alike raised a cheer and a hope.

For the record, Lincoln's response to Congress surely goes beyond the level of a mere white lie, but still and only rises to the level of a venial and not a mortal sin.

Were their presence recognized, the recalcitrant Democrats would have had the excuse needed to cloud and gum up the works in advancing the 13th Amendment. Lincoln's motive was honorable in that outlawing slavery in the United States before they laid their weapons down, was, in so very many ways, what it had all been about to begin with.

In truth, the Confederacy and their armies and the death rattle had already become acquainted, so their bargaining position was so very weak, but there was still something to be said for saving what lives they could and not adding to the already incomprehensible and horrific death toll.

Representing the Union were Lincoln and Seward whose mindsets were well known both to engaged citizens at the time and to all today who study this history. Here is the policy of the United States, as presented in Lincoln's own hand:

> *As to peace, I have said before, and now repeat that three things are indispensable:*
> *The restoration of the national authority throughout the United States.—No receding by the Executive of the United States on the slavery question from the position assumed thereon in the last annual message, and in preceding documents.—No cessation of hostilities short of an end of the war, and the disbanding of all forces hostile to the government.*

All propositions coming from those in rebellion against the United States would have to respect the above, but they were without any such authority to do so.

What interests us is that they were a rather strong and honorable bunch whose intentions were good. To a man, they mourned the war and sincerely and humanely longed for it to cease. The 3-man delegation included Alexander Hamilton Stephens, the Vice President of the Confederate States of America and a once friend of and former boarding room house mate of Abraham Lincoln when they served in Congress together, John C. Campbell, a once Associate Justice of the United States Supreme Court and Assistant Secretary of War for the Confederacy and Robert Hunter, former Speaker of the United States House of Representatives, United States Senator, and Confederate Secretary of State and Senator.

None of them were ever rebel zealots or firebrands. In fact, all of them struggled with secession, had long been interested in negotiating peace and had their open wars with the leadership of Jefferson Davis.

They truly wanted peace, but in what was a 4-hour meeting, there was literally no 'there –there.' We know that all were cordial, that Lincoln did what he typically did to lighten the conversation with stories and quips and that while holding fast to the central issues of sovereignty, authority and the fact that slavery was done, all due liberality as to compensation, repatriation, etc. would be afforded. There are many who allege that both Seward and Lincoln discussed prospective give-backs on the slave question which I believe to be impossible, as the ends going in for Lincoln and Seward were most assuredly the ends going out.

And yes, Lincoln did perceive it as a fruitless endeavor in that the main obstacle was the obtuse and 'blind to reality' president of the Confederacy, Jefferson Davis. In Lincoln's December 6, 1864 *Annual Message to Congress*, he wrote, "*Davis would accept nothing short of severance of the Un-*

ion—precisely what we will not and cannot give. His declarations to this effect are explicit and oft-repeated. He cannot voluntarily reaccept the Union; we cannot voluntarily yield it. . . . the issue between him and us can only be tried by war and decided by victory." So it was said and so it had to be, the good intentions of these fair minded and 'tried by and tired of war' peace delegates notwithstanding.

While David Herbert Donald, Lincoln biographer, assuredly knew far more than I, I am loathe to accept his contention that Lincoln went to Hampton Roads to 'play the peace delegation,' so to speak, in a public relations stunt to sow the seeds of discontent against Davis and rouse tired and beleaguered southerners who were sick of the war, but neither did he go to make peace. Davis had long been doing all he could on his own to spread those seeds of discontent among southern masses longing for peace; and what Lincoln could best do at Hampton Roads was to simply continue being Lincoln. Hampton Roads was but an obligatory courtesy call.

As to peace, he had said so often and simply that it required nothing more than the laying of their weapons down and submitting to the national authority, matters that were to be resolved in two months or but a short time in the lifetime of this awful war.

Seward later took offense to Senator Hunter's contention that all they were left with was "unconditional submission" when, in fact, they would be freely and without humiliation welcomed back into a Union with all civil and political rights; and Lincoln went so far as to inform him that he had the power to pardon, to restore seized property and to award compensation where circumstances might warrant, powers that he promised to exercise with the *"utmost liberality."*

The New York Herald of February 8, 1865 reported that *"Old Abe was a giant among pigmies."* The article defended his position as "impregnable" and reaffirmed the fact that there could be neither final victory nor peace, short of "the expulsion of Jeff Davis from Richmond and the defeat of and dissolution of Lee's army."

Some points of interest:

There is much to cobble out of the Lincoln-Stephens belonging, from their friendship in Washington, to their December 1860 and January 1861 correspondence to Stephens' later speech memorializing Lincoln in D.C. Also of interest is that there is no way that Stephens would ever have suffered those 5 months imprisoned at Fort Warren in Boston Harbor had Lincoln and his "utmost liberality" lived.

Even after Hampton Roads, Campbell continued to meet with Lincoln in the interest of peace. He was a true southern 'warrior for peace' who was extremely dismayed by what Lee would come to refer to as *"further fruitless slaughter."* And while I have yet to read it myself, it is on my bucket list of publications to procure and so I refer it to you—Mann's 1966, "*The Political and Constitutional Thought of John Archibald Campbell*."

While Senator Hunter was indeed dismayed by his experience at Hampton Roads, Lincoln, in his final days, personally reached out to him to discuss Virginia's re-entry into the Union. Also of note is the fact that General Richard Garnett, one of Pickett's Brigadiers was his first cousin. As Garnett's wounded leg was bad and Stonewall Jackson had once wrongfully accused him of cowardice, he alone rode, upon his black charger, into that mad torrent of Union fire on that incredible 3rd day at Gettysburg. Truly unfit for duty, he would not stand down, fell early in the battle and his remains were among the many never recovered. Forever committed to be one of the many '*Ghosts of Gettysburg*, his brother, Robert also fell in the service of the Confederacy.

Can't help but note the obvious at this juncture, which is the simple fact that the study of any point of or person in history spirals out in a fascinating myriad of directions and tangents. It all becomes kaleidoscopic and so wonderfully fascinating and ultimately impossible to fully discern. Try as we might, we are always left to wonder.

Should Matt ever get his wish to go back in time and sit in at Hampton Roads, I can't wait to get the skinny on all that was truly said on the question of slavery, or rather and far more importantly, the end of slavery.

APRIL 4, 1865

Our friend, *Bob Willard* once took an incredible walk through the Land of Lincoln, from his birthplace in Hodgenville, Kentucky to all the varying Lincoln stops in Indiana and Illinois, to New Salem and Springfield and other ports in Illinois that are proud to lay claim to Lincoln. Having long and often labored in Washington D.C., the final Land of Lincoln, he has often walked in Old Abe's footsteps there as well.

As to his imagined conversation, he opts, as many have, to both listen and question, and also, as many have, he opts for a particular moment in time. He chooses to walk again, joining Lincoln on what well may be his most famous walk, the one he took through Richmond on an unseasonably hot April 4, 1865.

Willard wrote, "I have challenged Lincoln buddies in a related way, where I ask if they could spend a single day with Lincoln (but could not interact or change anything), what day would it be? It's a fun exercise. My own answer for many years has been April 4, 1865, as he walks the streets of Richmond and "occupies" Jefferson Davis' home."

Yes, just to be in his company on that remarkable and blessed day, as he would have loved to ask him the questions that this one day inspired.

"What did he think about the freed slaves' reaction to his being there," I'd ask? "And why had it taken so long and why did he bring Tad (especially considering the possible danger)? Did he have goose bumps? I do whenever I think of this extraordinary stroll he had in Richmond on that day of days"!

I take the liberty here of calling an audible and relating my own first visit to Richmond. Given my own deep dives into the lives of Confederate leaders like Lee, Jackson, Longstreet and others, I could well have been drawn to it in its own right. But that was not the case and what rather inspired me to go there was Lincoln. He was going back to Richmond, you see, at least by way of a David Frech bronze sculpture, a work that was to rise in a park where the historic Tredegar Iron Works on the banks of the James River once fed the Confederacy's very ability to wage war.

Notably, he was to be well removed from their celebrated 'Canyon of Heroes' and placed on the outskirts of town.

I went because I picked up the news feeds as to the burgeoning controversy surrounding it. The Sons of Confederate War Veterans were mightily objecting for Lincoln historically, they insisted, came to Richmond, not in peace or in the interest of harmony and reconciliation, but rather and only as a conqueror who wished to pile it on by doing a celebratory end zone dance. The *New York Times, Newark Star Ledger* and *Washington Post* were all covering the controversy. I, for whatever reason, remember the Post headline, *Another Rebel Stand*.

They couldn't stop him on April 4, 1865 but 138 years and 1 day later, April 5, 2003, they were determined to do so.

I even got my wife, Maggie, to consent to joining me and we planned a long, four day weekend. While I visited some of the 7 Days battlefield sites, the Museum of the Confederacy, Jefferson Davis' house and church and what was once the home of the Confederate Congress on Thursday and Friday on my own, Maggie joined me for the big day and the big deal on Saturday, Lincoln's return to Richmond.

She was most surprised by the gauntlet of Confederate soldiers and erstwhile Confederate women (reenactors) who were screaming at us and all who were entering. But there were plenty of police on hand and it was no big deal.

What was, however, was the prop plane that began buzzing the crowd with a large trailing sign, heralding the words, "*Sic Semper Tyrannis.*"

Back and forth, it went throughout the ceremony, consistently interrupting the speakers and leaving the audience a bit confused. Our own Harold Holzer was, I recall, one of the honored guests and presenters that day.

I left puzzling 'my puzzler' as to the fact that the war philosophically and absurdly goes on. And while I'm tempted to add ignorantly, I freely admit that the protest was far more emotional than thoughtful. Even today, 17 years removed from that dedication, the "*Bind up the nation's wounds*" that is inscribed on the low lying wall behind the peaceful image of father and son on a park bench is greeted on social media with "What garbage this is" or "Lincoln was a war criminal and this is more salt in the wounds of southerners everywhere" or "War criminal and tyrant Lincoln should have no place of honor in . . ." and so on and so forth.

As it happened that April 4th, while Lincoln strolled through Richmond, Bobby Lee and his *Miserables* were on the run and while they held on to the forlorn hope of escaping to the Carolinas, their prospects were dim and Lincoln knew this.

He also knew, more than anyone outside of Grant, that the Army of Northern Virginia had long been the fighting soul of the Confederacy. From its inception, it fought against overwhelming odds; and no matter how much territory the Union army occupied, so long as this Confederate army was active in the field, the rebellion was still spiritually alive. Through four years of bitter conflict, the Army of Northern Virginia and its longtime commander, General Robert E. Lee, became the stuff of legend. But on April 4, as Lincoln disembarked from the boat, he had the confidence that came from knowing that their last days were at hand.

It would be soon. Of that, he had no doubt.

As such, it is my guess, Bob, that Lincoln's mind would, on that day alone, be focused upon the glorious fact that the end had finally come, an end that had often been in doubt. There would be time the next day and in days to come to ponder the "why so long" and "why so great a price," the "what ifs" and "might have beens." But not on that day.

It was an extraordinary and striking scene in Richmond, as a haggard, weary President Abraham Lincoln stepped off a Navy barge with his son, Tad, to visit the now devastated city of Richmond.

Notably, it was Tad's 12th birthday.

Word spread quickly among Richmond's African Americans and Lincoln was mobbed. "*Glory hallelujah!*" people cried. "*I know that I am free, for I have seen Father Abraham!*" Lincoln slowly walked the streets, took off his coat in the warm weather and in the embrace of the swarming crowd.

When they knelt before him, Lincoln said, "*Don't kneel to me, kneel to God only and thank him for your liberty,*" according to historian, Burke Davis' account.

"*My poor friends*," the president told the crowd. "*You are free—free as air. You can cast off the name of slave and trample upon it. It will be yours no more.*"

So as to your second question, Bob, I imagine that he had to be a bit shocked but elated by their reception. Uncomfortable with the praise, to be sure, but at peace with the fact that something great had been accomplished, something lasting and noble.

He was caught in that box. Humbly, he didn't see himself as extraordinary - never saw himself as extraordinary and yet he had accomplished a most extraordinary thing.

By the way, the Marine squad that Admiral Porter sent to protect the President and Tad never quite caught up with them and he and Tad were ridiculously and dangerously on their own in what was, up until the day before, the capitol of the Confederacy. But that he was in grave danger never appeared to cross his mind. Richmond, after all, had, to him, always been part of his United States of America.

He simply didn't see that he was placing Tad in danger and I think he brought him because it was his birthday and doting father and son needed each other.

As to those few whites who were on the streets of Richmond that day, we are told that remnants of, or officials of, the Confederate Government, the few who did not board the train to Danville and run with their president the night before, were on hand and reportedly pleased with the words that Lincoln shared. If Bob's "what if" should ever come to pass, he might kindly fill in the blanks for us.

But of this, we can be certain, magnanimity and Lincoln were old friends.

Accordingly when General Godfrey Weitzel asked Lincoln for guidance as to how to handle the conquered people, he responded, *"If I were in your place, I'd let em' up easy – I'd let em' up easy."*

Again, the newly freed, black citizens teemed outside and they longed to pat Lincoln on the back, to touch him, to celebrate him and as you might guess, he was taken aback by the adulation. It was their first day of freedom and so very strangely, the world had turned upside down, leaving them both elated and lost at one and the same time.

On this day, however, the wonder and excitement subdued the fear.

The 'what would become of them tomorrow' could wait.

"The slaves seemed to think that the day of jubilee had come," wrote H.S. DeForest, chaplain of the Union's 11th Connecticut Regiment. *"How they danced, shouted and shook our hands . . . and thanked God for our coming. . . . it is a day never to be forgotten by us, till days shall be no more."*

African American troops entered the town, the 28th USCT. Its chaplain was the Reverend Garland H. White, who had been born a slave in Richmond, before escaping to the North.

"It appeared to me [that] all colored people in the world had collected there," he recalled. Some of his men later brought him an old woman, who questioned him at some length and then joyfully said: "This is your mother, Garland, whom you are now talking to, who has spent twenty years of grief over her lost son."

There, in the midst of it all was Lincoln who came to embrace an American city that had been lost and was now found, a city where the cries and the weeping of Southern women whose husbands and sons had died, whose livelihoods and way of being and city had all but crumbled went unheard by him. Imprisoned behind the red and brown bricks of the stately Richmond homes that still stood, they huddled in fear for what had become of the life and world they knew.

Had he the chance, I imagine Lincoln would have tried to toss them a measure of hope as well.

After all, hope was why he came.

"*With malice toward none and with charity for all*," he had come not to gloat but to reconcile and reclaim.

A victory dance, hell no, he came out of respect, he came because he mourned with those who mourned, cried with those who cried and celebrated with those who shouted, *Jubilee.*

Goose bumps, Bob, no doubt. As measured and controlled as he was, on this day, all bets were off.

Life went on, as the few magnolias, tulips and April blossoms he passed attested to.

RACE, BIGOTRY, LOSS AND "WITH MALICE TOWARD NONE"

Edna Greene Medford of Howard University, had a small laundry list of pointed subjects that she would like to discuss with him.

These included his personal views on race and why it was that while demonstrating kindness to free African Americans personally, he so indiscriminately told racial jokes with racial slurs; and why it was that he treated Frederick Douglass one way and Sojourner Truth another; and just why and when he decided that he had the power to make men free (or "*at least, some of them*"); and then too and finally, what it was that gave life to the extraordinary thinking and emotional power behind the near sanctity of those magnanimous words of forgiveness, "*With malice toward none, with charity for all.*"

"Of course," she wrote, "I would be interested in talking to Lincoln about his views on race, for I have always found his statements and views regarding African Americans to be contradictory. I would ask him why he thought it was okay to tell racial jokes while showing kindness to individual people of color. I would want to know what he really thought of Frederick Douglass and why he was able to treat him with respect while considering African Americans socially inferior. I would ask why he responded to Douglass differently than how he responded to a visit from Sojourner Truth. And I would want to know when he first decided that he did indeed have the ability to declare enslaved people free (at least some of them)."

Please understand that Medford, who I revere, is a historian who discovers and inspires and I but a lifelong student of history who does not do the hard primary research but rather reflects, ponders and posits upon the same. It is, by the way, no small thing to tie disparate pieces together and affirm the deeper truths. There is something to be said for the fact that I go deep and long and hard and reverently at this, but in the end, my work is what it is, a search for the deeper truths and the wonder of the same.

I also know each of Medford's observations as to race and *Lincoln, the Enigma* to be valid and worthy of exploration. And while I too have thought about some of the issues that she raises, I still do not pretend to have hard answers. What I do have are visceral reactions and intuitive reflections to share. Some might well look upon them as excuses and look upon me as an apologist for Abraham Lincoln and while that may certainly be a possibility, I do not believe it to be.

Abraham Lincoln came to the White House and Washington as an imperfect work in progress. Like anyone, he was a product of his place and time and culture and, to a degree, of its inherent bigotries and ignorance. *"He was born in the slave state of Kentucky and he was part of the white diaspora that steadily migrated from the south into Indiana and Illinois. Among these emigrants, many no doubt did so to get away from the slaves themselves as much as the slavery. He was no abolitionist. We know this as he both said it and wrote it."* (Thank you Matt Lakemacher.)

These imperfections notwithstanding, it is again instructive to remember that in the greening and youthful spring of his life, he did not run with the pack and was among a distinct minority who voted against the bill affirming the sacred right of Southern States to their slaves.

However flawed, he was an anomaly, for there was never a doubt or a question as to where he stood on the institution of slavery and the amoral and inhumane depravity of it. And while he ever believed that the slaves ought to be equal before the law and entitled to eat the bread that they make, it wasn't until he was well into his service as President of the United States of America, I believe, that his prejudices and bigotries as to their being equal in all things were finally overcome.

Despite his friendships with people of color or the fact that he lived in harmony with free African Americans in his Springfield neighborhood, he was still surprised and humbled by his own ignorance upon discovering that African Americans and once slaves clearly viewed America as their own country as well. His '*Buy Out the Slaves and Support their Emigration Elsewhere, either to Liberia or Haiti or Chiriqui (Grenada) Plan*' was to go nowhere. Out of touch at the time, he spoke to 5 delegates about it at an April 14, 1862 meeting in the White House. All 5 were leaders and prominent clergymen in the African American community of Washington D.C. and they politely listened to Lincoln speak of the perceived benefits of the separation of the races upon the emancipation of the whole.

But Edward Thomas, Delegation Chair and community leader, John F. Cook Jr., founder of the 15th Street Presbyterian Church, Benjamin McCoy, the founder of the all African American Asbury Methodist Church, John T. Costin, a recognized leader of the African American Freemasons and Cornelius Clark would politely consider, recognize that there were indeed some of their own peers arguing for emigration as well, and yet, in their pointed failure to ever officially respond to Lincoln, loudly condemn the idea with their profound silence. Notably, their Southern Civic Statistical Association documented the economic contributions and strengths of that city's African American community and presented a strong case for citizenship, in that they would, in and around Washington, clearly expect to thrive in freedom.

Lincoln would never again publicly press the emigration-colonization argument.

That was it—one meeting and done. Their silence spoke volumes and he would never again raise the issue.

As to the above information, one definitive source is *The African American Delegation to Abraham Lincoln: A Reappraisal by* Kate Masur, published by Kent State University Press. Interestingly and bringing it home to this humble effort, Masur first acknowledged and thanked our own Edna Greene Medford for her contributions to her study.

Of course, Lincoln was taken by Frederick Douglass and so too, I believe, by Elizabeth Keckley *"who gave her own son to the war"* and by William Slade, the *"keeper of the keys"* to his White House and by the personal sacrifice of Elizabeth Thomas and by the goodness of his old friend, Billy deFleurville and by the noble gentlemen above who rejected emigration and, yes, even by Sojourner Truth and other African American freedom fighters and later, and without question, the 180,000 African American soldiers who would courageously fight to save his Union.

As to the free men and women of color who touched Lincoln, who befriended him and who had to have been forces in shaping his thinking upon the issue of equality in all things, a telling source, however romanticized, is *They Knew Lincoln* by John E. Washington, published in 1942. Among these, most notably, were the aforementioned William (Billy) de Fleurville, Elizabeth Thomas and William Slade, all of whom touched Lincoln's heart as well as his soul.

Haitian born and by way of Baltimore to New Orleans to Illinois, Billy the Barber first met Lincoln in 1831 in New Salem. Lincoln solicited clients for him and when they both relocated to Springfield, Billy's Barbershop, directly across from the Illinois State House, became a social center and a *"second home"* to Lincoln where he would tell his stories and jokes and help lure customers in for his friend.

According to Lloyd Ostendorf, a local newspaper editor, "*Only two men in Springfield, his law partner, William Herndon and his barber, William de Fleurville understood Lincoln*," the two *Billys* in his life.

When Lincoln walked in on the day of his wedding and asked Billy for a shave, he was told that a wedding shave was different and that it would cost a whole dollar, to which Lincoln replied, "*Alright, Billy, I suppose I ought not to dance without paying the fiddler.*" When Lincoln left Springfield, it was Billy who was entrusted with taking care of his property, a task that he faithfully fulfilled, going so far as to advise Willie and Tad that their dog, Fido, was being well taken care of. In late December of 1863, he wrote Lincoln a lengthy letter of encouragement that was, to me, fascinating. In it, he wrote of oppression and freedom, of the war and sacrifice and of his vision that "*The nation will rejoice, the oppressed will shout the name of their deliverer, and generations to come will rise up and call you blessed.*"

As for William Slade, who was, for the record, the president of Washington's SCSA, he was the ever present head of the staff at both the White House and the Soldier's Home. Faithful, diligent and true, he managed all events, took care of all needs and came to lay out the very clothes that Lincoln was to be buried in. Willie and Tad played with his children at both the White House and at the Slade home on Massachusetts Avenue and it was Slade who delivered Lincoln's private messages to cabinet officers and other officials. He was trusted with Lincoln's plans before anyone else in Washington.

When the home of gentle Elizabeth Thomas was, via eminent domain, commandeered for the erection of Fort Stevens, designed to protect Washington from an attack from the North, we know that Lincoln comforted and commiserated with her and promised her that she would be compensated for her sacrifice. The soldiers used her barn to set up a temporary home for her and so it was that she was still there on site on the foreboding days of July 11 & 12, 1864, when General Lee's "*Bad old Man,*" General Jubal Early and the 2nd Corps of the Army of Northern Virginia threatened Washington. While busy volunteering and supplying the soldiers with ammunition and supplies, it was Elizabeth Thomas who cried out, "*My God, make that fool come down off that hill and come in here*" (*They Knew Lincoln*) upon spotting Lincoln, top hat and all, standing upon the parapet.

In the all of this and more, and this was Lincoln's great strength, he never kept discovering, evolving and growing. Lincoln was ever in a state of becoming and on the issue of race and equality in all things, his lifelong prejudices were indeed finally and fully tamed. It may have taken him time, he may have been slow but he did grow up to the realization that just as he had turned around, so too could his nation, however difficultly, do so.

He delivered an almost perfect sermon on this subject on March 4, 1865.

Again and for most of his adult life, he did not believe in the equality of the races (few abolitionists did), but he fought for their freedom and for *raising them up in the race of life.* Regardless of his bigotries, it was he, as early as 1838 in his *Lyceum Address*, who condemned the madness of mob violence (i.e., the murder of abolitionist editor Elijah Lovejoy in Alton, Illinois); he who wrote the *Emancipation Proclamation*; he who laid the groundwork for and fought so very hard for the *13th Amendment*; he, in his *Last Public Address*, who opened the door to the franchise for once slaves and then free citizens; he who invited Frederick Douglass to be an honored guest at the White House; and he, who urged the freed slaves in Richmond on April 4, 1865 to give thanks to God only and not to him. He, who told them, "*You are free, as free as air.*

In the end, it is his actions that speak for him.

And yes, as to Sojourner Truth, their October 29, 1864 meeting may not have been as warm as his sessions with Douglass were, but still, Sojourner, according to Lucy Colman, in the immediate wake of that visit, described the two of them as "*fellow freedom fighters whose mutual respect and admiration surpassed both gender and color lines.*" It also is my understanding that when she told Lincoln that she did not know of him before his rise to the presidency, he softly smiled and told her that he did indeed know of her and her work, which was, at the very least, a demonstration of respect. He also was pleased to show her the Bible that had been presented to him by 'people of color' in Baltimore. Clearly, he must have been motivated to do this to tangibly demonstrate his connection to those she fought for.

Still, no doubt, he was at ease, free and even jovial with Douglass and I am without explanation. Beyond the basic acknowledgment of the fact that Abraham Lincoln was ever more comfortable with men and uncomfortable and awkward with women. Tall, gangly and anything but handsome (at least that's how he saw himself), he was self-conscious and not as laid back as he was with men. Anne Rutledge, the crying wives and mothers who begged for the lives of their husbands and sons and maybe Elizabeth Gurney were among the exceptions to this rule, but remember, even his marriage to Mary was deemed by him to be a "*matter of profound wonder*" that he did not fully comprehend.

I point this out only because it was true of him, recognizing that it in no way excuses or lets him off the hook.

Then too, where may his head have been on the day that he met with Sojourner. Was he at all worried about the soon to be November 8 election, or the Siege at Petersburg, or of the progress being made on the fight for the 13th amendment in the House of Representatives, or on the hope of making an end of his horrific war, or on the mother who just pleaded for her son that day or the wife for her husband.

And while none of these actions were necessarily earth shattering, there were that day anti-guerilla movements on the Mississippi and skirmishes in the Shenandoah, at Winchester, near Fort Donelson and at Nonconnah Creek in Colliersville, Tennessee. General Thomas, the *Rock of Chickamagua,* had ordered a Cavalry reconnaissance near New Market, Virginia and Confederate General John Bell Hood had just crossed the Tennessee River near Bainbridge on his way to join forces with General Beauregard. The war went on and even on the quietest of days, his boys in blue contributed their individual *"last full measures of devotion."*

After Lincoln passed, the road ahead for the finally freed was to be extremely difficult, harsh, rugged and wholly unacceptable, and it would likely have been less so had Lincoln lived, for in his death, both the South and those once enslaved lost the one man who might have made some difference. More than likely, the madness of Jim Crow, separate but equal and the vile hate and cruel bigotry that gave rise to it was sadly inevitable. But still the question of what Lincoln, whose leadership skills had been well honed and who was so obviously of a mind to grant these challenged and newly free citizens a start '*in the race of life,*' dreamers are left to ponder the 'might have been and the what could have been' in them.

What is certain is that Lincoln would never—ever—have tolerated the vigilantism and the violence that both Presidents Johnson and Grant did. He would have fought for justice and fairness for them, as my collaborator, Douglas Egerton, also strongly asserts.

To Lincoln, this would have been a priority. To those who followed him, it was not.

And just like Medford, whenever *"With malice toward none, with charity for all"* is heralded, how can we not be amazed. No matter how many times, stunned. Just imagine what it would have been like to hear it in the moment, to be there as Lincoln rose from his seat and approached the crowd. Imagine being there as the bright sun suddenly burst through the clouds on what had been a rainy and dreary day up until then. It was as if God blessed his address and his intentions.

As the ever present Noah Brooks recorded. *"Just at that moment, the sun, which had been obscured all day, burst forth in its unclouded meridian splendor, and flooded the spectacle with glory and with light."*

It was not lost on Lincoln who told Brooks the next day, *"Did you notice that sunburst? It made my heart jump."*

Upon writing the above and questioning myself as I did, I can't help but wonder is it true because it is true or is it my truth simply because that is what I will it to be? The subjective in our historical meanderings forever prods and tempers, and every once in a while, actually illuminates the objective. The all of which reminds me of two telling lines about the nature of history.

The infamous Napoleon Bonaparte noted that *"History is a set of lies agreed upon"* and Samuel Butler, erudite soul that he was wrote, *"God cannot change history, though historians can."* Oh, there were many, once upon a time, who wrote history as they wanted it to be, including those who promoted the mystical and ethereal Sainthood of Lincoln. But that trend wound down long ago and Lincoln scholarship today is spot on and profound.

Long ago, Theodore White, who gave us that *Making of the President* series back when the office demanded that the victor aspire to high honor and dignity, argued in his *In Search of History* that it is a search for the tidal waves that change the world and our way of being in it forever. That's no longer true either. Certainly not with Lincoln scholars, who are today probing the tiniest of ripples. And still he stands, firm, honorable, strong, gentle, kind.

General Robert E. Lee also once waxed poetically about history and concluded, *"It is history that teaches us hope."* And when a young woman at a reception at Washington College in Lexington, Virginia asked him what she must do to live a good life, he cupped her hands in his and said, *"Deny yourself."* Profoundly moving, I hear Lee's words and go right back to Lincoln, for whom denial was a life force and hope a gift given. (Fritzky, *What Must Needs Come*)

Edna Greene Medford and her work also teaches me hope. My 45 collaborators teach me hope.

As to the all of this, Lincoln and our still vast unfinished business and social and racial justice today, *Black Lives Matter* gives me hope, football players who kneel on sidelines to call attention to injustice gives me hope and even the opening of the Lynching Museum in Alabama gives me hope. For only the truth, only the truth of our history and a reckoning with it will ever enable us to heal, to reclaim and, finally-finally, build that better world where justice for all is finally and fully manifested. And if we don't do full justice for George Floyd and others dead by cop like him, indeed I tremble as to what will become of us. It must end, now and forever.

JUSTICE AND JUST WHAT THE HELL WAS WITH DAD ANYWAY

"For years, I always responded to the thrilling prospect of a conversation with Lincoln by suggesting that I would ask, 'What's with you and your father anyway.'"

Tongue in cheek or not, having already briefly gone there in this effort, it is an important question posed by *Harold Holzer*. It's personal and there are limits but still it fascinates, for while the impact upon what Lincoln achieved may have been minimal, it could just as well have been monumental.

For this relationship shaped the man who shaped the America that shaped us.

While there are many tributaries worth exploring, the most compelling is to what degree Thomas Lincoln's lack of ambition and palpable disdain for education, drove his son's insatiable appetite for knowledge and the determination to rise and to serve and to leave his mark. They were thesis and antithesis, the yin and the yang.

And while Thomas may never have taxed his mind or explored its depths, his ability to spin his own tales and stories speaks to his own inert ability to retain information. That, at least, begs the question as to what genes may have worked their magic in giving his son a mind that seemingly retained all information. Eidetic, photographic or simply Lincoln's unique genius, he never forgot what he read, what he witnessed or the 'who, what, why and when of it all.'

This was extraordinary and maybe just maybe, exactly, '*What was with him and his father anyway.*'

Begging the question of the great debt that may possibly be owed to Thomas Lincoln.

"*But it's hard to know what I would actually blurt out if, say, I had only one minute and one question,*" continued Holzer. "*Maybe I'd ask, ideally, as he was on his way to Ford's Theatre, how he actually envisioned the American future in terms of racial equality and long-deferred justice.*"

He opens up the same box as Medford in the end,, for it was centuries of already long deferred justice. Edna Greene Medford's prospective conversations already drove us to explore where Lincoln's mind was on the same in his own day and time. And I can only imagine what a limitless array of opinions, perceptions and arguments Holzer's question to Lincoln might invite.

I know that on his last day, Lincoln knew that the process of "righting" a 300-plus year wrong, as if that were even possible, had only just begun. He knew that there was no immediate way forward to exact even a meaningful measure of justice, much less full justice, but still, he believed it possible. And he would set out on that journey towards full justice.

The way forward lied with the franchise, with what would soon be memorialized in the 14th and 15th amendments and with the ability of the nation to grow and prosper in a way that would provide the opportunity for all to rise.

And while the horrific violence of the war and what he long knew of the threat of the mob and of man's inhumanity to man, i.e., his 1838 *Lyceum Address*, had to be playing on center stage in his mind, he could not possibly have conceived of a near century of Jim Crow and separate but equal and harsh bigotry and brutal lynchings and no equality and no justice—nor of the slow crawl forward a century later with Brown v. Topeka and Martin Luther King's crusade and Civil Rights and Voting Rights and Affirmative Action and Offices of Economic Opportunity and Wars on Poverty and Malcolm and Stokely, *Black is Beautiful* and *Black Power*—and nor of the election of President Obama, the later rise of *Black Lives Matter* and our recent descent into an abyss where justice is dispensed only to the rich and people of color, all colors, be damned.

155 years and counting. 155 long years and Neo-Nazis and white supremacists are still on the playing field and a president demeans and defames those who kneel for justice on the field.

We know, we know, but still.

Lincoln could never have foreseen this. Not in the deepest recesses of his mind.

That he knew the road to true equality and justice was to be difficult and long and that hatred and bigotry and even violence would be in the offing, yes, but he had too much faith in our institutions, in the rights that we wrap ourselves in and in our capacity for goodness to ever have conceived of what came to pass. A quarter century, a half century, maybe but never this, never so great and so monumental a struggle.

For once they were lynched and today, all too many rot in prison or continue to live in inner cities *"devoid of the colors, the scents and the textures of living things"* (Barbara Ward), devoid of the opportunity to be "raised up in the race of life."

What we do know, for certain, Harold, is that "Neither a slave nor a master be" has long been rendered settled truth. But, "In honor or dishonor" is forever tossed to the vagaries of the wind.

> *Take your place on the great Mandala . . . We are free now, we can kill now*
> *We can hate now, now we can end the world*
> *We're not guilty, he was crazy*
> *And it's been going on for ten thousand years!*
> —Peter, Paul and Mary

Kathryn Harris, for long the president of the Abraham Lincoln Association of Springfield, Illinois, joins both Medford and Holzer in focusing upon this issue of race, the evolution of Lincoln's thinking on the same and then too, his hopes for racial harmony in the future.

"*My conversation with Lincoln would address how his views on race evolved*," she wrote. "*I would like to hear him speak to the pivotal events or actions that prompted change in him.*"

"*Of particular interest to me*," she added, "*is his quote regarding neither being a slave nor a master.*"

Prompted by Edna Greene Medford and then again by Harold Holzer already, we have been mining this field but there is always more and now, I am, with head bowed, reminded of a Sergeant Lucien Parkhurst Waters, who

I first met in the Summer 2009 edition of *The Journal of the Abraham Lincoln Association* (Harris' own organization), via a compelling submission by Elizabeth Brown Pryor entitled *Brief Encounter: A New York Cavalryman's Striking Conversation with Abraham Lincoln.*

In going here, I open up a Pandora's Box, but our Lincoln must be taken whole. It is more about Waters than it is Lincoln but it sheds one of those lights on him that is not at all becoming and brings to the fore, the backwoodsman who lived where the bigotry and racism were taken whole and plain.

Formed early by a Colonel James Swain, Waters' cavalry regiment, what was often referred to as Scott's Volunteers (Assistant Secretary of War Thomas Scott, at whose behest Swain organized), was officially designated as the 11th New York Volunteer Cavalry and assigned to the 1st US Cavalry. Against his better judgment at the time, which was to serve his country by going to the Sea Islands of South Carolina to teach African-Americans who had swarmed into the Union lines, Swain charmed Waters (see the Lucien P. Waters Papers of the New York Historical Society) into joining his regiment instead.

A young supervisory mechanic and the son of a Presbyterian minister, Waters was fiercely opposed to slavery and he went to war to set other men free.

Literally!

To him, saving the Union was the secondary consideration.

Early on, Waters was elevated to the rank of Sergeant with responsibility for upwards of 100 men.

This 11th New York Volunteer Cavalry was assigned to scout, to surprise and to intercept civilians aiding the rebels, and also to interrupt irregular behavior by Union troops. A secret service of sorts, their eyes were fixed upon that which troubled Lincoln greatly, "the fire in the rear," as they broke up "*secesh* rings and tribunals." Assigned to Camp Relief, just north of the capitol Building, they also were charged with providing escort service for President Lincoln whenever he traveled around the city or to and from the Soldiers Home.

Lincoln resented and often grumbled about the need for this, about the invasion of his privacy and about wasting the time of good men who had better things to do. Still, he treated the soldiers with great respect, conversed with them and when circumstances permitted, even regaled them with a story. As for the men, they were taken by Lincoln's politeness, by what was referred to as his "oddities" and as Waters himself noted by "his solemn and awkward" bow. They were especially taken by the fact that he not only listened to but acted upon their complaints, from the quality of their equipment to the quality of their rations to their uniforms. Once outside the Soldiers Home, Lincoln was said to have taken a pair of army issue socks, ripping them apart with his bare hands and personally bearing witness to their poor quality. More than anything else, they were taken by the access that he afforded them.

One among them, noted Waters, said, *"The great man, bending beneath the weight of the Republic and its gigantic war, found time amid all his cares to be just to the common soldier."*

Avowed abolitionist that Waters was, he was an impatient Lincoln man who told his parents that he believed God frowned on the nation while it indulged in the *"damnable stinky curse of protecting the institution of Slavery"* and that his own resolve to fight for a true land of liberty was doubled. *"The issues are becoming sharper,"* he exclaimed, *"and it behooves the people of the North to awake from their sleep and to save, what I hope in the future we may call 'great freedom's land,' but which at present does not answer to that name."*

His duties and responsibilities were many and yet he found time to fight his own personal war for freedom. To him, it was not only about freedom for the slave but also freedom for the nation which had long been strangled by the veritable "straightjacket" of slavery. Waters began to personally seek out slaves in southern Maryland and northern Virginia who he might be able to help. A true believer in emancipation, he became a freedom fighting vigilante. Pryor wrote that "He used secret paths and hideaways known to the bondsmen and encouraged many to run away, smuggling some to Washington aboard U.S. gunboats that plied the Potomac River. He wrote false passes, told tall tales to slaveholders, and collaborated with like-minded sailors to conceal his freedom-seekers."

Freely plying his own morality, he dismissed any and all laws protecting the institution of slavery and he did so, Pryor also noted, while "mistakenly thinking he was pursuing his Moses-like mission with the blessing, indeed, under the orders, of his commander he called, "Uncle Abe."

And yet ironically, while in sync with Water's overarching goal, Lincoln's mind at the time was conflicted. He had already privately resolved to issue his *Emancipation Proclamation* at the end of the year, should a victory or excuse for a victory be available to him. But he also was preoccupied with worry about his precious border states that must be held for the Union and about perceived or imagined impacts upon the morale and the mindset of his soldiers who must save his Union.

Notably, Waters acknowledges that Lincoln appeared exhausted on the day he approached him, for it was just too damn hot and he was being pressured and picked apart and outside of Grant in the west, few had gone on to "win him victories."

On the humid morning of August 12, 1862, the state of Lincoln's state was frazzled, when Sergeant Waters seized the opportunity to present his President with a written petition for a furlough, the details of which you are free to investigate and are well documented by Pryor. Lincoln drew one of his classic, comedic poses as he dropped down, leaned his back against the portico column and drew his knobby knees up to his chin. Unaware and wholly without pretense, Pryor artfully captured the essence of the moment, *"There sits Abraham Lincoln, with a familiarity almost unimaginable today, legs folded and tall hat in place, looking for all the world like a cricket perched."*

A cricket perched, now there's a metaphor worthy of remembrance.

And then, without even opening the document, the testy response that shook Waters and contemporary readers alike, Lincoln's sudden, *"Probably has something to do with the damned or eternal niggar."*

"That spoke volumes to me," Waters wrote and it still shakes us.

That Lincoln never wrote the word is telling and so too is the fact that he did not use the term in the company of people of color, but that he could be coarse and crude and abrupt does. Pryor wrote, "Waters was offended, but he did not chastise the president, though he admitted that he would have liked to give him "a 'right smart' talking to."

Although it was only the briefest of exchanges, Pryor tellingly suggests, *"Waters experienced the president in all his complexity: the crude back-woodsman; the harried public servant; the dedicated champion of American-brand democracy who passionately believed that the people must have access to power; the hard-headed politician; the gangly, near gargoyle of a man."* Waters thought perhaps he should have taken Lincoln to task, but he was astute enough to perceive the great pressure under which the president was laboring and ultimately rationalized and forgave the outburst."

There can be no doubt that Lincoln was pressed by myriad and conflicting opinions and pressures and while determining to carve out his own and to stand firm, he was moving far too fast for some and far too slow for others. From that fire in the rear to the fervent abolitionists like Waters to the Democrats to Senator Charles Sumner and Congressman Thaddeus Stevens and Senator Orville Browning and the infamous Clement Vallandigham. Some conspired with his cabinet and others with his military leaders and there were insurrections that Lincoln had to put down and just one month earlier, his mighty Army of the Potomac, under the command of the irreverent General George McClellan, had been blown off the Virginia peninsula by Lee's Army of Northern Virginia.

Above all, there, hanging over his head, was the compelling question of the social issue or co-existence of the races. Tempered by his devotion to and oath to uphold the Constitution, by his contention that public opinion must be with him if he were to move the mountains and by the loud and conflicting voices surrounding him, the heart and soul may have been ready but the man and the public leader was still reticent. Conflicted! Capable even of betraying racist sentiments.

Only 10 days after he coldly snapped at Sergeant Waters and uttered the term "damned, eternal niggar," he notably, in the context of all here discussed, wrote his famous letter to Horace Greeley in response to his angry, open letter to Lincoln in the *New York Tribune*. In it, Greeley had criticized the president for not taking advantage of the emancipation provisions of the only recent July 17 passage of the Second Confiscation Act.

It is fair to assume that you have read his letter to Greeley and, more than likely, read it often. In it, the conflict and the questions and the ultimate resolve enjoin, but not that which he also had, in secret, already resolved to do about slavery only 5 months later. *He had already penned his Emancipation Proclamation, what would be a first step.*

Here he was, still bobbing and weaving with Greeley and the public, while having already determined to boldly move.

In the Greely letter, duty and obligation and intention were on center stage, but not the hope and will attending to his "*oft expressed personal wish.*" Yes, the Union, but exactly one month later, in just 31 days, he would pronounce his intention to issue the Emancipation Proclamation should the rebel states refuse to lay their weapons down, a refusal that was a foregone conclusion. Antietam, the bloodiest single day in a most bloody conflict, a day on which Robert E. Lee performed brilliantly on the field and a day on which the Union suffered more casualties and more deaths than their counterparts, yet still a day that gave Lincoln victory enough to hang his executive order upon. Numbers aside, it was truly a draw at best, but it was the Army of Northern Virginia that left the field and so, it enabled a beleaguered President, who was finding victories hard to come by, with the wiggle room he needed to act boldly and change the very paradigm of the war.

A conflicted man in a most convoluted time, Sergeant Waters couldn't have been pleased with the Greeley letter either. But he had no idea that his president was already setting wheels in motion to address what he most cared about. We, lovers of Lincoln, honor the brilliance of the writing and the sheer force of the message and even forgive its ambivalence on slavery, but we shake and bow our heads when we consider his unkindly and bigoted utterance to Waters. Yeah, yeah, yeah, I can conjure up all kind of rationales and while we understand that this was our Lincoln too, still, it's just not our Lincoln and that hurts.

For those who might argue that all we have is one man's word, be assured that this one man admired Lincoln, used stationary with his image on it and was so taken by his moment with the "Great Man" that he penned a sketch of Lincoln and he together for his brother and confirmed just what happened in letters home.

And just like us, he too wished that he had never heard those words.

To be fair and objective, the truth is that there are other incidents of Lincoln's using that term while in the White House, but almost exclusively in the early years. He was caught in the pangs of growing up and dusting off the remnants of bigotry.

"*As I would not be a* slave, *so I would not be a* master," was, according to the editors of his *Collected Works*, penned by Lincoln on August 1, 1858. The scrap of paper upon which it was written, went on to read, "*This express-es my idea of democracy. Whatever differs from this, to the extent of the difference, is no democracy.*" Accordingly, Lincoln believed that democracy could, in no way, tolerate or embody the concept of masters and slaves, as the relationship between the two was inherently undemocratic.

Continuing with this theme, originally raised by Medford and picked up by both Holzer and Harris, Rebecca Morris, Christopher Oakley and Eileen Patch also weigh in, in lockstep with them as they too focus on reconstruction.

Rebecca Morris wrote:

> I would talk to him about his plans for reconstruction after the war's end. How would he translate his simple instruction to Grant to "Let 'em up easy" into practical policies that reunited the states but kept in place the gains that had been made in ending human bondage? Certainly his actions would have been very different from those of his successor but would he have been able to prevent the birth of the myth of the "Lost Cause," the implementation of the black laws that negated emancipation and the post-war violence that became so prevalent in the south? Would his vision of limited equality for the African American race have evolved into a fuller acceptance of blacks as full, contrib-uting members of American society and would he have been able to lay the groundwork for an integrated culture that might have avoided the loss of civil rights in the first half of the 20th century.

Christopher Oakley, like Morris, goes to reconstruction as well, after first noting, "*I feel as if I have actually been having an extended conversation with Lincoln throughout my adult life and I talk to him today about strategies to unite our divided nation now*" or what is the subject of our final question.

"I'd like to speak with him about his plans and hopes for reconstruction. What trouble did he expect? What objections? How did he plan to deal with the oh so many people and factions who were to do battle with him and what did he see in 5 years or 10 years down the road"?

Morris then joined Oakely in going to "reconstruction and how best to save democracy from its current onslaughts today."

As to the great philosophical and sociological divide that threatens Amer-ica today and a president who blatantly assails sacred precepts of democracy and who goes so far as to celebrate the victories of thugs who win sham elections in foreign lands and to congratulate one, in a most un-democratic land, upon being named *president for life*, there will be more later.

But as to your very thoughtful questions for Lincoln about reconstruction, maybe, just maybe, he would have said something like this: "At least, during the terrible war, we could put direct aim and fire upon the enemy, in the field in our front and upon the government in Richmond. My boys in blue and theirs in their assorted grays and browns. But when the enemy became nothing more than blind, irrational, ugly hatred, we could do no more than respond to the violent brushfires that arose, hoping against hope that the madness of bigotry would dissipate in time."

I am, Rebecca, taken by a couple of your points, i.e., "fuller acceptance," "contributing members of society," "limited equality" and "the loss of civil rights in the first half of the 20th century."

After more than 300 years of "I am master and you are slave," 300 years of I am superior and entitled to all things and you but a servant who is entitled to nothing, the tidal wave of anger over the lost cause and the inherent and deep-seeded bigotry and racism were destined to explode. Hate, especially blind hate, can be a terrible force and the 'good old boys' in the South hated both the government of the United States and the emancipated for the purported sin of not being theirs any longer, so much so that they would demean the emancipated as 'Boys' for more than a century.

I respectfully take aim at your reference to *limited equality,* as I believe and have already argued that his years in the White House helped him to come full circle on this issue. While enjoying his precious respite of laughter while watching *Our American Cousin* on that dark and fateful Good Friday, he had long been at peace with the notion of full citizenship and equanimity. He had moved beyond mere "equality before the law" unto "equality in all things."

Oh, there was much more to come, but he had signaled his intention in his *Last Public Address.* The finally freed, given the 13th amendment, would freely integrate with their white brethren. Soon to be followed by the 14th and 15th, guaranteeing them the full flower of citizenship and the equal protection of the law.

Or so it was hoped, but as we all well know, it was not to be. White America and its holier than thou, cool, calculating dark racism spoke loudly. It barred the door and said, "No"! And it said, "No," for a very, very long time.

Oh, over the years, there were glimpses, moments in time that were rich with promise and possibility, and yet, even now, 155 years removed, nothing has been finally fulfilled, as there has been no final ascension as a nation where all, free and equal and together, are being raised up in the fullness of life.

While heralding the melting pot, welcoming the "tempest tossed" and insisting that our diversity is our strength, one race of Americans or group of races of Americans has forever insisted upon putting other races down, be they the Irish, the Italian, the Polish, the Jewish, the Hispanic, the Asian, the Arabic and, always and ever, the finally freed of 1865.

"*In honor or dishonor*," Lincoln once said and would, I believe, *Eileen Patch*, so say again, for despite the high ideals of so many great men and women over the years, of those who so valiantly gave their last full measure, in wars both just and unjust, of those who elevated our culture and our art and our literature, dishonor it remains.

And sadly, rarely more so than today when our president, the one who sits where Lincoln sat, loudly bullies and defames entire races of people and individual Americans and foreign leaders and newscasters and truth-tellers and law enforcement agents and public servants. Devoid of conscience and never more overtly or disgustingly than with his "Send them back" chant at a North Carolina rally.

Justice, equality, we have shouted. But today, African Americans are 6 times more likely than whites to be imprisoned and they egregiously wallow in poverty as the wealth/wage gap separating the two is as stark now as it was when Martin Luther King, 52 years ago, climbed the mountain, saw the light and claimed the victory.

Rebecca, you focus upon *the early 20th century*, but the racist rampage ran through the entire 20th century and the early 21st century as well. The 21st, where the George Floyds are still being lynched.

At this juncture, Lincoln would be stunned by the existence of the Neo-Nazis and White Supremacists, the torch holders of the KKK that was formed in the latter 19th century. Yes, stunned by the staying power of perverse ignorance and deep seeded bigotry, stunned by the threatened violence and abhorrent behavior and maybe even more stunned, not by this overt madness, but rather by the covert, quiet indifference to sustained injustice.

One hundred years after Lincoln and now 52 years after Martin and Bobby, who were uniquely focused upon this very injustice, no one has picked up the entirety of the moral mantle that fell when they fell, not even, despite his gentle decency and goodness, the African American who did the impossible and went to the White House himself.

In fairness, he tinkered on the edges and dived headlong into health care, but there was more glimmer than gain, more 'by my example than by my action.' And so, we continue to fall short and poverty escalates and the old Clinton Crime Bill and mandatory minimums assure us that many young African American and Hispanic men and women will continue to find their home to our increasingly 'for-profit' prisons. And how can schools in places like the South Bronx and Harlem teach when their students are homeless or going without heat in winter or without plumbing or electricity in substandard housing. How, when their neighborhoods are besieged by violence and gangs and drive by shootings and the untimely deaths of their own. How, when the only good meal they may get each day is the school lunch that

President Trump proposes to eliminate or how when no policies or programs are forthcoming to address their communities, their way out, their economies, their jobs, education, hope. Nada, nothing.

Which is why I for one looked to Bernie to pick up the torch and fight the fight,.

Yes, I think Lincoln would be stunned by this, by our virtually ignoring the "death by cop" of far too many young black men. It's mad and it's sad and it's callous and make no doubt about it, "Black lives did and would ever matter" to Lincoln. He would be puzzled by our having a problem with it, by our having a problem with dignity and justice for all.

Lincoln long worried about the issue of integration, about how white America, the majority and black America, the minority would come to coexist. He understood that there would be issues to resolve, so much so that he originally looked to avoid the same via emigration. He knew that it would take time to assimilate, to accept, to lay one's bigotries down, to be fair and true and honorable—one to the other—to extend the hand of friendship and that of basic human decency.

But he would be blown away by the fact that this is still not finally fulfilled and that the darkness within us has so tightly held on and been sustained these many years.

"And I'm proud to be an American where, at least, I know I'm free," they sing at our president's rallies today. Really, they do. Proudly, they do. Oh so very sadly, they do.

For freedom isn't free.

DINNER AND THE CRAFT OF WRITING

Douglas Egerton is another "dinner conversation" dreamer who suggests that he is open to all possibilities and to wherever Lincoln might like to take the conversation. His particular interest, however, is asking Lincoln for a primer on writing.

"I would like to talk with him about how he mastered the craft, about how he was able to hone in on the powerful and brief statement that spoke volumes, moved mountains and forever changed lives." Like so many of his peers, Egerton is amazed by Lincoln's rich poetic prose where the muted voices of Defoe and Gray, Burns and Knox, Dickens and Shakespeare and so many other poets, playwrights and novelists found refuge and higher purpose.

Alleging that he has never mastered the brief statement or the attendant power of it, there is much, he insists, that Abraham Lincoln could teach him about that particular art. In asking for this, Egerton elaborated upon the two most memorable dinner conversations that he had experienced, two that had a tremendous impact upon him and bore witness to the richness and wonder that one with Lincoln might realize.

As to the two reverently remembered, one was with Doctor and Professor John Hope Franklin, the Dean of African American History and the other with former United States Senator from South Dakota and 1972 Democratic nominee for president, George McGovern, who rose out of the maelstrom of race, Civil Rights and opposition to the Vietnam War in the late sixties.

Just another one of those eras in which America seemed to be '*coming apart.*'

Egerton wrote, "Professor Franklin was quite old at the time, and so he had a long lifetime of amazing stories, from coming to know Dr. W.E.B. DuBois to helping the NAACP overturn the Plessy v Ferguson decision with Brown v. Topeka and the recognition that separate but equal was inherently unequal. "Nobody wanted to speak, and people just kept asking Professor Franklin to tell stories about this and that, and it made for a fascinating evening. Perhaps, I would enjoy the same kind of evening with President Lincoln."

Interestingly, as to his dinner with George McGovern, they did speak of McGovern's 1972 race against President Nixon, but believe it or not, Egerton said, "*We mostly chatted about Abraham Lincoln.*"

Self-deprecatingly, Egerton closed out his generous and telling response by affirming the fact that Lincoln was the master of the brief statement. "*The Gettysburg address* and *the Second Inaugural* are only two examples of his ability to cut to the heart of the matter in just a few words. Clearly he knew his Shakespeare and Dickens, both of whose voices are echoed in his prose. But I find that the older I get and the more I write, the longer my books become, a problem for my editor, I admit and I would love to take lessons in how to craft a sentence as elegant as most of his."

Truth is, what writer wouldn't want to take lessons from a man who painted masterpieces with words. But I fear such creative genius is not extrinsic, but rather intrinsic, in that it was born in the deep recesses of Lincoln's well-worn, tell-tale heart and soul.

Jack C. Waugh joined Egerton, as he too longed to speak with and pick the brain of Lincoln the writer, the craftsman, the artist, the poet.

"I would want to talk to him about writing," he said. "Lincoln was not only one of the greatest, very likely the greatest, of our presidents, a skilled politician and statesmen. He also was a giant in American Literature. He knew how to write, and as one writer to another, I would like to talk to him about how he did it."

We have briefly explored this, making the case, as Waugh does that Lincoln and the best of American Literature are bound together. As to how he did it, I believe Lincoln could well instruct great writers like Waugh and Egerton and lesser writers like me, as to his reliance upon logic, structure, reason, the use of figurative language, repetition, rhyme and inversion, the use of great literature, great poetry, the Bible and the impactful, short and lyrical statement.

But then, he also had that something that could never be taught or passed on. For his gift as a writer was, I believe - and to great degree - the byproduct of a rare and unique creative genius. He so easily bound his mind's rare appreciation for structure, geometric precision and reason with his spirit's embodiment of the poet's heart and the saint's soul. For him, it wasn't about writing well, it was about writing perfectly.

While *Mel Maurer* also chimes in about his interest in Lincoln's take on people, both friends and enemies, whom he encountered, what he would most like to speak with Lincoln about was his writing.

"I would like him to introduce me to his thought process as he prepared to write," he wrote. "I admire so many of his works, especially his moving *Farewell Address* before departing Springfield, his courageous *House Divided Speech*, both his *First and Second Inaugurals* and, of course, his immortal *Gettysburg Address.* Each of the above and so many, many others are what I refer to as Lincoln's poetry-prose that must be studied and not merely read. He had a rare gift."

As to Lincoln's extraordinary way with words, we all agree—Mel, Douglas Egerton, Jack C. Waugh, you, I and the millions who share our keen, never quite satisfied interest in him. On these questions and your collective interest, I come up short, but I did come across an article that I believe all of you might be interested in.

Theodore C. Sorensen, another man whose way with words is to be admired, who wrote all of President John F. Kennedy's major and moving speeches, has something to offer us. In 2008 or 45 years after he wrote for JFK, he wrote a piece *for the Smithsonian* entitled, *"Lincoln Had the Best Speechwriter—Himself."*

I but share these excerpts from this great Sorensen piece about Lincoln, the writer:

- Abraham Lincoln, the greatest American president, was also in my view the best of all presidential speechwriters.
- I did not learn much from all of those speeches President Kennedy asked me to read (except for FDR's first inaugural), but I learned a great deal from Lincoln's ten sentences.
- Seward recommended that Lincoln add this to the conclusion of his *First Inaugural* -- "The mystic chords which proceeding from so many battle fields and so many patriot graves pass through all the hearts . . . in this broad continent of ours will yet again harmonize in their ancient music when breathed upon by the guardian angel of the nation"

- Lincoln graciously took this and gave us, "*The mystic chords of memory, stretching from every battlefield and patriot grave to every living heart and hearthstone all over this broad land, will yet swell the chorus of the Union, when again touched, as surely they will be, by the better angels of our nature.*" Just amazing!
- Now, that's genius, pure unadulterated genius!
- Lincoln's success as an orator stemmed not from his voice, demeanor or delivery, or even his presence, but from his words and his ideas. He put into powerful language the nub of the matter in the controversy over slavery and secession in his own time, and the core meaning for all time of this nation as "The last best hope of earth."
- With his prodigious memory and willingness to dig out facts (as his own researcher), he could offer meticulous historical detail, as he demonstrated in his antislavery *Peoria Speech* of 1854 and in the 1860 *Cooper Union Address.*
- His two greatest speeches—the greatest speeches by any president—are not only quite short (the *Second Inaugural* is just a shade over 700 words, the *Gettysburg Address* shorter still), but did not deal with facts or policy at all, but only with the largest ideas.
- Lincoln lived in an age of print. He spoke to readers of the printed page. His words moved voters far from the sound of his voice because of his writing skills, his intellectual power, his tight grip on the core issues of his time and his sublime concept of his nation's meaning.
- He had a talent for getting to the point.
- Lincoln avoided the fancy and artificial. He used the rhetorical devices that the rest of us speechwriters do: alliteration ("*Fondly do we hope—fervently do we pray*"; "*no successful appeal from the ballot to the bullet*"); rhyme ("*I shall adopt new views so fast as they shall appear to be true views*"); repetition ("*As our case is new, so we must think anew, and act anew*"; "*We cannot dedicate, we cannot consecrate, we cannot hallow this ground*"); and—especially—contrast and balance ("*The dogmas of the quiet past are inadequate to the stormy present*"; "*As I would not be a slave, so I would not be a master*"; "*In giving freedom to the slave, we assure freedom to the free*").
- He used metaphors, as we all do, both explicit and implicit: think of the implied figure of birth—the nation "*brought forth,*" "conceived"—in the Gettysburg Address. He would quote the Bible quite sparingly, but to tremendous effect. See how he ends the monumental next-to-last paragraph of the second inaugural: "*Yet, if God wills that [the Civil War] continue until all the wealth piled by the bondsman's two hundred and fifty years of unrequited toil shall be sunk, and until every drop of blood drawn with the lash shall be paid by another drawn with the sword, as was*

said three thousand years ago, so still it must be said, 'the judgments of the Lord are True and Righteous Altogether.' "

- He was aware of the right rhythm and sound. An editor of the *Gettysburg Address* might say that "Eighty-seven years ago" is shorter. Lincoln wrote instead, *"Four score and seven years ago."*
- And, finally, he had the root of the matter in him. Speeches are not just words. They present ideas, directions and values, and the best speeches are those that get those right. As Lincoln did.

Breaking down Sorensen, the second greatest presidential speechwriter ever, into a few words, Lincoln applied research, great thought, preparation, big ideas, core issues, pointed focus, great use of rhetorical devices, figurative language, rhythm and rhyme and not just mere ideas but deep, abiding and enduring values.

JUST LISTENING AND SECRETARY SEWARD

For her part, *Michelle Krowl* would like to sit back and listen to Lincoln share whatever stories or jokes of his that bring him joy. Only later, would she begin to pepper him with a few specific questions. Among them, which copy of the *Gettysburg Address* did he use and if the Nicolay Copy, then why and what of his *Blind Memorandum*? Finally and maybe most importantly, she would ask him the questions that are often asked of her about his documents and his words that she is unable to answer.

As the Civil War and Reconstruction Specialist in the Manuscript Division of the Library of Congress, she gets to be intimate with some of the most precious documents in the history that we here engage.

"If I had the opportunity to have a conversation with Abraham Lincoln," she wrote, "I would want it to be one full of jokes and storytelling. While there would, of course, be so many more important issues to discuss with Lincoln given the weighty problems of his era, I would first want to witness his eyes sparkling with delight at a good joke. I would want to hear just how he told a story, and if he really said, 'That reminds me of a story' as often as observers later said that he did.

She continued, "Outside of the smelly cigar smoke in the air, I think it would be wonderful to spend an evening in William Seward's house on Lafayette Square as Lincoln, Seward and John Hay bounced humorous stories off of one another. Beyond genuinely wanting to experience Lincoln as a storyteller, I would not want to waste a precious moment of time with him discussing anything that would cause him a moment of additional pain."

Historians today, she noted, have so many questions about the papers that he produced during his lifetime that the state of our best forensic science cannot decipher. As to the "Nicolay Copy," by the way, she would ask if the work on it began in Washington, D.C. and the alternative ending in Gettysburg, as we now think likely. That understood, she would ask, 'when was the "Hay Copy" produced?

"Imagine, going to the source for answers and guidance," said Krowl. "Wouldn't that be a trip? Those questions satisfied, I would hold on to him for as long as possible and ask him to tell me another story and have our conversation go in a humorous and joyful direction once again."

I am taken by the fact that she places him in the Seward house on Lafayette Square, taken because I, in my historical meandering, have long come to look upon Seward's parlor and Seward himself, in a very real way, as Lincoln's *'safe harbor.'*

Not unlike Speed's store or New Salem's Rutledge Tavern or Billy's Barbershop or the inns he frequented on the 8th Circuit, the laughter in Seward's parlor and the friendship of Seward himself were wellsprings of adrenaline for Lincoln.

Oh, Seward and his 'higher law' and his contention that *"We are the stewards"* of the *"Creator of the universe"* - Seward whose friendship and trust, like Secretary Stanton's, became sacrosanct—Seward, the one who was to have been king who would, day by day, be moved by Lincoln and come to speak of him *"in the strongest terms of praise."* Oh yes, he was, *"Just the man for the crisis"* (Henry J. Raymond) and one who was *"above the pale of ambition."* In a very real way, Seward was at his best in his drawing room after supper, comfortable in his easy chair and surrounded by billowing smoke from his always black cigar" (David Herbert Donald's *"We Are Lincoln Men" Abraham Lincoln and His Friends*, p. 160).

From utterly different walks of life, they were kindred spirits. Seward, interestingly, cared as little as Lincoln did about appearance or apparel or his disheveled hair and he was the only one in the cabinet who enjoyed listening to Lincoln's tales as much as Lincoln enjoyed telling them.

From the rough-hewn log cabins of the frontier and the more refined streets of Orange County, New York, they came and they could go toe to toe with one another, as they were, in a very real way, cut from the same cloth. Seward didn't win the arguments but he served as the filter via which Lincoln clarified his.

Our own Frank Williams in his *Judging Lincoln,* reports that it was Seward who secured the Democratic operatives, led by Mr. Bilbo who did the hard lobbying to undermine the Democratic opposition to the 13th amendment. It was Seward who historian, Walter Stahr, so appropriately labeled *Lincoln's Indispensable Man.* It was Seward who Lincoln confided in and listened to and trusted. Ever his own man and his own mind, still Lincoln deeply respected Seward and, much more often than not, took his thinking into account.

Lincoln did not go to the elaborate dinners at the Seward home on Lafayette Square for they were not alike when it came to fine wines and fine foods and fine *airs*. Nor when it came to Seward's fine cigars and brandies in the parlor. But they were alike in their good humor and in their stories and in their laughter and in their mutual respect and in what, without question, became bonds of genuine affection. Abraham Lincoln tolerated the swarming cigar smoke in his parlor just to be with him, to release and to smile a bit on many a dark day.

Yes, that Michelle chooses to hear Lincoln tell his stories did not surprise. Not at all! But that she chose Seward's parlor as the venue did. It shouldn't have for it is the perfect place, but it did and I found myself longing to be there as well. And unlike Lincoln, I would have enjoyed one of Seward's fine cigars and a bit of the brandy as well. It was the ever present Noah Brooks, I believe, who told us that Seward's cigars were always of the highest quality.

Old softie that I am, I have long been deeply moved by the last encounter of these two giants and so memorialize it here. A solemn day under solemn circumstances, there would be no laughter that day. For Lincoln had been to Richmond and Seward had been grossly injured in a carriage accident and he lay in bed with severe and painful wounds.

Upon his return to Washington after his visit with Grant at the front and his walk through Richmond, Lincoln went to see his friend and trusted secretary. It was late and where there had typically been raucous laughter, there were but whispers as the gaslights had already been turned down low. Lincoln quietly entered his bedroom, crouched down and leaned across the bed, resting his head on his elbow so as to get close to his friend. Lincoln did most of the talking for even uttering words was difficult for Seward.

Lincoln told him that he thought the end was near and gave him a moving account of his experience at the front and of his walk through Richmond, but while Lincoln was still with him, Seward, simply drifted off to sleep upon which Lincoln reported to his son, Fred, before quietly taking his leave.

Some ten days later, as John Wilkes Booth cried out, "*Sic Semper Tyrannis*," his co-conspirator, Lewis Powell viciously assaulted Seward's son, Fred and then knifed Seward himself repeatedly as he lay in bed.

Seward who would remarkably recover, would not be told of Lincoln's passing, but he would notice the flag over the War Department flying at half-staff and so he knew. "The President is dead," he told his male nurse. "If he was alive, he would have been the first to call on me." (Noah Brooks, *Mr. Lincoln's Washington*, p. 459).

Indeed, Seward was right. Lincoln, most certainly, would have been the first. We will never know where the secret currents of his thoughts then took him, nor the toll that they exacted upon his ravaged body and spirit. But the limits of history notwithstanding, we can well imagine.

That imagining, by the way and fascinatingly, is as much a part of our historical sojourns as is our discovering.

JUST TERRIFIC STORIES AND HOMESPUN WISDOM

Among the other collaborators who chose to spend their time with Lincoln simply listening to him tell stories were *Richard Brookhiser, David Sullivan, Mike Movius, Steve Raymond* and *Robert Brugler.*

Richard Brookhiser wrote, "I wouldn't expect anything from a conversation with him other than terrific stories – just terrific stories. If I knew him as well as Joshua Speed, I would ask him about his Step-Mother."

David Sullivan wrote, "I think it would be so fine to spend a casual afternoon sitting with Abraham Lincoln. It would be a real treat to hear a few of his favorite stories and I'm sure he'd be happy to oblige. But I'd also sure like to listen to him read those inspiring 270 words of his 'Gettysburg Address.' I would like to talk to him about his thoughts as he wrote it."

Mike Movius wrote, "I would like to talk to him about how he developed his story-telling abilities and how he so often merged that skill with the sharing of moral musts. And while his sense of humor was not always appreciated by his audience, I so love the fact that he laughed uproariously at his own stories. I'd like to talk to him about that as well."

Steve Raymond added, "It would be very difficult for me to have a conversation with Lincoln because I would not want to speak, but rather and only listen. If I was very fortunate, I might hear the same eloquence that his neighbors in Springfield did when he gave his impromptu *Farewell Address.* And oh to hear the great rhetoric of his inaugurals or the incredible expressions and thoughts conveyed in his many letters to newspaper editors or the mothers and widows of war victims and, of course and above all, to hear him share his 'Gettysburg Address.'"

Robert Brugler wrote, "If I could speak with Abraham Lincoln, I would appreciate having him tell me about the multiple decisions he had to make during the war. A close second would be to hear him tell stories; especially the ones that were used to prove a point and move a mind. Finally, I think it would be more than enough to just sit back, watch, listen and respond accordingly."

Five collaborators weigh in specifically on listening to his stories, but each with a twist.

As ever, *Brookhiser's* response was cryptic but loaded. That he wonders about knowing him as well as Joshua Speed is to suggest knowing him better than anyone. Speed was his best and closest friend, the one he trusted above all others. Followed by his 'only if or then, would I ask him about his Step-Mom.' The all of which was followed by my why. Why would you need to know him as well as Speed to do that and why this paramount conversational interest in Sarah Bush Johnston Lincoln?

And then it struck me that Lincoln, according to Jeff Oppenheimer in his *That Nation Might Live – One Afternoon with Lincoln's Stepmother*, insisted that Sarah, his Step-Mom, had been "*the best friend he had in this world.*" So what we actually have here is a 'best friend' on the one hand and a 'best friend' on the other hand gig, where Joshua Speed, BFF #2, speaks with Lincoln about his Stepmom or BFF #1. In the head of the one into the heart of the other.

Why this paramount interest in her? Likely because, she, according to Oppenheimer, "humanized" Lincoln and his world by insisting upon the wooden floor and the whitewash and livability upon her arrival at Pigeon Creek, Indiana. Likely, because she picked up where his "Angel Mother" left off in encouraging his reading, his intellectual pursuits and his very belief in his capacity to be something more than a rail splitter or frontier farmer.

Then too, maybe because "*She recognized a boy of tremendous talent and saw the diamond when virtually everyone else around this gangly, awkward boy saw the rough.*" (Oppenheimer- *That Nation Might Live*). Maybe because she made all the difference!

We are well familiar with his Stepmom's "*Scarcely one woman—a mother—in a thousand can say*" and her "*He never told me a lie in his life—never evaded, never equivocated, never dodged,*" but there is ever so much more when one dives deep into the depths of William (Billy) Herndon's account of his visit with Lincoln's Stepmom at Goosenest Prairie, Illinois on September 8, 1865, less than 5 months after Lincoln died.

There, through her eyes, you engage Lincoln as a babe in his yellow flannel petticoat, cuddled in the arms of Nancy, under the warmth of a bearskin. There, the roaring fire in the Lincoln's small cabin by Nolan Creek in "Kaintuck." There where Sarah, who little knew that she was destined to become his Stepmom, came to visit upon hearing that Thomas and Nancy had given birth to a son.

How I love Sarah's, "*Babies weren't as plenty as blackberries in the woods of Kaintuck.*" How I love her, "*That was the first time I set eyes on Abe. I can scarcely say, even from his very first, he was mighty good company, solemn as a papoose, but interested in everything. Abe never was much for looks. Looks didn't count them days no how. It was strength and work and daredevil.*"

But above all, I love Nancy's response to Sarah's question about what he was to be named and what is the only testament we have to this. From Oppenheimer via Herndon via Lincoln's Stepmom, we hear Lincoln's 'Angel Mother' respond, "*Abraham. After his grandfather that come out to Kaintuck with Daniel Boone. He was mighty smart and wasn't afraid of nothing, and that's what a man has to be out here to make anything out of himself.*"

There you have this precious gathering of both of his mothers on the day after he was born and their thinking about what he had to be or what they hoped he would be. In so very many ways, they nailed it on the first full day of his life. "Solemn, interested in everything, mighty good company, mighty smart, afraid of nothing, daredevil." Their words, not mine and not ours. Their thoughtful, pointed, spirited words that so wonderfully square with what we write.

And so I humbly withdraw my question about Brookhiser's paramount interest in Sarah Bush Johnston Lincoln who shaped the man who so shaped and reclaimed our democracy. For it was not my friend Davy Crockett who "patched up the crack in the liberty bell." It was Sarah's Stepson.

As to *David Sullivan's* and *Steven Raymond's* understandable interest in his extraordinary speeches, we will dive into that in our next chapter.

Then too, *Mike Movius* and *Robert Brugler* are right to connect Lincoln's homespun tales and even his jokes to the proselytization of moral musts, but this was not new with Lincoln, as the most ancient of stories were similarly fashioned to advance the good, the wise and the virtuous. Before man had the ability to communicate in even symbols or in art, this was so.

In all of Lincoln's tales, from *Metamora* to the *outhouse that Ethan Allen visited in England* to the *total abstinence principle* and *unbeknownst to me* and the *cowardly legs,* his *'no vices -no virtues,'* his *one fixed rule regarding Fox River* and hundreds more, there were ever and always morals, instructions for living, rich wisdom.

TODAY

Wendy Allen threw us a curve.

Having singularly focused upon painting Abraham Lincoln, spectacularly and brilliantly, she taps her "what if" to paint him in person. Interestingly in her time or our time and not in Lincoln's own time. Her miracle or fantasy or dream is to bring our 16th president, whom she has spiritually, and for long, bonded with, into the heart of her own world.

Having for so long, kept him vibrantly alive for us, she certainly has the standing.

She plans to introduce him to our Brave New World where he would be slapped in the face by 155 years or 56,575 days of alleged progress. And not necessarily to our politics and travails which drives this work, but rather to the wonders, grand achievements and toys of our day.

"My conversation with the President would be entirely selfish," she wrote. "Now that he has all the time in the world, I would ask him to sit for countless life portraits.

I would dress him in comfy contemporary clothing and show him my world. I'd put him on an AirBus380 and whisk him away to some place far off and neon like Shanghai. During those long transoceanic flights, I'd try my best to bring him up to date with all that he has missed. I'd let him learn to use my iPad and phone. I'd teach him how to drive.

She would take him to visit today's D.C. but only if he wanted to.

If a time limit were imposed, then a tour of California would be in order first. And when the winds of time came to take him back, I'd say goodbye on the cliffs of "the greatest meeting of land and sea in the world," Point Lobos, California."

It's her own heart and spirit that she'd extend to him, everything from her rare creativity to her appreciation of the wonder and beauty of this earth. She certainly got me to put Point Lobos on my bucket list but I'll pass on neon Shanghai, which I imagine to be another witness to her artistry, bright, colorful, intense and compellingly moving. Out of the darkness or void, a kaleidoscope of brilliant color and imagining.

ALL IN THE FAMILY

After first catching up with Lincoln on family matters, *Marilyn Krowl Rexilius,* has a long litany of issues that she would appreciate discussing with him including his relationship with his soldiers, the Emancipation Proclamation, the horrendous body count, his suspension of the writ of habeas corpus, his jokes, his stories and more.

"I love thinking about having a conversation with Abe" she wrote. "Naturally, I'd first enjoy catching up with him on the family. I would be nervous and forget what to ask, I'm sure, but I would show him my charts and photos like you do at any family reunion or gathering and draw the connections.

"I would then try, in some completely inadequate way, to express my gratitude for all that he did to and for my country. I would ask him to share some of the difficult moments that he had, while making critical decisions or bearing with the news from the many fronts in the field. I would ask him where his head was and what fears he may have had when he called for the 75,000 troops after the fall of Fort Sumter.

Relentless, she continued and continued.

"Philosophically, spiritually, practically, what of the ever mounting and unimagined body count? How did he manage to survive that strain or sense of responsibility is anyone's guess, but that he did so amazes and were he willing to talk about it, that too, no doubt, would also amaze.

"Given the magnitude of it all, how was it that he was able to remain so kind, pleasant, funny and magnanimous?

So many questions, but she's a cousin who just might know that never in his public life, did Lincoln shy away from any question asked of him, no matter the belligerence or animus behind it.

In stark contrast to the majority of our public leaders today, he responded directly and forthrightly simply because he never had anything to hide. As to where he stood, he was an open book. Oh sure, he understood that executing new policy had to be tied to the vagaries of public opinion and he understood the art of timing and public relations, but that never precluded or stopped him from giving an honest answer about any issue, no matter how sensitive, when freely asked.

Again, the issue of his suffering:

Long Nine Legislator Robert Wilson, Mentor Graham, Billy Herndon and Joshua Speed were among the many who bore witness to the extent of Lincoln's melancholy and depression. And while the case can be made that it tempered over time, as the awful weight of duty and responsibility claimed him, the dreaded specter of it always haunted.

There were so many instances reported where he had to fight like hell to sustain life and sanity. We see it in his stunted relationship with Mary Warren and in his skipping out on his eventual wife the first time around and in those many moments where friends reported him retreating into an almost catatonic silence and sinking into the black hole where he battled his demons or the hypo.

But in the White House, where duty and responsibility overwhelmed, such moments were largely reserved for the dead of night. To temper it by day, he relied heavily upon homespun tales, good humor and the tonic of laughter, no matter the darkness of the latest telegram or the weighty policy and storms that were constantly brewing.

It is often said that "*Action is the antidote to despair.*"

From the moment he was elected, Lincoln lived in action, as we related earlier, steady and relentless waves of action, the action that was demanded by a great divide, secession and Sumter and Bull Run, by the Peninsula Campaign and the ever growing body counts and Antietam, by the suspension of Habeas Corpus and Generals who repeatedly failed and the 'fire in the rear,' by dueling Cabinet members and his concerns about his Emancipation Proclamation and Fredericksburg and Chancellorsville, by the 100 other battles and by the fight for the 13th amendment and the use of a pen that put sacred words on paper that reclaimed and celebrated the American Republic and democracy and the fashioning of a plan for Reconstruction.

Action, duty and responsibility shadow-boxed with melancholy and despair and claimed the victory.

But as to how he lived, here is a piece from Doris Kearns Goodwin's *Team of Rivals* that I love. It speaks not to the angst and depression, but rather to Lincoln's innate and inherent kindness and goodness, to his spirit and light. In it, she brilliantly juxtaposes the dueling natures of Stanton and Lincoln in their 'opposites attract' miracle of a working relationship. She wrote:

> *The secretiveness which Lincoln wholly lacked, Stanton had in marked degree; the charity which Stanton could not feel, coursed from every pore in Lincoln. Lincoln was for giving a wayward subordinate seventy times seven chances to repair his errors; Stanton was for either forcing him to obey or cutting off his head without more ado. Lincoln was as calm and unruffled as the summer sea in moments of the gravest peril; Stanton would lash himself into a fury over the same condition of things. Stanton would take hardships with a groan. Lincoln would find a funny story to fit them. Stanton was all dignity and sternness, Lincoln all simplicity and good nature.* (p. 560)

There he stands, one, who no matter the sinking ship, would lift up the one who was drowning and find the raft to lay him upon.

EVERYDAY TALK WITH A HABEAS CORPUS TWIST

Joan Chaconas wrote, "Lincoln was very brave and wise to suspend the writ of Habeas Corpus which is still a bone of contention with some people today but as I see it, he had no other choice."

While everyone's contentions and numbers vary, I buy into the rough assessment that virtually one-third of all folks residing in Washington, D.C., upon Lincoln's arrival there either sympathized with or outright supported the Confederate cause. After all, it was a southern, slave- holding city. It wouldn't be until April of 1862 that the District of Columbia Compensated Emancipation Act moved forward.

In a more recent time, pre-Trump of course, the belated question of reparations for the ancestors of once slaves was, at least, being academically debated and it's popping up again among Democrats who would be president in 2020, so it's hard to imagine that the prevailing concern in the early 1860s had to do with rather compensating slave owners for their loss.

While many sympathized with the Confederacy, Washington and Baltimore were cities replete with anti-Union zealots, outright traitors, would-be spies and many men who would go on to serve in the Army of Northern Virginia. And while Clement C. Vallandigham was all the rage, the fire in the rear that Lincoln often spoke of rang out throughout the North.

In Article I, Section 9 of the Constitution, it states that "the privilege of the writ of Habeas Corpus shall not be suspended, unless when in cases of rebellion and invasion the public safety may require it." There lies the suspension clause that Lincoln acted upon, given a clear and certain public safety issue of monumental proportions. Lincoln never wavered on this and ignored Chief Justice Taney's ruling, regarding the military arrest of John Merryman in Cockeysville, Maryland, for recruiting, training, and leading a drill company which was to fight for the Confederacy. Taney's southern sympathizing court, unsurprisingly, ruled that the president had no such power, as it resided in Congress alone.

On July 4, 1861, Lincoln delivered a message to Congress on this issue:

> *Now it is insisted that Congress, and not the Executive, is vested with this power. But the Constitution itself is silent as to which, or who, is to exercise the power; and as the provision was plainly made for a dangerous emergency, it cannot be believed the framers of the instrument intended, that, in every case, the danger should run its course, until Congress could be called together; the very assembling of which might be prevented by the rebellion. No more extended argument is now offered, as an opinion will probably be presented by the Attorney General. Whether there shall be any legislation upon the subject, and if any, what, is submitted entirely to the better judgment of Congress.*
> (Journal of the Abraham Lincoln Association – James Dueholm, *Lincoln's Suspension of the Writ of Habeas Corpus: An Historical and Constitutional Analysis*, Volume 29, Issue 2, 2008)

As to this, Dueholm interestingly noted, *"While Lincoln talked and acted, Congress talked without acting."* In fact, it wasn't until March 3, 1863 that they did and then positively so, authorizing Lincoln to take the action that he took two years earlier. Better late than never.

In early 1862, according to Dueholm, Horace Binney, an 82-year-old lawyer, published an article that provided strong scholarly support for Lincoln's claim to a constitutional power to suspend the writ of Habeas Corpus. After a detailed, lengthy and exhaustive paper, he came down on the side of Lincoln.

"The difference between Lincoln and Binney is that the former goes on for another fifty pages. This is not to criticize him (except for prolixity). His role differed from Lincoln's, and 'he could no more be expected to stop at two pages than Edward Everett at Gettysburg could have been expected to stop at two minutes.' But Lincoln's simple argument is more compelling, truer to the Constitution, and less open to attack than Binney's more reasoned discourse. As a lawyer pleading his own case, no less than as politician and statesman, 'the president is," as Secretary of State William Seward said, 'the best of us.'"

Dueholm's piece is a gem.

THE PERSONAL, THE EVERYDAY, THE ORDINARY

While others have dabbled into the 'personal, every day and ordinary' waters as well, they also had more pressing matters to discuss, but not *Anne Moseley*.

She wrote,

> This is a hard question because I would be star struck and wouldn't know what to say. The questions I would have for him would be about his family, personal interests and what he thought about being labeled as one of our greatest presidents in history.
> I would like to ask him the questions historians today are debating about his relationship with Ann Rutledge, the wrestling match with Jack Armstrong, and his relationship with his wife Mary. Whether or not I would have the courage to ask him these questions is another thing entirely. But it would be nice to just sit and talk with him as a friend, about everyday things, and get to know him as a person."

Our friend, *Dave Wiegers* is on the same page as Anne.

He wrote,

> This question is often asked of historians and scholars and I can understand that they might want to converse about his views on slavery, the war, his law career and so much more. Me, I think I'd simply like to talk about life in general. Talk about the things that all people like to talk about, family, children, daily life, what challenges them, what makes them mad, what gives them joy.

No matter our preoccupations with the politics, the great debate, the war, the sacrifice, the slaves, the redemption, we all appreciate where Anne and Dave's heads are, in that Lincoln's is ultimately the story of a man, just a man, a man who carried a ton of baggage and doubts and insecurities with him. Just like any other man and just like we all do, with the exception of these three which made all the difference for Lincoln, rendering him so very special and so unlike most.

That he determined in his earliest of days to leave a mark, to make a contribution, to render himself worthy of remembrance.

That he had a mind, a gifted mind, one with a steel trap that absorbed all he read and enabled him to apply systemic reasoning to the resolution of grave problems.

Finally and most importantly, I believe, that he had a poet's heart, a poet's spirit and a poet's ability to craft words that moved, inspired and healed, words that no other leader in all of history was capable of crafting, words that no other writer in the public realm has ever been capable of crafting.

As to your commentary, Anne and Dave, I believe he saw himself exactly as you do, 'as an everyday man trying to live each day out as best he knew how.' He never saw himself as being of more worth than any other. His considerable abilities notwithstanding, abilities that he was well aware of, pride was altogether foreign to him.

No matter his height, he looked up at everyone and never down.

As to your questions, Anne, I understand that you can't go to Lincoln without diving into the gauntlet that he ran with his wife, Mary, who often lived on the outer edges or brink of civility and sanity. After reading Michael Burlingame's remarkable biography, I was shook and found it impossible to continue looking for the good in her. But not Lincoln who rather amazingly, despite her hellfire, still treated her with respect and warmth, ever affectionately, calling her "Mother."

I also am with you when it comes to longing to know more of Anne Rutledge. Because all of the once doubts and 'doubts no more' notwithstanding, this was love and longing, this was romance and tenderness and innocence, this was hope and possibility. And yet, I fear that we have, post Burlingame, reached the outer limits of historical inquiry here.

It's the 'what ifs' of history that fascinate. Here Lincoln's first love and maybe his greatest love and maybe the one woman with whom he did not feel awkward or lacking, the one with whom he may have found pure happiness. His Anne with her blue eyes and auburn hair, who invariably was described as sweet, kind, beautiful, gentle and loving, Anne who died too young and too soon on August 22, 1835, some 25 years before her beau was elected president of the United States.

As to Mary, we understand that he might never have become president without her. And yet with Anne, with whom we assume he may have been truly happy, we acknowledge that he may never have been president at all and then what of all his contributions and what of us. What a conundrum in the 'what if' world to consider, for we are, at once, ever on his side, saddened by his loss of Anne and happiness and yet cognizant of the greater loss that might well then have befallen us.

Anne or Anna Mayes Rutledge or Annie, yours is a loss that we lovers of your Lincoln still mourn. I never got to her dueling graves, largely because I doubted my wheelchair could ever have taken me over the valley and through the glen to the Old Concord Cemetery in Petersburg, where she was laid to rest and where the backside of a modern stone reads, *"I could not think of her out there alone in the storm*—A. Lincoln." As to the front, her name and the dates, the witness to her all too brief 22 years and the words, *"Where Lincoln Wept."*

It is as much his grave as it is hers.

Ridiculously in 1890, in an effort to make their cemetery more inviting, her remains were removed to the Oakland Cemetery when in point of fact, all that was removed were the 4 pearl buttons that they found and some dirt. There today, on a stone in need of refurbishing, the famed Edgar Lee Masters' maudlin poem, *"I am Ann Rutledge who sleeps beneath these weeds, beloved of Abraham Lincoln, wedded to him, not through union, but through separation. Bloom forever oh republic from the bust of my bosom."*

Interestingly, Anne Moseley, your friend, Jack Armstrong's stone lies right next to that of Anne in the Old Concord Cemetery and Edgar Lee Master's is not far from the remnants of our sadly, reinterred Anne in the Oakland Cemetery.

Not long ago, when visiting the restored New Salem, I spent more than half my time there in the restored Rutledge Tavern imagining, wondering and mourning the loss of our great friend's great loss. There I thought of Lincoln's reply to an old New Salem friend, Isaac Cogdal, who visited him upon his election to the presidency in 1860 (David Herbert Donald's *Lincoln*) and asked him if he thought of Anne still. His reply was, " *I did honestly and truly love the girl and I think often, often of her now.* " There and then, while letting imagination run wild, a palpable emotion, depth of feeling and spiritual essence filled the room. It was so thick around me that I could reach right out and touch it. In your face, tangible, true, powerfully moving. The stuff that matters that never truly dies.

JUST DINNER

Frank Williams also is a member of the "Let's Have Dinner with Lincoln" Club. He wrote that he just wants him to be his guest at Dinner, one that he'd cook. He claims to be very, very good at it which is good enough for me, so while Lincoln relaxes and regales him with stories and his celebrated humor, he'd cook.

"I like to cook and bake, wrote Williams, and I recall when the magazine, Bon Appetite asked its readers, 'Who would you most like to have dinner with,' so many responded Abraham Lincoln. I was genuinely shocked to see how many aficionados of Bon Appetite, those who fancy themselves great chefs like me, went to Lincoln, who unsurprisingly was, without doubt, the leader in the *Bon Appetite's* 'unfortunately deceased' guest category.

"It struck me then that I would just love to have had that opportunity as well." No preconceived notions. Frank stressed the fact that he would let Lincoln take the lead, respond accordingly and simply enjoy.

Can't help but comment that Frank might not have to go all out in his preparation, in that Lincoln was a man of very simple tastes. A biscuit and a boiled egg and the occasional piece of fruit generally satisfied. Anything in the pantry or fridge would do. Perhaps some crackers and cheese.

HOW AND AGAIN — THE BURDENS AND THE STRENGTHS

Michaela Wieties, winner of the Lincoln Forum scholarship years ago, *Rich Thompson,* Lincoln artist and *Win Anderson*, High School history teacher from Minnesota joined hands with those who longed to speak with him about how he managed to find the strength to bear the mighty burdens, to persevere and to remain so fully human no matter the darkness.

Long familiar topics, for with the very earth crumbling around him, he stood firm. Though the mountains shook and the earth opened up and the skies fell, he stood firm.

Rich Thompson would dive into the pain, the 630,000 lost, the personal heartbreak, the bearing with and so would *Win Anderson* and *Michaela,* but she also would ask him about how to persevere in our own difficult times today to find the inspiration with which to make one's difference in the face of it.

Michaela, I believe he might well have said something like this:

> You do this by determining to do so, by determining, as he did, to leave a mark for good, by being brave enough to stand up for your own beliefs and freely articulate them, by volunteering with non-profits and legitimate organizations that address them and/or by engaging political organizations or candidates who, in a most positive and explicit way, speak for you. There is a great divide and too much bitterness today, so this is not easy, but it is oh so necessary. Write, comment, reflect, debate, speak, engage in whatever way suits you.

Be you! Don't hide!

Or he might tell you, as he once told others:

- *"Be sure you put your feet in the right place, then stand firm.*
- *"You are not bound to win but you are bound to be true.* You are not bound to succeed, but you are *bound to live by the light that you have. You must stand with anybody that stands right, and stand with him while he is right, and part with him when he goes wrong.*
- "You have to do *your own growing no matter how tall your grandfather was.*
- *"You must have faith that right makes might; and in that faith, dare to the end, to do your duty as you understand it.*
- *"Towering genius disdains a beaten path, it seeks paths hitherto unexplored.*
- *"As our case is new, so we must think anew and act anew."*

Rich Thompson also wrote, "I'd be interested in hearing more about his cabinet and a staff where so many tried to undermine his actions and decisions. A specific question would certainly revolve around the reasons he had for keeping McClellan on as commander of the Army of the Potomac for as long as he did.

And finally, If you could do three things differently what would they be and why"?

As to his management of cabinet members, congress and political factions, he was a master political strategist with a keen understanding of people. As such, he was rarely fooled and he also knew how to bring prospectively opposing forces together by focusing upon the one or two issues, among the many, where they were of one mind.

Indeed when he held his first meeting with his cabinet, there wasn't a man in the room, besides Lincoln, who didn't think that they were the better man, the better educated, the more refined, the more presidential and certainly the more worthy of being president.

But he tamed most of them in short order, outfoxed and outplayed the one who never stopped trying to play him, established positive working relationships with all and extremely close, personal friendships with two.

There's a line from a silly song that describes the quintessential old miser in the movie, *Scrooge*, starring Albert Finney—"Duplicity, deceit and subterfuge and no one's worse than Ebenezer Scrooge." It always puts me in mind of Salmon Chase, Lincoln's brilliant, effective but ever conniving Secretary of the Treasury.

He schemed from the first day until his last, when Lincoln finally accepted his resignation. But Lincoln outplayed him at every turn and brought him back from the political dung-heap to make him the Chief Justice of the United States Supreme Court. Magnanimous to a fault again, Lincoln trusted him completely, knowing that he would firmly protect what had been accomplished as to abolition and the rights of these newly freed citizens.

Can't help but share this sweet piece from presidential bodyguard, William Crook's *Reminiscences* as shared by Margarita Spalding Gerry. For having recently quoted Doris Kearns Goodwin as to the Lincoln-Stanton belonging and fierce bond. What a gem it is.

> *The President's relationship to Secretary Stanton was another instance of Mr. Lincoln's marvelous self-control. Where the good of the nation was involved he didn't even see things that related to himself alone. Secretary Stanton was a strong man and devoted to his country. I believe, too, that he loved the President. But while he recognized Mr. Lincoln's greatness and was loyal, those traits of Mr. Lincoln's which was antipathetic to his character irritated him sometimes almost beyond endurance. Mr. Stanton was not a man of much self-control. The President's tenderness of heart seemed to him weakness. The fondness for reading and for jesting, which every day restored the balance in the President's overweighted mind, seemed to Mr. Stanton something approaching imbecility. He was furious once when Mr. Lincoln delayed a cabinet meeting to read the witticisms of Petroleum V. Nasby. When the President,*

*during hours of anxious waiting for news from a great battle, was apparently
absorbed in Hamlet, Mr. Stanton, whose invectives were varied, called him, I
have heard, 'a baboon.'* (Margarita Spalding Gerry, *Through Five Administrations: Reminiscences of Colonel William H. Crook*, p. 33)

Petroleum V. Nasby, you can't help but love it.

Petroleum, by the way, was a fictional cartoon creation of David Ross
Locke, a 'n'er do well' champion of the Confederate cause who got drafted
by the Union and promptly deserted to join the Confederacy. He displayed a
distinct lack of courage and was wise enough to fight in fictional battles only.
More than anything else, he was an opportunist, an always half-drunk and
phony preacher who largely quoted the Bible verses that explained why it
was that slavery was a moral necessity. Jon Grinspan in a June 11, 2012
piece for the New York Times, referred to him as the *"Stephen Colbert of the
Civil War,"* that's the former, pre *Late Show* version of Colbert, where he
played the part of a smart but ridiculous conservative foil.

Locke and Colbert applied sarcasm at its best and most impactful - as an
art form.

As to the three things, were he to have a 'do over,' Rich, how about these:

First, to have relieved McClellan after the basic organizing and training of
the troops was realized (maybe 4-months plus), which was the only military
skill set that he had of any value; and to have elevated either General John
Reynolds or General Winfield Hancock or even General Sedgwick to command, rather than Generals Pope, Burnside and Hooker. Imagine no Peninsula Campaign, no 7 Days, no "Slows" and just Generals who were smart
enough to realize that victory lied not in taking Richmond but in taking the
Army of Northern Virginia. And hey, no Peninsula Campaign and no fallen
General Joe Johnston and maybe, just maybe, Bobby Lee gets stuck with Jeff
Davis in Richmond for another year or more. Oh, what a gift and wonder that
might have been to the Army of the Potomac.

I believe my command choices would never have been blindsided by
Longstreet at Second Bull Run and nor would they ever have been stupid
enough to attack Marye's Heights.

Second, to have issued a direct order to General George Meade to expedi-
tiously pursue and attack the then defeated Army of Northern Virginia on the
heels of their victory at Gettysburg. With their backs up against a flooded
Potomac, Lee was oh so vulnerable and unable to escape. Damn, if they
didn't give him and his 'fighting soul' of the Confederacy two more long
years.

They had successfully fought on the defensive at Gettysburg, but despite
their great success, Meade was still afraid to go on offense against an army
that had already and forever been stripped of the opportunity to go on the
offensive or to be audacious or bold itself. Lincoln knew this, he mourned

this, he wrote the scathing letter to General Meade but too gentle, too kind, too generous, he would not offend and so, threw it in the drawer.

And finally, pre 13th amendment, given that 180,000 former slaves were already fighting for his Union, to have brought Frederick Douglass and/or other admired African American Community Leaders in D.C. into the fold of his administration to take steps to fashion policies and processes that would assist freed slaves, that would educate them as to their rights, that would provide pathways to opportunity that would help with Reconstruction and send a clear and certain message that they were free and free forever and as empowered as all of their fellow citizens. There was a desperate need that he would have seen in time, but sadly, even if he had seen it earlier, President Johnson would no doubt have pulled the plug on it

There you have it, Rich, 3 prospective Lincoln *'should have dones,'* which were, of course, empered by that was done.

ONE POLICY

Steven Koppelman poses a straightforward, simple and important question.

He wrote, "Were I to have an actual conversation with him, I would most like to discuss how he was able to seemingly foresee the future and intrinsically understand that saving the union of American states really was the paramount issue and that slavery, which of course caused the war, ultimately needed to be eradicated. Were these always one and the same thing to him? And, what in his mind caused him to have such a deep and absorbing love of the Union."

Were the saving of the Union and the eradication of slavery one policy?

From the moment he read the draft of his *Emancipation Proclamation* to his cabinet and before he even wrote his famous "I would Save the Union" letter to Horace Greeley, they most certainly became one. Saving the Union, after all, and making it worthy of the saving were ultimately contingent upon removing the cause of the separation.

As to his love of the Union and his ability to see beyond his own time, Steve, both observations-slash-questions are, in and of themselves, moving.

As to the love of, my thoughts immediately turn to our friend, Richard Brookhiser and the mere title of his first book on Lincoln, *Founder's Son*. He was moved by the founders, by Washington, Paine and Jefferson, and he revered, respected and honored their work and their legacy of which he was now a part. He appreciated the minds of the men who forged a living Constitution and he tied his war to a reverence for the political philosophy as expressed by Thomas Jefferson in the *Declaration of Independence*.

They inspired him as did the American political experiment itself and the Democratic Republic that they gave rise to. The Union, his Union, the one that he had a duty to preserve and protect, was but the byproduct of a great experiment testing whether or not people were going to be free, truly free, to govern themselves.

Experimenters and explorers all, both they and he!

America was still in its infancy and he, like Washington, was just another sailor on a ship, navigating in uncertain and uncharted waters. And so very, very much was at stake. His mere thinking and the resonance and beauty of the phrase, "*The Last Best Hope of Earth*" tell us all we ultimately need to know both about his rich reverence for our past as well as his faith and hope in our future destiny, free of the horrid stain of slavery.

I can imagine a laughing Lincoln shaking his head at the lot of us.

Kent Gramm, you wrote that "We need conversations with him." We took you seriously and well imagined; and while we may have fallen short, he somehow never does.

Figure 3.1.   By his Summer Cottage, it stands and in it, you cannot help but see the lines etched into his face by the compelling sadness and the harsh toll exacted by his awful war. *Source:* Lincoln at the President's Cottage in D.C. - by Evan Schwartz, EIS Studio 2008. Photographed by Dave Wiegers.

Chapter Four

The Turn of a Phrase

I am reminded of a provocative line in Daniel Mark Epstein's *The Lincolns: Portrait of a Marriage.* So simple and so telling, *"Everyone knew him. No one knew him."*

There it is, my friends. In life and in memory, we know him so very well, but!

What we do know, absolutely know and can faithfully and fully trust beyond his actions taken, however, are his pen and his words, his vast reservoir of words, both spoken and written. Frederick Douglass was among the first to assure those in his company who doubted Lincoln that they could always and ever trust his word.

Words have consequences. Words have power. Once said or written, they become timeless. They move, mold and guide. They impact, they inspire. Heroes, heroines, movers and shakers, philosophers, poets and visionaries, they all die, but the words they leave behind take on everlasting life. While most of us have either great faith or some measure of faith in the immortality of spirit and soul, here on earth, it is the words drawn from our history and our literature that are most certainly immortal.

Homer and Socrates and Aristophanes and Cicero and Jesus and Justinian and Galileo, Locke, Dickens, Wilder, Twain and even my Peter Paul & Mary, James Taylor, Harry Chapin, the Beatles and tens of thousands of other voices live on in me and in you. They and their moving, powerful and often beautiful words. Muted or loud. Sung, disparaged or celebrated.

And so it is the words spoken or written by our friend, Abraham Lincoln that resonate with and move us in this short chapter. A simple exercise, but also a brightly illuminating one, as the collaborators who have kindly driven this work and are intimate with Lincoln, weigh in on the words of his that continue to ring most loudly in their ears today.

Lincoln's sample size is, of course, vast and what *Harold Holzer* refers to as his '*Greatest Hits*' are familiar, well honored and understandably so, but it is in the 'nooks and crannies' or crevices of his comings and goings and meetings and writings where he can most astound. Even in the most non-descript of letters and with the everyday and ordinary, he painted with words in much the same way a Renoir or Van Gogh painted with oils.

He well knew that words can both sing and soar and he beautifully placed them in position to do just that.

So, there is this vast, truly vast array of passages of Lincoln's that have impacted my worldview for some 60 years. And so it is with Jack Waugh and with all of our collaborators and with you, no doubt. We reach for the big, better, best of them here, which may well be a fool's errand.

In an earlier or first draft of this piece, with an almost limitless array of quotes in mind, I opined that no matter the response of each collaborator, I'd no doubt be affirmatively shaking my head in a full on "Oh Yes-I agree" mode. For when it comes to Lincoln and words, what's not to like. I was in full throttle "all hail" anything and everything that came out of his mouth and mind. But then it hit me and I stopped myself in my tracks for indeed, there once were lines of Lincoln's with which no one today ought to be in sync.

And so this brief caveat before diving into the good stuff.

Abraham Lincoln's earlier views on race and 'equality before the law and/or equality in all things' disappoint. Especially over the course of the 1858 Senatorial campaign with Stephen Douglas. Given Lincoln's pointed anti-slavery stance, Douglas constantly played on the overt and absolute racism of the day in an attempt to paint Lincoln as a radical who would dare threaten their sacred, 'lily white' social order. Oh yes, devoid of context and understanding, quote after quote can be pulled that will leave you shaking your head, because he did not then believe that the two races were, in fact, equal in all things or, for that matter, even able to coexist.

Indeed, he, a product of his day, time and culture, often bore witness to a racist mindset. He still had much growing up to do. Far more open minded than the masses, he always viewed the slaves and free African Americans compassionately and empathetically, as fellow human beings and never as lesser beings. Entitled to freedom and entitled to reap what they sow and to the fullness of life, they were, as he ever steadfastly proclaimed. And so too, all he personally encountered were treated with unpretentious dignity and the ready hand of friendship.

Past ignorance and societal prejudices and cruel racist and bawdy jokes aside, he would deal with his demons as president of the United States of America and come full circle to embrace both equality in all things and an America that would freely embrace all.

So we ruggedly forgive him these considerable faults and rather focus upon the greater goodness in him. We do this, for while his perceptions and worldview may once have been jaded, his inherent goodness and decency ultimately determined his life, his contributions and his fate and not his once prejudices.

So forward, we go.

Lincoln left us one 'hell of a' lot of words or what might more accurately be considered a body of literature. From the youngest of ages, he sought to debate, to convince, to enlighten and to 'make 'em laugh.' As a young boy, with humorous and stylistic flare, he would mimic and poke fun at the dire warnings of hellfire and damnation Calvinists after Sunday services. In the Old and New Testaments that he acquired a photographic memory of, it is the light of Jesus of Nazareth that shines in the former, while the metaphorical hinge to which we attach all conveyed by Lincoln also is a light that shines— Lincoln's light. For it is not the sun or the stars, o'er the years alone that generated light for us, but also the contributions and words of those who moved the mountains for us.

In the passionate and powerful poetry of Lincoln's words and arguments, that light still beams. For he took the English tongue to war and to redemption and changed the world with it.

His objective was never to persuade alone, but rather to fashion belongings, connections and spiritual bonds. Inherently humble, and in truth, humble to a fault, he wrote up as it were and never down. He did not come down from on high and rarely threw stones. He applied fact, consideration, thoughtfulness and reason.

There would be no boast or brag with him as his words dripped with compassion and empathy. He was civil, honorable, respectful, tolerant and understanding. He wrote, as only the greatest of poets do, with an inherent and unparalleled stylistic wizardry and out of the blood, sweat and tears of a deep spiritual reckoning with the world.

Out of the depths of grief, loss and pain.

Out of a harsh and impassioned struggle to reconcile himself to life.

There was always one foot in the grave and the other in the stars, while heart and soul were inevitably and firmly placed on the ground, in the "primordial sympathies" and struggles and in the never ending battles to build that better world. Out of the vortex and wonder of the all of this, comes the deep, soulful richness of both the man and his prose. As to his craft, he has invariably been described as anything from an artist to a carpenter, an architect, a smithy, a craftsman. What amazes is that he could convey missives to the masses, as if he were communing with each and every individual personally.

Intimately!

He mastered the short statement and said more with less. i.e. Edward Everett's, "I should be glad, if I could flatter myself, that I came as near to the central idea of the occasion in two hours, as you did in two minutes." He did the homework and the research as he was ever determined to get to the truth, a truth that the long tide of history bore out. And genius, why of course, genius, he had and applied that in spades.

Lincoln's words were neither bloated nor static nor empty and given their extent and their wealth, we do not study Lincoln in a vacuum, quiet and alone, but up close and personal and together. His words challenge us, cry out to us—even demand us to do our own bits to not only remember, but rather preserve and protect what he secured for us. While, at one and the same time, advancing the line for good.

155 years removed, through and in his words, Lincoln's beating heart still beats and calls upon us to sustain and to advance.

We begin with *Harold Holzer* who wrote, "As to those of Lincoln's own words I treasure most, beyond what might be called the 'greatest hits' and particularly in fraught times like now, it would be the seemingly casual, but in fact brilliantly expressed question from his *First Inaugural Address*: "*Why should there not be a patient confidence in the ultimate justice of the people. Is there any better or equal hope in the world*"?

Yes, the people, the passage of time, another election cycle, another chance, another hope and in fact, yet another inadvertent response to our compelling fifth and final question.

We appropriate Holzer's "*Greatest Hits'* to include the most recognized and widely celebrated of his speeches, i.e., *Second Inaugural, Gettysburg, First Inaugural, Cooper Union, House Divided, the Farewell Address*, the *1854 Preoria Address,* select letters, two Messages to Congress, portions of the *Lyceum Address* and select passages from the great debates with Douglas.

My friend, *Jack C. Waugh* went long. To our simple, "What words of his speak most loudly to you and why," he generously responded:

"There are so many things Lincoln said and said so well. He said he wrote so that a 12-year old could understand him. He broke from the florid prose so prevalent in his time. He wrote short sentences. And he reached for the sublime. His best works are pure prose poetry.

The selections below of his words that speak to me so vividly are but a sampling of his powerful eloquence. I could pony up many more. I could just as well quote in full the entire documents from which these were excerpted and call them all sublime."

FROM THE FIRST INAUGURAL ADDRESS, 1861

In your hands, my dissatisfied fellow countrymen, and not in mine, is the momentous issue of civil war. The government will not assail you. You can have no conflict, without being yourselves the aggressors. You have no oath registered in Heaven to destroy the government, while I shall have the most solemn one to 'preserve, protect and defend' it. We must not be enemies.

Though passion may have strained, it must not break our bonds of affection. The mystic chords of memory, stretching from every battlefield and patriot grave to every living heart and hearthstone all over this broad land, will yet swell the chorus of the Union when again touched, as surely they will be, by the better angels of our nature.

FAREWELL ADDRESS, SPRINGFIELD, 1861

My friends: No one not in my situation, can appreciate my feeling of sadness at this parting. To this place, and the kindness of these people, I owe everything. Here I have lived a quarter of a century, and have passed from a young to an old man. Here my children have been born, and one is buried. I now leave, not knowing when or whether ever I may return, with a task before me greater than that which rested upon Washington. To his care commending you, as I hope in your prayers you will commend me, I bid you an affectionate farewell.

From his Letter to Horace Greeley, 1862, "*I shall try to correct errors when shown to be errors, and I shall adopt new views so fast as they shall appear to be true views.*"

From his Second Inaugural Address, 1865, "*With malice toward none; with charity for all; with firmness in the right, as God gives us to see the right, let us strive on to finish the work we are in; to bind up the nation's wounds; to care for him who shall have borne the battle, and for his widow, and his orphan—to do which may achieve and cherish a just and lasting peace among ourselves, and with all nations.*"

From his "House Divided" Speech, 1858, "*We are now far into the fifth year since a policy was initiated with the avowed purpose of putting an end to slavery agitation. Under operation of that policy, that agitation has not only not ceased, but has constantly augmented. In my opinion, it will not cease until a crisis shall have been reached and passed. 'A house divided against itself cannot stand.' I believe this government cannot endure permanently half slave and half free.*"

From his Cooper Union Speech, 1860, "*Neither let us be slandered from our duty by false accusations against us, nor frightened from it by menaces of destruction to the government, nor of dungeons to ourselves. Let us have faith that right makes might, and in that faith, let us to the end, dare to do our duty as we understand it.*"

GETTYSBURG ADDRESS, 1863

But in a larger sense, we cannot dedicate—we cannot consecrate—we cannot hallow--this ground. The brave men, living and dead, who struggled here, have consecrated it, far above our poor power to add or detract. The world will little note, nor long remember what we say here, but it can never forget what they did here. It is for us the living, rather, to be dedicated here to the unfinished work which they have, thus far, so nobly advanced. It is rather for us to be here dedicated to the great task remaining before us—that from these honored dead we take increased devotion to that cause for which they gave the last full measure of devotion—that we here highly resolve that these dead shall not have died in vain—that this nation, under God, shall have a new birth of Freedom—and that this government of the people, by the people, for the people, shall not perish from the earth.

From the Peoria Speech – 1854,

When the white man governs himself that is self-government; but when he governs himself, and also governs another man, that is more than self-government—that is despotism. If the negro is a man, why then my ancient faith teaches me that all men are created equal; and that there can be no moral right in connection with one man's making a slave of another.

THE ANNUAL MESSAGE TO CONGRESS, 1862

The dogmas of the quiet past, are inadequate to the stormy present. The occasion is piled high with difficulty, and we must rise with the occasion. As our case is new, so we must think anew, and act anew. We must disenthrall ourselves, and then we shall save our country. Fellow-citizens, we cannot escape history. The fiery trial through which we pass will light us down, in honor or dishonor, to the latest generation. In giving freedom to the slave, we assure freedom to the free, honorable alike in what we give, and what we preserve. We shall nobly save or meanly lose, the last best, hope of earth. Other means may succeed; this could not fail. The way is plain, peaceful, generous, just—a way which, if followed, the world will forever applaud, and God must forever bless.

From the Letter to James C. Conkling, 1863, *"The signs look better. The Father of Waters again goes unvexed to the sea. Peace does not appear so distant as it did. I hope it will come soon, and come to stay; and so come as to be worth the keeping in all future time. It will then have proved that, among free men, there can be no successful appeal from the ballot to the bullet."*

From the *Letter to A. G. Hodges, 1864, "I am naturally antislavery. If slavery is not wrong, nothing is wrong. I cannot remember when I did not so think, and feel."*

THE LAST DEBATE WITH DOUGLAS AT ALTON, ILLINOIS, 1858

The real issue in this controversy, the one pressing upon every mind is the sentiment on the part of one class that looks upon the institution of slavery as a wrong, and of another class that does not look upon it as a wrong.

That is the issue that will continue in this country when these poor tongues of Judge Douglas and myself shall be silent. It is the eternal struggle between these two principles—right and wrong-throughout the world. They are the two principles that have stood face to face from the beginning of time; and will ever continue to struggle. The one is the common right of humanity and the other the divine right of kings. It is the same principle in whatever shape it develops itself. It is the same spirit that says, 'You work and toil and earn bread, and I'll eat it.' No matter in what shape it comes, whether from the mouth of a king who seeks to bestride the people of his own nation and live by the fruit of their labor, or from one race of man as an apology for enslaving another race, it is the same tyrannical principle.

Don't know about you, but the words referred to by Jack above—all of them and there are many more—never get old or tired. You read them, hear them, say them and you want to stand up and cheer.

"There are a number of words of Lincoln's that speak loudly to me, and it varies by situation as to which ones speak the loudest at any given time," wrote *Michelle Krowl.* "I am moved by the simple beauty of many of his words, such as those in the *Gettysburg Address* or the *Second Inaugural* and one line in the July 14, 1863 letter that Lincoln never sent to General Meade after Gettysburg which stays with me because of the anguish behind it":

It read, *"Your golden opportunity is gone and I am distressed immeasurably because of it."* Lincoln well knew that if Meade had crushed General Robert E. Lee's Army of Northern Virginia after Gettysburg (as he believed he could have), at the same time Vicksburg fell, that the war might come to a speedier end and lives would be saved. As it happened, the war was prolonged indefinitely and the reader grieves with Lincoln in his despair, while knowing that Lincoln chose to subsume his own feelings and spare Meade.

Lincoln included a passage in his *July 4, 1861 Message to Congress* that speaks to the continuing promise of the United States: '*This is essentially a people's contest. On the side of the Union, it is a struggle for maintaining in the world, that form, and substance of government, whose leading object is, to elevate the condition of men, to lift artificial weights from all shoulders, to clear the paths of laudable pursuit for all, to afford all, an unfettered start, and a fair chance, in the race of life.*"

Instances in which Lincoln employed logical reasoning to make important points remain compelling. To address a Union rally in his hometown of Springfield, Illinois in August 1863, Lincoln asked his friend James Conkling to read remarks on his behalf. The *Emancipation Proclamation* remained unpopular, and some Union men balked at fighting on behalf of African Americans. In two sentences, Lincoln slashes and burns their position and moves on to the larger point of the need to win the war, regardless of their individual motivation to fight. He wrote, "*You say you will not fight to free negroes. Some of them seem willing to fight for you; but, no matter. Fight you, then, exclusively to save the Union. I issued the proclamation on purpose to aid you in saving the Union. Whenever you shall have conquered all resistance to the Union, if I shall urge you to continue fighting, it will be an apt time, then, for you to declare you will not fight to free negroes.*"

Some of Lincoln's words, or words ascribed to him, speak loudly to me only in that I find myself using them. When I have nearly finished a number of tasks or get to the end of something, I sometimes think to myself *I am 'down to the raisins'* after a remark Lincoln made to David Homer Bates in the War Department telegraph office. Having reached the end of the new telegraphs to read. Lincoln told the story of a little girl who ate all too much, finishing with raisins. After she became violently sick, the doctor proclaimed her nearly cured when she got "down to the raisins."

Frank Williams reverently wrote, "The speeches or portions of papers of Lincoln's that resonate with me are—his *Lyceum Speech* in Springfield in 1838 which calls for '*reverence for the laws*' and eschewing violence—also, his special *Message to Congress* on July 4, 1861 after the firing on Fort Sumter when he calls the war of rebellion '*a people's contest*' and asks Congress to ratify actions taken by him as president while they were not in session—his '*Are all the laws but one [suspension of the writ of habeas corpus] to go unexecuted, and the Government itself go to pieces, lest that one be violated'*?—the final *Emancipation Proclamation* on January 1, 1863, you know the one that Professor Richard Hofstadter said had all the moral grandeur of "*a bill of lading*" with the President's ringing, '*henceforward and forever free*'—and then there is Lincoln's *Corning letter* where he defends his administration for its policies relating to civil liberties, the arrest of critic Clement Vallandigham, suspension of *habeas corpus* and trial by military commission—'*Must I shoot a simple-minded soldier boy who deserts, while I must not touch a hair of a wily agitator who induces him to desert'*?—of course, the Second Inaugural—all 702 words of it and the best in our history—for empathy, read his sympathy letter to Fanny McCullough, whose father, a friend of Lincoln's, died in battle—his '*In this sad world of ours, sorrow comes to all; and, to the young, it comes with bitterest agony, because it takes them unawares*—and his '*perfect relief is not possible, except with time.*'

Karen Hawbecker wrote, "Some of Lincoln's words that speak most loudly to me are found in the *Conkling letter*, written on August 14, 1863, in which he addresses those who wanted him to settle for an unholy peace. I saw the original letter when it was on display in the Smithsonian Institution to mark Lincoln's 200th birthday in 2009. Just hear these simple stirring words":

> *Peace does not appear so distant as it did. I hope it will come soon, and come to stay; and so come as to be worth the keeping in all future time. It will then have been proved that, among free men, there can be no successful appeal from the ballot to the bullet; and that they who take such appeal are sure to lose their case, and pay the cost. And then, there will be some black men who can remember that, with silent tongue, and clenched teeth, and steady eye, and well poised bayonet, they have helped mankind on to this great consummation; while, I fear, there will be some white ones, unable to forget that, with malignant heart, and deceitful speech, they have strove to hinder it.*

"From my perspective," she continued, "Lincoln is foreseeing a future in which he hopes free elections will have been successfully defended once and for all from those who would impose their will through violent compulsion. He intends it to be a lesson to all future generations as he gave singular emphasis to this profound defense of freedom when reading the above to his secretary, William O. Stoddard. His final line still resonates for us today in our continuing efforts to keep the peace and freedom that these black men and former slaves helped secure, "*Still, let us not be over-sanguine of a speedy final triumph. Let us be quite sober. Let us diligently apply the means, never doubting that a just God, in his own good time, will give us the rightful result.*"

Now most would say that we are at peace. Generally speaking that is. And yet, we are still engaged in the Middle East and we, quite remarkably, have active duty troops placed in nearly 150 countries, with the bulk in places like Japan, Germany, Italy, Afghanistan and South Korea and as little as a handful or two in places like Estonia, Latvia or Luxembourg. But we're bitterly divided at home where Republicans and Democrats, more often than not, excoriate one another. And racial tension is red hot and furious, as the ancient battle for true justice for all rightfully rages on. We long for peace and understanding and more *'you before I.'*

"I love the *Second Inaugural Address*! I have incorporated it into almost every talk I've ever given," wrote *Paula Hopewell*.

"The thoughts expressed in this speech are thought-provoking, generous and forgiving. Yes, they are the work of a master politician, but they reach beyond the practicalities of the Reconstruction that lay ahead to a fair assessment of slavery and its evils. The Address attempted to reinforce what we had in common as *"both sides read the same Bible, both sides pray to the same God—let us judge not—with malice toward none—let us strive on to finish the work we are in."*

"Why do these words speak to me? Kentuckian by birth, I have lived in one other Border state (Maryland) and one slave state (North Carolina), as well as three Northern states (Ohio, Minnesota and Connecticut). I am Southern enough to feel the judgment and prejudices of the North, even as they exist today. I have heard many opinions that start with "Down South . . ." and end with any number of opinions and attitudes, some of which I find unfair. The South does not have a monopoly on racism or the unfortunate history of supporting slavery.

"I applaud the recent trend by major universities to acknowledge their role in slavery, most recently Columbia and Georgetown.

"In May of 2015, there was a long-overdue ceremony in Hartford, at our state Capitol. The regimental flags of Connecticut's Colored Troops were brought up out of the basement and given a place of honor on the main floor, along with all the other Civil War flags that were already there. I had the good fortune to attend that ceremony, which included direct descendants of those African American Troops."

"There are so many of Lincoln's words that speak loudly to me," added *Steve Koppelman,* "indeed to all of us. Some that stand out, in chronological order, would be *'Let us have faith that right makes might'* from his Cooper Union address; *'Fellow-citizens, we cannot escape history. The fiery trial through which we pass, will light us down, in honor or dishonor, to the latest generation'* from his Annual Message to Congress in December of 1862; *'I now wish to make the personal acknowledgment that you were right, and I was wrong'* from a letter written to Ulysses S. Grant after his Vicksburg campaign in July of 1863; *'That government of the people, by the people, for the people, shall not perish from the earth'* which of course is from the Gettysburg Address; *'I claim not to have controlled events, but confess plainly that events have controlled me'* from a letter to Albert Hodges in 1864; and finally, *'It may seem strange that any men should dare to ask a just God's assistance in wringing their bread from the sweat of other men's faces; but let us judge not that we be not judged'* from his Second Inaugural Address. Of course, these are all rather famous and well-known individual quotes, but taken altogether, in my mind, they show the essential and true Lincoln, each speaking to me at full volume."

Steve's choices certainly speak to and reaffirm the position carved out at the outset of this Chapter that Lincoln's words live and live loudly and continue to move. They lift and elevate. Still upfront, still personal, still empowering.

"I'd like to be there with him to discuss *'the better angels of our nature,'*" wrote *Matt Lakemacher.* "I'd like to expound upon the idea that *'the Almighty has his own purposes'* and *'the judgments of the Lord are true and righteous altogether.'* I'd like to be there to discuss his *Meditations on the Divine Will* or to consider grief with Lincoln in the Bardo, after the death of Willy and the carnage of Civil War. *'The will of God prevails,'* even if *'God's purpose is different from our purposes and his ways beyond our understanding.'* Like Job, sometimes we just have to accept that he is God despite our circumstances and like Elijah we have to listen for that still small voice.' Those are the moments and conversations that I'd like to share with Father Abraham."

Oh what a loaded paragraph. Matt's chosen excerpts and commentary all ultimately speak to the rough-hewn resolution of Lincoln's lifelong shadow-boxing match with God. In Saunders' supernatural *Lincoln in the Bardo*, which Matt references, the all of this clash and the wonder of Lincoln's almost desperate search for understanding is on full dress parade.

Here *Robert Brugler's* preferred quotes and brief commentary:

"We are not enemies, but friends. We must not be enemies. Though passion may have strained, it must not break our bonds of affection. President Lincoln was attempting to speak to the Union loving people of the South, assuring them that they had nothing to fear from his administration."

"Fellow-citizens, we cannot escape history."

"The last best hope of Earth." The few Democratic Republics in the world were struggling. Kings and Queens, Princes and Potentates controlled nations. If the Union failed, the nobles would be very pleased.

"His address at the dedication of the *Gettysburg National Cemetery*, loudly speaks to me today.

"With malice towards none and charity for all. To those who fought against us, he said, we must let them up easy. Treating the Confederates as a conquered people would be injurious to the Nation's reconstruction.

"Today, I keep coming back to oh so many Lincoln's thoughts, words and deeds. Donald Trump is the antithesis of Abraham Lincoln. In our time, Lincoln's wisdom, insight and temperament are sorely needed as our president has not attempted to *"get right with* Lincoln as he should."

Amen to that, Robert.

This from our great friend from Germany, *Angela Mayer:*

"As to his words, I am a big fan of the conclusion of his *First Inaugural Address*. Having read Secretary Seward's first draft of these proposed changes and how Abraham Lincoln turned them into this masterpiece demonstrates what power words can have when so very well used. Also, there are the communications between Lincoln and Grant. I'll quote two - *"I now wish to make the personal acknowledgement that you were right and I was wrong"* after Vicksburg. The way Lincoln put himself into Grant's hands impressively demonstrates how he was able to build trust with but a few words. It paved the way for this wonderful line, *"Let nothing which is transpiring change, hinder or delay your military movements, or plans."* His simple use of words paved the way in building a historic relationship of respect, trust and understanding. "

THE QUICK HITS

Douglas Egerton—As already conveyed and here emphasized—"Maybe as a writer, I would wish to talk to him about how he mastered that craft. In a time of long-winded speeches and essays, Lincoln, of course, was the master of the brief statement; the *Gettysburg Address* and the *Second Inaugural* are only two examples of his ability to cut to the heart of the matter in just a few words. Clearly he knew his Shakespeare and Dickens, both of whose voices are echoed in Lincoln's prose. But I find that the older I get and the more I write, the longer my books become, a problem for my editor, I admit and I would love to take lessons in how to craft a sentence as elegant as most of his."

Edna Greene Medford—"I am astonished by the final statement in his *Second Inaugural Address: 'With malice toward none, with charity for all.'* Given the end of such a destructive war, this was a truly profound and generous statement."

Bob Willard—"My big three. I call them the jewels of Lincoln's oratory, the *Second Inaugural, Gettysburg* and *Farewell Addresses* are probably universally cited in answering this question. But if I had to pick something else, my choice would come from his acceptance speech upon being nominated as the Republican candidate for Senate in 1858, the *House Divided* speech. But I would not focus upon the words at the end which we all recall. I rather love the opening line, '*If we could first know where we are, and whither we are tending, we could then better judge what to do, and how to do it.*' For anyone who has ever been involved in strategic planning, these words should be imprinted on the top of every page they produce."

Mike Movius—"Lincoln's fascination and reliance upon the *Declaration of Independence* and the line '*a new nation, conceived in Liberty, and dedicated to the proposition that all men are created equal*' interests me in that it is not law, but rather the basis of the American character. So, for me, it must be the beginning of his 1863 *Gettysburg Address* and his echoing the words of Thomas Jefferson. That thought led to the *Emancipation Proclamation,* the induction of black Americans into the Union army and, was of course, the compelling cause of the great conflict in the first place."

George Buss—The *House Divided Speech.* "I did it in the Old State Capitol for the 150th Anniversary. It was standing room only and electric. To have people hang on every word is all consuming. Now, I have the honor of delivering the *Gettysburg Address* on Remembrance Day in Gettysburg, after Jim Getty's 40-year run. I am humbled to be channeling Lincoln in that sacred setting. I recall Jim introducing me to author, Jack Waugh in 1996. He said, 'Jack, this is George Buss, he does a fine Lincoln. I never want to disappoint Jim."

When I write that Lincoln's words and thoughts live, I am being figurative, while George does so literally and powerfully. Indeed, *"He does a fine Lincoln!"* Sadly, Jim Getty passed in 2015, leaving a great big hole in the Gettysburg community.

Dennis Perreault—"As a teacher, Lincoln's November 5, 1855 letter to Isham Reavis has always stood out and spoken to me about the importance of working hard and being committed to self-improvement regardless of your personal circumstances."

In that Dennis here pulled a 'rabbit out of the hat,' a lesser known effort of Lincoln's, we share it in full. Young Isham had asked if he might study the law with Lincoln's aid.

> *I have just reached home, and found your letter of the 23rd. I am away from home too much of my time, for a young man to read law with me advantageously. If you are resolutely determined to make a lawyer of yourself, the thing is more than half done already. It is but a small matter whether you read with anybody or not. I did not read with any one. Get the books, and read and study them till, you understand them in their principal features; and that is the main thing. It is of no consequence to be in a large town while you are reading. I read at New-Salem, which never had three hundred people living in it. The books, and your capacity for understanding them, are just the same in all places. Mr. Dummer is a very clever man and an excellent lawyer (much better than I, in law-learning); and I have no doubt that he will cheerfully tell you what books to read, and also loan you the books.*
>
> *Always bear in mind that your own resolution to succeed, is more important than any other one thing. Very truly your friend.*

Steven Raymond—"Fortunately, I can imagine hearing the profound eloquence of his *Farewell Address* to the people of Springfield and the great rhetoric of his Inaugurals. Then too, there are the words he used in so many letters to newspaper editors and to the mothers and widows of war victims, and of course, again, the *Gettysburg Address*."

Dave Wiegers—"I think you ought to read the *Gettysburg Address* and his *First* and *Second Inaugurals* to hear Lincoln at his best and most profound."

Michaela Wieties—"Lincoln was a master at putting words together to create such beautiful, powerful speeches. His quote that has most inspired me is *"That some may achieve great success, is proof to all that others can achieve it as well."* He struggled and worked hard and achieved such tremendous success. He inspires me to work harder and strive for my own success."

Joan Chaconas—"It seems to me that we are still struggling with Lincoln's hope of building a nation where "all might truly be equal" and with the thinking expressed in his *Gettysburg Address*. While our world is ever so much more advanced in most ways than the one Lincoln knew, we still deal with people and their prejudices.

We still know turmoil as so many see themselves as more equal than others. And so we strive and we hope and we stand, as Lincoln did, when he said, "*I shall not surrender this game, leaving any available cards unplayed.*"

Another rabbit out of the hat. But permit me to expand upon this quotation of Joan's. It was May of 1862 and Lincoln was riding in a carriage with Secretary Seward and Secretary Welles on the way to the funeral of Secretary Stanton's son. He startled both of them when he said, "*I have about come to the conclusion that we must free the slaves or be ourselves subdued.*" After they expressed surprise, even shock, at what appeared to be a major change of position, it was then that Lincoln intoned the words above—"*I shall not surrender this game, leaving any available cards unplayed.*"

Two months later in July of 1862, Reverdy Johnson, a Union Senator from Maryland, traveled to Union-occupied Louisiana and reported to the president that southern Unionists in the state were upset with General John W. Phelps's policies regarding fugitive slaves, leading to this response from Lincoln:

"*I distrust the wisdom if not the sincerity of friends, who would hold my hands while my enemy stabs me. This appeal of professed friends has paralyzed me more in this struggle than any other one thing.*" Indeed he had determined to play every available card, including and most notably, the *Emancipation Proclamation.*

Mel Maurer—"His well-chosen words in his *Farewell* at Springfield, first and especially and then the *Second Inaugural Address*, the *House Divided* speech and, of course, the *Gettysburg Address*, I consider these as poetry-prose which should be read and studied by all."

Were these *Greatest Hits* , in fact, as Mel proposes, studied by all, maybe just maybe, we would be a kinder, gentler people and a greater nation.

Christopher Oakley—"*The better angels of our nature*" is one of the most eloquent phrases in the English language. But my favorite shall always be "*Government of the people, by the people, for the people, shall not perish from the earth.*"

Jim McGrath—"He was a story teller, a humorist, a communicator. He wrote one-liners that punched and he was, most importantly, I believe, able to put what we feel in our hearts into words. His humble origins, his natural compassion and his empathy always shone through. Among my favorites are the passages in the *Lyceum Address* where he focuses upon violence and mob law and what it is that will check that or reason, law and the people. This and his "*neither a master nor a slave,*" the very Definition of Democracy.

Kathryn Harris—"Of particular interest to me is his quote regarding being "*neither a master nor a slave*" and his comments on this quote. There is an endless array from which to choose, but I find this so enlightening and it stands out."

JUST QUOTES

Richard Brookhiser—He shared two quotes, without any commentary whatsoever. Both are gems, worthy of an explanatory word or two. Neither were flagged by anyone else, which again attests to the richness and depth of the Lincoln library.

> *Our republican robe is soiled and trailed in the dust. Let us turn and wash it white in the spirit if not the blood of the Revolution." and "I have sought His aid--but if after endeavoring to do my best in the light which He affords me I find my efforts fail, I must believe that for some purpose unknown to me, He wills it otherwise.*

The first quote is from yet another extraordinarily powerful and impassioned speech, delivered in the wake of the passage of the Kansas Nebraska Act which pulled Lincoln back into politics. It was delivered in Peoria, Illinois on October 16, 1854. A brilliant effort, Lincoln was back and he was back to stay.

Shortly after he voiced the above line that Brookhiser flagged, he added this clarion call:

> *Let us return it (slavery) to the position our fathers gave it; and there let it rest in peace. Let us re-adopt the Declaration of Independence, and with it, the practices, and policy, which harmonize with it. Let north and south—let all Americans—let all lovers of liberty everywhere join in this great and good work. If we do this, we shall not only have saved the Union; but we shall have so saved it, as to make, and to keep it, forever worthy of the saving.*

With the second quote, Brookhiser references a somber and almost surreal sentiment that Lincoln shared with Eliza Gurney and 3 other Quakers in the wake of their October 26, 1862 prayerful and moving meeting at the White House. All of the whys and wherefores of this meeting, which took place as a driving rain fell in Washington, will never be known, but we do know this, Eliza Gurney truly got to Lincoln, touched him, moved him, comforted him. Somehow, someway, she took a bite out of his grief and his suffering. Eliza and her fellow 'Friends' came, unlike almost everybody else, not to ask for anything of their president, but rather and kindly and simply to give, to console and to pray and to let him know that they were in it with him. In leaving, Eliza assured Lincoln that her prayers for him would be sustained throughout the great conflict and beyond.

It may well have been as good as any White House meeting ever got for him.

Anne Moseley—Here, the words of Mr. Lincoln's that speak to me, "*Die when I may, I want it said of me by those who knew me best to say that I always plucked a thistle and planted a flower wherever I thought a flower would grow.*" Francis Carpenter, the painter, is the source of this wonder.

While recalled by him, I believe Lincoln said this to his great friend Joshua Speed, who was visiting and sat through a meeting that he had with a number of women who had come to plead for the lives of their husbands and sons. Just one of many such encounters where the demand of military discipline was tossed aside by this president and compassion and forgiveness rather manifested. In speaking to them of his intentions to release their loved ones, Lincoln famously told them, "*I believe I will turn out the flock.*"

Anne added Lincoln's, "*Character is like a tree and reputation like a shadow. The shadow is what we think of it; the tree is the real thing.*"

Attributed to, of course, but of unknown origin. On the plus side, it's certainly very Lincoln like, as it is the tree that is the real deal while the shadow bends and shifts and rushes in and out. The tree sustains itself in the darkness which the shadow cannot abide.

Then this, "*The cause of civil liberty must not be surrendered at the end of one, or even, one hundred defeats.*" —Abraham Lincoln to Henry Asbury, November 19, 1858

Please note that this was said on the day Lincoln accepted the Republican nomination for United States Senate and delivered the *House Divided Speech* in the Old Statehouse in Springfield.

"*I say 'try.' If we never try, we shall never succeed.*" —President Lincoln to General McClellan, October 13, 1862

While this letter was sent less than a month after the draw and purported Union victory at Antietam, the one that the *Emancipation Proclamation* was hinged to, Lincoln's latent and longstanding frustration with McClellan's "slows" would soon lead him to again remove him as commander of the Army of the Potomac.

Another telling line *that I'd like to add* from the letter Anne references is: "*Are you not over-cautious when you assume that you cannot do what the enemy is constantly doing? Should you not claim to be at least his equal in prowess, and act upon the claim?*"

"*Determine that the thing can and shall be done, and then we shall find the way.*" —Abraham Lincoln's speech in the United States House of Representatives on Internal Improvements on June 20, 1848.

President Polk, with whom Congressman Lincoln was ever at odds, had just vetoed an Internal Improvements measure, basically arguing that such was the province and responsibility of the states and not the federal government. He weakly contended that there was no Constitutional grounds to justify the same.

In the beginning, Lincoln was a Henry Clay Whig, the political hero of his who picked up Alexander Hamilton's neglected *Report on Manufactures* and ran with both it and its strong contention that government must invest in transportation projects in order to drive the economy, jobs and opportunity.

Thank you, Anne for going deep and carving out gems.

Rich Thompson—"There a number of quotes that I enjoy and often refer to. They include:

"*As our case is new, so we must think anew, and act anew.*" and "*Always bear in mind that your own resolution to succeed, is more important than any other one thing.*" and "*Let us have faith that right makes might.*"

"My favorite speech, which I'm sure is true for so many, is the *Gettysburg Address*. It never fails to move me."

Jonathan Sarna—The quote that resonates the most with me, heard and cited by Isaac M. Wise after meeting Lincoln reads, "*To condemn a class is, to say the least, to wrong the good with the bad. I do not like to hear a class or nationality condemned on account of a few sinners.*" (*Lincoln & the Jews*, p. 118)

David Sullivan, in one brief line, simply wrote, "*The Gettysburg Address* always speaks to me most loudly."

MY TURN

It's my turn and while the Lincoln library is so extensive and rich that one can go on and on, the attention of my collaborators has, given the specific question asked, necessarily been devoted to absolute favorites or to the particularly relevant to our struggle in America today. So I am taking the liberty of going long, like my friend, Jack Waugh, and of stretching my own responsorial limits, while at the same time, trying to remain somewhat respectful of the same.

In that my laundry list of beloved Lincoln works and/or recorded words is enough to fill a book, viewed through another lens, this response could just as well be considered an opening salvo. Consequently, an 11-point summary of Holzer inspired "*Greatest Hits*" here follows a brief sojourn through a sampling of the colloquial and conversational, the everyday and the ordinary.

The "*Greatest Hits*" require no elaboration while I'll enjoy teeing-up and briefly commenting upon the everyday and ordinary.

On the skinny, we'll look at a short 1848 letter to Herndon, a handful of telling comments and one great story while Lincoln was waiting to take office in what he called "*The very Garden of Gethsemane,*" an even wider array of expressions as he busied himself pardoning condemned soldiers and later opting for forgiveness rather than vengeance, a wonderful passage from one of his *Thanksgiving Proclamations*, some of his perfect stabs at humor, a brief telegram to Stanton, a single line from his famous letter of sympathy to Fanny McCullough, an excerpt from his poetry, and a classic quote, no longer attributed to him, a fact that I simply choose to ignore in that it is so him, even if debatably not of him.

Because Congressman Alexander Stephens of Georgia was to become the Vice President of the Confederate States of America and was as good a friend as Lincoln had while In Congress, this February 2, 1848 missive of praise to Herndon about him is haunting, "I just take up my pen to say, that Mr. Stephens of Georgia, a little slim pale faced consumptive man, with a voice like Logan's, has just concluded the very best speech, of an hour's length, I ever heard. My old, withered, dry eyes are full of tears yet. If he writes it out anything like he delivered it, our people shall see a good many copies of it."

Here, a portrait of Lincoln, post-election and before taking office, bearing witness to the tenor, tone and honorable resolve that will define his presidency.

What follows is passed down by Walt Whitman, who lived in Washington D.C. during the war years. He paid very close attention to Abraham Lincoln, recording much of what he witnessed and heard on both the streets and in its many hospitals, where he was as frequent a volunteer as any.

"Almost everyone was asking him, with evident apprehension if not perturbation, wrote Whitman, "what is to be the issue of this Southern effervescence? Are we really to have Civil War'? He responded in substance as follows:"

> *Many years ago, when I was a young lawyer and Illinois was little settled, except on the southern border, I, with other lawyers used to ride the circuit; journeying with the judge from county-seat to county-seat in quest of business. Once, after a long spell of pouring rain, which had flooded the whole country, transforming small creeks into rivers, we were stopped by these swollen streams, which we with difficulty crossed. Still ahead of us was Fox River, larger than all the rest; and we could not help saying to each other, 'If these streams gave us so much trouble, how shall we get over Fox River? Darkness fell before we had reached that stream; and we all stopped at a log tavern, had our horses put out, and resolved to pass the night. Here we were right glad to fall in with the Methodist Presiding Elder of the circuit, who rode it in all weather, knew all its ways, and could tell us about Fox River. So we all gathered around him, and asked if he knew about the crossing of Fox River. 'Oh yes,' he replied, 'I know all about Fox River. I have crossed it often and understand it well; but I have one fixed rule with regard to Fox River; I never cross it till I reach it.'*

He would, of course, certainly and soon reach it and no matter the darkness, the sadness, the danger, he indeed crossed it.

While in limbo, waiting to take the oath of office, Lincoln sadly witnessed the nation he was soon to govern begin to come apart at the seams. Many Republicans, members of his own party, joined a host of others, in the face of secession and deferentially wavered on key issues (popular sovereignty- extension of slavery into the territories-etc.) in the face of secession. Can't help but love this poignant observation of Lincoln's as the great madness took hold:

"Have none of it. Stand firm. The tug has come . . . On that point, hold firm, as with a chain of steel."

We remain fascinated and moved by Lincoln's propensity to forgive rather than punish, his extensive use of the pardoning power and his corresponding determination to *"Let the rebels up easy."* He would treat with neither vengeance nor malice, humanely and gently and with his eyes firmly focused upon the bright light of the coming dawn.

On this subject, we open with a few telling observations from his secretary, John Hay:

"I was amused at the eagerness with which the president caught at any fact which would justify him in saving the life of a condemned soldier. He was only merciless in cases where meanness or cruelty were shown. Cases of cowardice he was especially averse to punishing with death. He said it would frighten the poor fellows too terribly to shoot them."

"I'll do it. I'll do it. By jingo, I'll do it."

"If a man had more than one life, I think a little hanging would not hurt this one, but after he is once dead we cannot bring him back, no matter how sorry we may be, so the boy shall be pardoned."

"If Almighty God gives a man a cowardly pair of legs, how can he help their running away with him?"

His other secretary, John Nicolay recalled and recorded this gem:

"Now this is a pretty story to come to me with, isn't it? Your son came home from fighting against his own country; he was sick: you secreted him, nursed him up, and when cured, started him off again to help destroy some more of our boys. Taken prisoner, trying to get through our lines, you now want me to let him off upon his oath" to now support the Union.—Now, I want you to understand that I have done this just to get rid of you."

And then this:

"Well, this is wonderful. I knew this man well. I have heard him preach; he was a tall, angular man like I am, and I have been mistaken for him on the streets. Did you say he was to be shot day after tomorrow? No, no! There will be no shooting nor hanging in this case. Henry M. Luckett! There must be

something wrong with him, or he wouldn't be in such a scrape as this. I don't know what more I can do for him, but you can rest assured, my child," turning to Mrs. Bullitt, "that your father's life is safe."

"Henry M. Luckett! No, no! There is no shooting or hanging in this case."

Near the end of the war, Lincoln had a conversation with General Sherman as to what would be done with Jefferson Davis. While not for publication, he said that he wished he would escape. There had been enough blood and in keeping with his extraordinary 2nd Inaugural, he wanted no more.

Lincoln related this homespun ditty to get to the heart of the matter:

> *A reformed drinker had taken the Total Abstinence Pledge. When offered whisky, he said, No more, no more, but his friend whispered, what if I just add a little to this here lemonade, to which our total abstainer responded, so long as it is unbeknown to me.*

And there we have it, please let Davis escape, *"So long as it is unbeknown"* to him.

Later, Secretary Stanton got word that Jacob Thompson, a rebel guerilla, was attempting to escape to Maine and from there to England. Stanton wanted to intercept and arrest him, but Lincoln famously said, *"I rather think not. When you have got an elephant by the hind leg and he is trying to run away, it's best to let him run."*

Here in the opening passage of an early 1863 *'Day of Fast & Thanks' Proclamation*, we discover this extraordinary piece, post Fredericksburg and *Emancipation Proclamation* and pre Chancellorsville and Gettysburg, Lincoln sees such wonder, in the throes of such carnage and uncertainty:

> *We have been the recipients of the choicest bounties of Heaven. We have been preserved, these many years, in peace and prosperity. We have grown in numbers, wealth and power, as no other nation has ever grown. But we have forgotten God. We have forgotten the gracious hand which preserved us in peace, and multiplied and enriched and strengthened us; and we have vainly imagined, in the deceitfulness of our hearts, that all these blessings were produced by some superior wisdom and virtue of our own. Intoxicated with unbroken success, we have become too self-sufficient to feel the necessity of redeeming and preserving grace, too proud to pray to the God that made us!*

On the circuit, he was a lawyer by day and a stand-up comic by night. Why is it that only those who go deep inside in a relentless search for understanding and meaning and know great sadness are somehow rendered capable of making us laugh?

The first piece is attested to by many:

Two Quaker women were discussing the great conflict and one says, "I believe that the South will win this war." The second asked "Why dost thou believe that?" "Because Jefferson Davis is a praying man," she said. "But so is Abraham a praying man," the second retorted. "Yes, I know, but God will think he is joking."

While the details have already been shared, I but remind you here of his stunning, '*Why Reverend Cartwight, I am going to Congress.*"

Because it was one of Lincoln's 'ever in the pocket, go to' stories and jokes, the Ethan Allen of Revolutionary War fame bit is special. After the dust of the fight for independence settled, he took a trip to England to visit family. In an attempt to get a rise out of their Rebel guest, his hosts planted a portrait of George Washington in their privy or out-house, in what was an intended affront to Allen's devotion to their common cause. When Allen first went to visit the privy, they anxiously awaited his return. But disappointingly unflustered, he simply didn't react at all and said nothing whatsoever about their ruse. Eventually exasperated by his silence, one of them finally asked him if he had seen the picture in their privy. "*Oh yes,*" he cheerfully responded. "*Just brilliant, absolutely brilliant, after all, nothing will make an Englishman shit faster than the sight of George Washington.*"

Among the most recognized of quips from the 1858 Debates with Stephen Douglas –was this oft-repeated gem: "*Judge Douglas says that I am two-faced. I ask you if I was, why would I wear the one that I have on now?*"

In 1838, on April Fool's Day, on the heels of his fiasco of a courtship with Mary Owens, Lincoln wrote this to Eliza Browning, wife of Orville Browning, both of whom he was at ease opening up to: "*Others have been made fools of by the girls; but this can never be with truth said of me. I most emphatically, in this instance, made a fool of myself. I have now come to the conclusion never again to think of marrying; and for this reason; I can never be satisfied with anyone who would be block-head enough to have me.*"

What follows now is but the briefest of telegrams, sent by Lincoln from City Point on April 3, 1865 at 5:00 p.m., to Secretary of War Stanton. The salient words are the final six, which remain poignant in our history, because they bear haunting witness to Lincoln's own recognition of the overarching concern that Stanton had for his safety and well-being. One can only imagine the certain apoplexy that Stanton was having back in D.C., the Capitol of the United States, upon receiving this choice bit of information that the president was soon to walk through the streets of the Capitol of the Confederacy.

"*It is certain now that Richmond is in our hands, and I think I will go there tomorrow. I will take care of myself.*"

On December 23, 1862, Lincoln wrote a letter of sympathy to young Fanny McCullough upon the fall of her Father. It may not reach the rhetorical heights that the Letter to Mrs. Bixby (now largely credited to John Hay) did, but then too and most importantly, it was meant for a child. What makes this one sentence that I cull out from it so important is that Lincoln knew what it was to be Fanny and to feel exactly how she must feel. "*In this sad world of ours, sorrow comes to all; and, to the young, it comes with bitterest agony, because it takes them unawares.*" Now I confess that I may well be moved by Lincoln's poetry simply because it is his, but the fact is that he moves me, hook, line and sinker, moves me and takes me on this melancholy and moving sojourn of his. The following is from his "*My Childhood Home I See Again.*"

> *My childhood home I see again—*
> *And gladden with the view—*
> *And still as memories crowd my brain—*
> *There's sadness in it too . . .*
> *The very spot that grew the bread—*
> *That formed my bones I see—*
> *How strange, old friend, on thee to tread—*
> *To feel I'm part of thee . . .*
> *Near twenty years have passed away*
> *Since here I bid farewell*
> *To woods and fields, and scenes of play,*
> *And playmates loved so well*

While no longer attributed to Lincoln, I hold tight to this quote anyway, because it so defines his career in public service, "*I am a slow walker but I never walk back.*" Just one more, because it so speaks to Lincoln's Constitutional clarity, his resolve and determination. "*There are not two Countries and there never will be two countries. Tell Davis if you treat for peace, it will be for this one country*" This to Secretary Stanton, a salient point, that he held tight to.

HERE FINALLY, THE STUFF THAT MADE ALL THE DIFFERENCE

As to his greatest hits, his formidable and incredibly moving contribution to both the country and its literature, this is my highly subjective and debatable *Top Ten*. Each must be taken whole as they never cease to astound.

> The Second Inaugural Address
> The Gettysburg Address
> The Farewell Address

The 1863 Letter to James C. Conkling:

> *Peace does not appear so distant as it did. I hope it will come soon, and come to stay; and so come as to be worth the keeping in all future time. It will then have been proved that, among free men, there can be no successful appeal*

from the ballot to the bullet; and that they who take such appeal are sure to lose their case, and pay the cost. And then, there will be some black men who can remember that, with silent tongue, and clenched teeth, and steady eye, and well-poised bayonet, they have helped mankind on to this great consummation; while, I fear, there will be some white ones, unable to forget that, with malignant heart, and deceitful speech, they strove to hinder it.

The 1862 Annual Message to Congress:

Fellow-citizens, we cannot escape history. We of this Congress and this administration, will be remembered in spite of ourselves. No personal significance, or insignificance, can spare one or another of us. The fiery trial through which we pass, will light us down, in honor or dishonor, to the latest generation. We say we are for the Union. The world will not forget that we say this. We know how to save the Union. The world knows we do know how to save it. We—even we here—hold the power, and bear the responsibility. In giving freedom to the slave, we assure freedom to the free—honorable alike in what we give, and what we preserve. We shall nobly save, or meanly lose, the last best hope of earth.

The July 4, 1861 Annual Message to Congress:

This is essentially a people's contest. On the side of the Union, it is a struggle for maintaining in the world, that form, and substance of government, whose leading object is, to elevate the condition of men—to lift artificial weights from all shoulders—to clear the paths of laudable pursuit for all---to afford all, an unfettered start, and a fair chance, in the race of life.

His Meditation on Divine Will:

The will of God prevails. In great contests each party claims to act in accordance with the will of God. Both may be, and one must be, wrong. God cannot be for and against the same thing at the same time. In the present civil war it is quite possible that God's purpose is something different from the purpose of either party.

The First Inaugural Address:

Why should there not be a patient confidence in the ultimate justice of the people? Is there any better, or equal hope, in the world?
In your hands, my dissatisfied fellow countrymen, and not in mine , is the momentous issue of civil war. The government will not assail you. You can have no conflict without being yourselves the aggressors. You have no oath registered in Heaven to destroy the government, while I shall have the most solemn one to preserve, protect and defend it.
I am loath to close. We are not enemies, but friends. We must not be enemies. Though passion may have strained, it must not break our bonds of affection.

The mystic chords of memory, stretching from every battle–field, and patriot grave, to every living heart and hearthstone, all over this broad land, will yet swell the chorus of the Union, when again touched, as surely they will be, by the better angels of our nature.

The Cooper Union Address:
See Jack C. Waugh above, as I reference exactly what he does.

The 1862 Letter to Horace Greeley:
All of it.

The 1835 Lyceum Address:

At what point, then, is the approach of danger to be expected? I answer, if it ever reach us it must spring up amongst us; it cannot come from abroad. If destruction be our lot, we must ourselves be its author and finisher. As a nation of freemen we must live through all time, or die by suicide.
Passion has helped us, but can do so no more. It will in the future be our enemy. Reason, cold, calculating, unimpassioned reason must furnish all the materials for our future support and defense. Let those materials be molded into general intelligence, sound morality, and, in particular, a reverence for the Constitution and laws; and that we improved to the last, that we remained free to the last, that we revered his name to the last.

The 1855 Letter to Joshua Speed:

I am not a Know-Nothing. That is certain. How could I be? How can anyone who abhors the oppression of negroes, be in favor of degrading classes of white people? Our progress in degeneracy appears to me to be pretty rapid. As a nation, we began by declaring that "all men are created equal." We now practically read it "all men are created equal, except negroes" When the Know-Nothings get control, it will read "all men are created equal, except negroes, and foreigners, and Catholics." When it comes to this I should prefer emigrating to some country where they make no pretense of loving liberty—to Russia, for instance, where despotism can be taken pure, and without the base alloy of hypocrisy.

In his De Naturum Deorum (On the Nature of the Gods), Cicero wrote, "Nemo igitur vir magnus sine aliquo adflatu divino umquam fuit" or "No great man ever existed who did not enjoy some measure of divine inspiration."

If most of the passages related above were not divinely inspired, then what words ever were?

Oh no, I believe that so inspired was our Lincoln that he inspires still. And however much he may have struggled with God, the God I look to certainly never struggled with him.

For great he was and great his work and great these words. Still living, still on fire, still so powerfully demanding that we ought to finally and fully open our eyes and build the America that we have for far too long pretended to be, the one he would have had us be.

The answer lies not in the flag that the president hugged so tightly and nigh on absurdly at a CPAC gathering of the pretenders, but rather in the sacred legacy that they rather toss to the vagaries of the wind, the legacy of Lincoln, who they sadly know not. Others demand that none be excluded and that all be raised up and given a voice, as did Lincoln. For with all due respect to E Pluribus Unum, it is not merely and simply, "Out of many, one" but also "Out of one, all."

Chapter Five

Let the Light So Shine

Abraham Lincoln's extraordinary humility was the bedrock foundation of a leadership style that precluded anything, however egregious the slight or the intrigue or the betrayal, from ever being taken personally by him. He may well have been president, but truly remarkably, nothing was ever allowed to be about him.

Although it often flies under the radar, this selflessness, more than any of his dozens of other admirable attributes and qualities, defined him.

While General Robert E, Lee, the legendary commander of the Army of Northern Virginia often said, "At least, they do not die for me," Lincoln never doubted that they died for him and for the preservation of the Republic and of a political system "dedicated to the proposition that all men are created equal." He carried each death upon his gangly but sturdy shoulders and in the battered recesses of his tortured soul.

He did so to fashion a nation reborn, one that politically and spiritually, long impacted for good, but one that is rather and regrettably under siege today.

Lincoln's national soul has been pierced and rendered what D.H. Lawrence once bitterly described as "hard, isolate, stoic and a killer."

We are a soul that no longer melts.

Against a present will, most of us still believe that we are destined to advance in the world and to improve our stations and to leave our children in a better place than we once found ourselves. We still hold fast to the imagery of "the light, the lamp, and the golden door." We remain the "tempest tossed," no matter the zero tolerance or the inhumane separation of mothers and children or the most recent dark executive order aimed at limiting the garnering of green cards to only those with the big bucks.

Despite the conflicts and all that separates us and all of the bigotries and hatreds that rear their ugly heads and yes, despite the ignorance that threatens, the American Mind is, as ever, the American Mind. To be free, to be able to stand up, to say yes, to advance and to dream. Our voices remain inexhaustible, the voices and spirits that will endure and resist until the light that shone so brightly when our ancestors so bravely fought for that "new birth of freedom," for a country "of, by and for the people" and for a land worthy of the 630,000 who gave their "Last full measure of devotion," shines for all today. What was at stake in that Civil War was our intent and our commitment to be true to that sacred promise, the same promise that has ever inspired men and women of good will to see us through our darkest moments, through Depression, through D Day and the horror of Bastogne, through the sadness of Vietnam and the horror of Little Rock, Memphis and Selma, through November 22, 1963 and April 4, 1968, June 6, 1968, September 11, 2001 and May 25, 2020 when George Floyd, for the sin of being black, was murdered in public view by the Minneapolis police and a people united cried out this stops now. No more! No more! No more!

United, all races, all colors, all creeds, we are a people born in and steeled by the sacred protections that are guaranteed in our "Bill of Rights."

We rely upon these gifts given to us by Paine, Jefferson, Washington, Madison, Thoreau and oh so many others. Never forgetting that it was Abraham Lincoln who reaffirmed them, in the midst of a horrifically harsh and bitter war, and sacredly secured them for posterity. At Appomattox, self-representative government was preserved and a people, long enslaved, were finally freed and this nation was imbued with a soul and a spirit that upholds the dignity of all, no matter the color of their skin, their sexual persuasion or their faith.

It just took us a hell of a long time to begin celebrating that.

THE 16TH AND THE 45TH

After considering the daily news and reviewing the responses of our collaborators, we cannot help but draw a pointed and stark contrast between Abraham Lincoln and he who dares tell us, "I am the greatest president, greater even than Abraham Lincoln." Our collaborators will drive the dialogue and the words of Lincoln and Trump alone will do the rest.

154 years removed, we in the face of Trump's assault on both our inherent values and Constitution, go to Lincoln, for he was light for us and for all time and we are living in muted darkness now. Lincoln's "Last best hope of earth" is under siege as we contend with the possibility of betraying formative principles. In the name of *America First*, we seem to have become the common enemy of all nations, save Israel and the places where "they take

their despotism plain," like China, Russia and North Korea. We berate and mistreat our closest allies in Europe and in Canada and Mexico; we betray our commitments to climate change and the Paris accords and Iranian Nuclear Disarmament; we peel back the foreign aid that we long delivered to struggling countries around the globe; and we deny safe harbor to the refugee and the 'tempest tossed' that we once wrapped our arms around. And the Lady in the Harbor in New York would most assuredly bow her head and cry had she the power. Empowered, the *'Know Nothings'* are running rampant again and *America First* serves only the rich and mighty and the underprivileged, the minorities and the poor and the dying vestiges and remnants of a once mighty middle class be damned.

The common and ordinary, after all, are not great. Neither, by the way, are the pawns who would make America great again, who still loudly echo the president's greatest hits at his ego-reboots and love fests. Sadly, they are all extras in his latest reality TV show which has room for only one star.

The "Lock her up—Build the wall—Drain the swamp—Send Them Back" greatest hits still reverberate, while he finds ever new ways to demean, bully and lie so as to keep throwing fresh meat to his voracious audiences. The non-Impeachment Trial put another victory notch in his belt and it just goes on and on, as a feckless band of once thoughtful and honorable Senators sold their souls to him and are left to pray for an absolution that may never come.

Trump the Greatest as opposed to the one who never—ever—bragged or boasted. Yes, the one whose humility and magnanimity oozed out of every membrane of his body and who achieved truly great things and aspired to even more.

Today, Trump's ego boasts of ever new and imaginary polls that designate him the greatest and "the most sound-minded president" to ever serve. A genius, a very stable genius, the greatest dealmaker, the 'big, better, best" of all, the brightest of all stars and constellations.

It is not merely the fact that his ego is so huge that is at issue, but rather that humility is both foreign and offensive to him. He is appalled by it as respect, reverence and deference are, to him, but the tired and worn vestiges of overt weakness.

I often think of a 2016 campaign rally, during which and in deference to the Evangelicals, he held up and proclaimed the *Bible* to be the only book better than his own, *The Art of the Deal*. When asked later about the biblical passage that meant the most to him, he, betraying his absolute unfamiliarity with it, simply responded, *'Oh, all of them.'*

Interestingly, not long after, he was asked what Abraham Lincoln's greatest achievement was, when he, in like fashion, uttered the same four words, "Oh all of them." That from a man who would be president and who as president betrayed the fact that he knew neither when the Civil War was fought nor what it was about.

These '*Oh, all of thems*' were among the many indicators of the fact that he would go to the White house with neither a spiritual foundation nor a historical one and, so very unfortunately, with neither God nor our fore-fathers in mind, heart or soul.

He was to be neither responsible to his Maker nor to the makers of the United States of America. Devoid of accountability to either a Higher Power or to a rich Heritage and Legacy: and, quite frankly, without any working knowledge of the Constitution of the United States of America, he was free to pay homage to his ego and celebrity alone. There, where he is comfortable and there, where he lives.

Sadly, in every day and in every way, it all begins and ends with him. He is tethered to neither faith nor to history. To neither ideology nor to belief.

As to the Constitution, the emoluments' clause is crazy and after all, what's wrong with shaking down a foreign power for dirt on a prospective political rival. And while impeachment was warranted and justified, all Re-publican Congressmen and Senators turned into shriveling '*nimoids*' who refuse to think and live only to shield and protect their master and their power. Co-equal branches be damned. He stepped on Congress and now goes after the Judiciary.

And there he stands, where Lincoln did, our Lincoln, in such stark and blazing contrast. Lincoln for whom everything, absolutely everything, began and ended with those he served. Lincoln who was hard wired to neither look down upon nor disparage anyone. Lincoln who was so profoundly humble.

Lincoln went to the White House with rich and compelling spiritual and historical foundations. He went to the White House with a chapter and verse, almost photographic familiarity with the Bible. He went to the White House with rich reverence for not only the *Maker of All Things* with whom he bobbed and weaved but also for a wide array of ministers of faith whom he had befriended over the years. He also went to the White House with rever-ence for the Sons of Liberty, the Revolutionary patriots and martyrs for the cause of liberty, the Founding fathers, his own Henry Clay, Daniel Webster and oh so many others who also saw the light that America could be.

Our earlier focus upon Lincoln's *Ever Fixed Marks,* what were the by-products of a humility so rare and extraordinary, said it all and said it loud-ly—he was as good as it gets—larger than life, simply extraordinary. But as Trump is devoid of humility, no such qualities can possibly thrive in him and the sad truth is that any manifestation of the same is but temporal pretense and shadow.

While the laundry list of contrasts that can be comprised is massive, these 3 are defining and they alone make all the difference—these 3 that Lincoln had in spades and that are nowhere to be found in the lexicon of the life that

Donald Trump has lived—these three, a sense of humility, a spiritual perspective and/or belonging and a rich reverence for the history, heritage and legacy of America's past.

It's hard to know where you ought to go if you have no idea where you come from.

As to this contention, in a now haunting piece in the April, 2017 *Washington Post*, Michael Gerson suggested that the bar was set very low for Trump but that he still failed to meet it. "Ultimately," he wrote, "Trump is failing because he has little knowledge of the world and no guiding star or moral principle. The best of our leaders—think Abraham Lincoln—have been sure about the truth and uncertain about themselves. Trump is the opposite. His mind is uncluttered by creeds. He knows what he wants at any given moment, but it can bear little relation to the next moment to come or the moment before for that matter."

In short, nothing with Trump is sacred, nor are there any settled truths.

And here's the rub, without settled belief, as Gerson also clearly notes, persuasion itself is impossible. Without a link to the past, without any real ideology, without any moral center, Trump is unhinged and adrift and devoid of any genuine interest in anything, beyond his own wealth, ego and, most importantly, his winning. For continued victory and bearing witness to his greatness is the alpha and omega.

That's all he's got.

Now don't get me wrong, for there can be no doubt but that he has well served corporate America, the moneyed interests, the investment bankers, Big Pharma, the fossil fuel interests for whom he has set fire to environmental regulations, the major banks, the arms manufacturers and anyone with enough scratch to have truly benefited from his top heavy tax cut.

There also is no point in arguing policy with Trump, because it is impossible to convince one without any convictions. And without conviction, one will, like Trump, seesaw back and forth on issues, in so far as it is perceived as helping him to win.

Again, the cold warriors and brutes in his nest, the ideologues and true believers once pressed him, but they have all been fired. Only those who genuflect and bow are left and Trump is free to turn on a dime.

In short, he makes it up as he goes along in tweet-storm after tweet-storm, driven by the latest advice from the latest star among his ever changing White House minions or by the dark whims of Rush Limbaugh or Sean Hannity or by the hate of the non-great or powerful. The prevailing source of advice is ever in the wind and in the dirt and in the dark corners. Rootless, his passions, beyond he, himself and that which his cheering base reaffirms at the latest rally are non-existent.

So when the going gets tough, he will make it up on the fly and when it gets really tough, he'll unleash the big lie, the "Obama had my wires tapped in Trump Tower just before my victory" kind of lie, the "Only the voting fraud prevented me from winning the popular vote' kind of lie. The Joe Scarborough is a murderer kind of lie and the Obama and Biden are both going to go jail for life because of their crimes kind of lie. For crimes that exist in his mind only. It is always about perception and the given days news cycle and never about governing or truth.

Just yesterday, he tweeted 44-times, of which the overwhelming majority were outright lies.

This in such stark contrast to Lincoln who never opened his mouth without knowing why, who always did his homework and often extensive research, who considered the historical, political and spiritual facets of both his words and policies, who often went down the 'road less traveled' because that is what honor and compassion and empathy demanded, who put the people first every time and never considered himself.

As to our collaborators, we begin with *Jack C. Waugh again,* who made his case, as did most others, quite some time ago and yet it well could have been written yesterday. Clearly and hauntingly, he embraces so many of the familiar truths and arguments today, while noting, so very somberly that if Americans only knew Lincoln in the first place, as they should, Trump's very election would have been an impossibility.

A critical difference in Abraham Lincoln's time and the crises and challenges of our own time is presidential. In Lincoln we were blessed with one of the greatest, if not the greatest, most competent president in American history. In our time, in Donald Trump we are saddled with arguably the worst and most incompetent in our history.

Lincoln saved what is the mother of all republics and democracies in world history. Donald Trump is well on the way to destroying it. Lincoln rose to the presidency with no executive experience. Trump had no political experience. Lincoln quickly became a shrewd chief executive. Trump as president is in over his head. He is inept and his administration in a shambles.

The personal chasm between these two presidents is wide and deep. Lincoln had compassion and a native kindness. Trump is a hater.

Lincoln was a thinker, taking his time to see a problem from all its angles and ramifications before acting. Trump is a quick-draw hip shooter, making important decisions and issuing them on twitter in the middle of the night with virtually no thought for their consequences.

Lincoln learned early in his political career that personal invective and insult were not only unkind, but self-destructive. Personal invective and insult, firing his late-night tweets as if from a Gatling gun is Trump's modus operandi.

Although Lincoln's direct attention was on winning a civil war, reuniting a nation, and in the end, abolishing slavery, he was widely admired by leaders of virtually every foreign nation. Trump with his insults and refusal to work with other nations on key issues such as world climate change has alienated and puzzled many of the world leaders.

Lincoln admired women, at one time proposing that they be given the vote. Trump gropes them and derides and bullies them, suggesting in his election campaign that his Democratic opponent, a woman, be thrown in prison.

Lincoln said and believed that if there must be a choice between man and money, It must be for the benefit of the man every time. Trump believes the opposite and will opt for the bottom line every time. Lincoln was so indifferent about the importance of money personally that for months at a time he would forget to deposit his paycheck.

Lincoln believed and said that government's proper role is to care for persons who cannot help themselves. Trump believes in cutting back services for the needy, to enhance more opportunity and to make the rich richer.

Lincoln believed in tearing down walls between peoples. Trump is building his ridiculous but ever so beloved wall over the objection of the United States Congress. He build walls to sever himself from African Americans, from Muslims, from Mexicans, from any and all people of color. And yes, sentient human beings.

Lincoln was a humble man who often told jokes at his own expense. Trump is a narcissist who admires himself above all others.

The difference in the quality of leadership of Lincoln in his time and Trump's in ours is clear. Lincoln took on the great challenges and won. Trump pretends they don't even exist.

Then Waugh added an addendum:

In Lincoln's time, one great shrill issue, slavery, dominated American politics. Now we have a canister of issues, some new, hugely political and divisive, some like climate change, income inequality and the erosion of the middle class, some driven by religious fanaticism, abortion, and gay and transgender issues. The world has been made more interdependent, closely linked by 21st century technology. But it is as divided as ever by political tension. In this country, the proper role of government in the lives of its people is constantly an issue. And wars still exist, on a world scale, more deadly than ever.

Some of these issues would be new to Lincoln, some wouldn't be. Political tension and war wouldn't. The growing environmental threat to the world, for instance, would be. But it is certain if he were president he would approach all of them with the welfare of the country and its people, and all the world's people, his uppermost priority. He would approach them all with sensitivity, without malice, and with great political skill.

As to the historical perspective that Jack Waugh shared, let us turn to an interview that Bob Woodward of the *Washington Post* conducted with Donald Trump early on, long before the construct of his book, *Fear: Trump in the White House* took shape and became a #1 Best Seller.

At the time, Trump described himself only as "Someone with a very good brain" and not necessarily as the "Genius" that being president made him. Of all people, the conversation was somehow steered to Lincoln and Woodward asked, "And why did Lincoln succeed? Thought about that at all"?

Trump's answer truly spoke for itself as his "Very Good Brain" had apparently skipped the classes on American History. Woodward actually noted that his response "would have made a third grader proud."

> *Well, I think Lincoln succeeded for numerous reasons,* Trump responded. *He was a man who was of great intelligence, which most presidents would be. But he was a man of great intelligence, but he was also a man who did something that was a very vital thing to do at that time. Ten years before or 20 years before, what he was doing would never have even been thought possible. So he did something that was a very important thing to do, and especially at that time.*

The *very vital* thing that he did, of course, went unmentioned, the Save the Union, Free the Slaves, Win the Great American Civil War, Emancipation Proclamation gig and all the rest.

When his campaign laid out a plan for him to actually channel Lincoln in a major speech near Election Day in Gettysburg, Pennsylvania, a speech billed as a major address. It was to be the substantive closing argument as to what he planned to accomplish as president, but he went off script right away. He would say nothing of Lincoln, nor of what he said there, nor of why his campaign was there, nor of Gettysburg, nor reference anything as to any policy. He laid out no vision for America, but instead reiterated his belief that the electoral process was rigged, that Hillary Clinton, the criminal, shouldn't be allowed to run for president and that the women who came forward to accuse him of sexual assault were all charlatans and fame seekers whose charges were all bogus. Rigged was one of his go to words.

History in his White House began with his excited determination to hold up Andrew Jackson as his hero, simply because Newt Gingrich and Steve Bannon had advised him that Jackson was a street fighter and brawler like him. What they missed or didn't care about was that Jackson also was an overt racist and bigot who gave us the vile Indian Removal Act, Trail of Tears and death of more than 4000 Cherokee who had been exiled from their Georgia. When the Supreme Court ruled that the Indian Removal Act was unconstitutional, Jackson in defiance of the Constitution and the separation of powers said, "Well, John Marshall has made his decision. Now let him try to enforce it."

Nor did it matter that when one of Jackson's slaves at the Hermitage had the temerity to escape, not only did Jackson offer the highest of bounties for the slave's return, but also a bonus of $10 per lash inflicted. The key was that the bonus was good for up to a maximum of 29 lashes or $290 more, upon the general assumption that the 30th lash could well be the killing blow, one that we might assume, he was, at least figuratively, saving for himself.

Then too, there was the raw incident during Black History Month in 2017 when a proclamation recognizing the contributions of Frederick Douglass was being signed. That was all well and good, but Trump actually spoke of him as if he were alive and active still. "Frederick Douglass is an example of somebody who has done an amazing job and is being recognized more and more," he said.

With him, came alternative facts, alternative realities and indeed an alternative past.

For next on his hit parade was, "People don't ask that question, but why was there the Civil War. Why could that not have been worked out," he asked. He went on to pose the same question this way, "People don't realize, you know, the Civil War, if you think about it, why?" He continued to suggest that it also was something that his adopted greatest American hero, Andrew Jackson was "really angry about" and could well have handled, i.e., "There is no reason

for this," the great Jackson reportedly cried. Thus implying that Jackson was alive and well despite having died 16 years earlier.

Paul Starobin, author of *Madness Rules the Hour*, incisively noted, "History is not tidy. Trump likes tidy. He likes slogans. History doesn't offer any." Going deeper, he suggests, "Trump seems almost uniquely ill equipped to process history, whether because of his lack of empathy, his allergy to complexity, or his tendency to keep distant from anything that might carry the whiff of defeat."

When the press understandably reacted to President Trump's manifesting historical inaccuracies, the White House shot back in a manner that it has grown accustomed to. It obfuscated and it diverted. They looked upon those reporting about his historical fictions as damned liberal, intellectual elitists again; and they reminded us of mistakes, far lesser mistakes by the way, that were made by Obama, i.e. that Black president; and they dumbed down history itself, after all that Lincoln was a mess, a fragile and depressed and even suicidal man who told "fart" jokes' or they cried that these reports were simply "Gotcha" journalism or fake news and that what the president was really saying was misinterpreted or taken out of context.

After all, Trump didn't do anything wrong, it was all the damn whistleblower's fault, he and that damn Hunter Biden.

In a Facebook post of our own *Bob Willard* that I happened to catch, he wrote, "I continue to be curious about and amused by our president's musings about my hero and his "Did you know, the first Republican president, Abraham Lincoln." At a record-breaking fundraiser on March 21, 2017 for his party's congressional campaign committee, held in the National Museum in D.C., Trump described his party as one of builders. Turning to the teleprompter, he started to discuss one of these builders."

Trump began his speech with "Our first Republican President, Abraham Lincoln, ran his first campaign for public office in 1832 when he was only 23 years old. He began by imagining the benefits a railroad could bring to his part of Illinois without ever having seen a steam-powered train. He had no idea, and yet he knew what it could be. Thirty years later as President, Lincoln signed the law that built the first transcontinental railroad, uniting our country from ocean to ocean." (And then, he tailed off-script) with "Great president. Most people don't even know he was a Republican. Right? Does anyone know? A lot of people don't know that. We have to build that up a little bit more. Let's take an ad. Let's use one of those PACs. Those PACs. You never know what the hell's going to come out of those PACs."

As to where we are today in America, *Harold Holzer* , the Dean of Lincoln Scholars began by plucking a timeless question out of Lincoln's *First Inaugural Address*: "Why should there not be a patient confidence in the ultimate justice of the people. Is there any better, or equal, hope in the world"?

Then eloquently, Holzer added:

> Well, as different as things feel today in terms of politics and government, I would begin my accounting of Lincoln's potential to inspire us today with the demonstrable truth quoted above. I would suggest that it could help us look forward to our future in a time of great anxiety about democratic institutions themselves, because the time will surely come again when we can routinely choose our leaders and, through them, our policy priorities. I don't want to use, or misuse, Lincoln to be any more specific than that, except to remind us that he cautioned against a house divided, implored us to show charity for all and urged us on to a new birth of freedom. It's painful that we have to live through an era dedicated to a darker vision before, one hopes inevitably, we have the chance to return to the Lincolnian values that guide us to reflect, more often than not, upon what he so memorably called the 'Better angels of our nature'

Holzer possesses an abiding faith and hope in the American people to, when push comes to shove, do the right thing. The sooner the better. And yes the 2018 mid-terms turned the bright lights of hope back on and ended Trump's hold on all instruments of governance in D.C., while 2020 and prayers and hopes abide

In his response to our final question, *Frank Williams* presented a laundry list of both stunning words and actions of Lincoln's that ought to speak loudly to us today. In sharing them, he appears to have added professorial robes to his judicial ones. He wrote:

"Let's start with '*Notes for a law Lecture,*' with Lincoln's 'Discourage litigation,' a good policy for mediation and restoring civility in this '*House Divided*.' Lincoln was mediating long before it was common practice. Again, his '*Lyceum Address*' speech and '*Let every American, every lover of liberty, every well-wisher to his posterity, swear by the blood of the Revolution, never to violate in the least particular, the laws of the country; and never to*

tolerate their violations by others. Lincoln speaks to the violence then beset-
ting the country with attacks against abolitionists and others."

As then, he still speaks to us today.

For Williams then looked to "The first Lincoln-Douglas debate at Ottawa,
Illinois on August 21, 1858 relating to reputation, the power of the press, and
the nationalization of our institutions and to "Lincoln's, *'Public sentiment is
everything. With public sentiment, nothing can fail; without it nothing can
succeed. Consequently he who molds public sentiment goes deeper than he
who enacts statutes or pronounces decisions'"* … and then to Lincoln's dig
at the Supreme Court for its horrific Dred Scott decision denying any chance
of citizenship for an African American and at Senator Stephen Douglas's
efforts to repeal the Missouri Compromise by passage of the Kansas-Nebraska Act, leaving to the citizens of a territory whether slavery is allowed . . .
And still to *Lincoln's letter to James Conkling, August 26, 1863* on the
powers of the presidency and emancipation: *'You dislike the emancipation
proclamation; and, perhaps, would have it retracted. You say it is unconstitutional, I think differently. I think the constitution invests its Commander-in-
chief with the law of war, in time of war. The most that can be said is that
slaves are property. Is there, has there ever been, any question that by the
law of war, property, both of enemies and friends, may be taken when
needed? And is it not needed whenever taking it, helps us, or hurts the
enemy?'* Here the President is defining the war powers of his office which
are not defined in the Constitution. One cannot help but mention the Second
Inaugural and its recognition that both North and South were responsible for
slavery and the war itself, as his plea for peace and reconciliation not only in
America but throughout the world. Now, if this message doesn't resonate for
today, then nothing does."

On quite a roll, Williams considers a multitude of wisdoms, the all of
which remain relevant today and shed perpetual light upon what America
truly is. Indeed as a lawyer, Lincoln urged settlement first, he urged mediation, resolution and what is commonly called peace. And yet as a nation
today, we are oh so divided and we do not look for common ground.

Williams also took us to Lincoln's recognition of the importance of the
power of the press, the same press that is today proclaimed to be the "Enemy
of the People." His sharing Lincoln's admonition that all policy relies upon
"public sentiment" begs the questions of just how loud the noise is today, the
dissonance, the denial of fact, the unwillingness to dig deep where the truth
lies; and yes, justice, but again, why not for all and not just the empowered
and mighty; and most importantly, the end of Lincoln's solemn *Second Inaugural* and the hope and call for reconciliation with all nations.

Lincoln's call for reconciliation with our sister nations today calls upon
us to consider Trump's September, 2018 speech to the United Nations General Assembly. There he, the anti-Lincoln bragged, boasted and rang the

"alarm bells" of his America First doctrine, rejected globalism, defamed the Human Rights efforts of the U.N., declared the International Court to be without any standing or power at all, criticized Germany (our ally), announced that there will now be a litmus test before the dispensation of foreign aid, preposterously and callously and cowardly balked on opening our doors to refugees, ignorantly suggesting that the answer to the refugee crisis is for the refugee generating countries to *make their own countries great again*. To all the nations of the world, his stark and clear message was that if you aren't with us, you are most certainly against us.

Why not? Pick yourself up by the bootstraps Syria, Yemen and you too, Afghanistan. That you and yours have, in recent memory, known only death and blood and drones and bombs and darkness is no excuse. No matter the evil afoot, both within and without that has driven the survivors from their homes, just be great again.

Has there ever been a more ludicrous pronouncement by any president in our history than his "Just make your own countries great again." To the starving millions in Yemen who have been devastated in a Saudi Arabia led war that the United States of America has shamelessly and amorally backed.

Todd Brewster, author, editor, historian, et al, submitted a compelling response to this

Question as to Lincoln's Light and our house divided today. Presented as submitted, it reads:

> *Lincoln's detractors* (in our own day and not in Lincoln's) *are correct to see his imprint on the nation today. We do live in Lincoln's America. But that is no error, it is a glorious achievement. I am not only speaking to his freeing of the slaves. As a description of Lincoln's legacy, that does not go far enough. No, Lincoln's entire presidency can be understood as a reconsideration of American identity.*
>
> *Wars are fought over the definition of boundaries but they are also fought over the definition of words and the American Civil War was, at root, a clash of competing understandings of the word "liberty." In Lincoln's day definitional skirmishes were everywhere. Was America the nation described in the slavery-embracing words of the Constitution or those of the equality centered Declaration of Independence? Was America one nation or a confederation of states? Was labor the product of unrestricted capitalism or should we see labor as "prior to, and independent, of capital"? Lincoln declared for the less recognized side of these equations – for the Declaration over the Constitution; for one nation over a league of states; for labor over wealth. But he often saw both sides of public discussion and was not willing to sacrifice "union" to get his way. In the end, that was his greatest achievement. The defense of the union meant the reassertion of the rule of law as a container for our arguments. One imagines a cartoon house, inflating and deflating while a fight goes on inside, yet the roof never blows. That was the way that Lincoln would have it.*

The arguments at the core of the Civil War have remained with us ever since. We still debate the division of power between the federal government and the states. The political discussion over jobs pits those who seek to free up capital resulting in more employment against those who seek safeguards that guarantee a living wage, access to health care, equality of opportunity and safe working conditions. We no longer countenance slavery, but racism is rampant and while equality is a well defended principle of our national creed, it is subject to the clash between those who would preserve only "equality of opportunity" and those who demand "equality of results." These are healthy arguments, well within the bounds of reasonable discourse and Lincoln might well have seen such debate as the sign of a durable republic. But the most disturbing echo of the past comes in the threat to "union," in the decline of civility and the drawing of rigid lines between political factions. That would surely have saddened Lincoln beyond measure.

Brilliantly and movingly assessing the issues, Brewster reluctantly but clearly invites us to consider the wholly unacceptable specter of disunion, of being entirely driven apart by faction. *E Pluribus Unum*, out of many and out of the all, one, we theoretically are, but having rigidly retreated into our own corners of the ring, both attention and healing are demanded. The very idea of America rests upon the Union—the all in for the one, the unique acceptance of and belonging to all others.

No matter how often the specter of the '*Know Nothings*' rear their amoral heads.

While it may well have fomented in the blood of our land and in the hearts and minds of citizenry and policy makers alike, this lack of civility and the rigid lines dividing partisans and segments of the population haunt us today. There can be no doubt but that Lincoln would have worked first, to raise up the people, rather than immunize the barons of industry and power brokers alone; and that he would by example and by deed, have sought to restore civility and find common ground wherever possible. Unlike his counterpart today, who via his own lack of civility, daily and blatantly invites it and regularly throws fresh dry logs upon what is an already massive and divisive conflagration.

He thrives on this division.

Steve Koppelman wisely wrote, "It is hard today (and specifically at the time I am writing this) to not look at our President and all of the things that he has said and that he appears to be doing and the great divide in our country that we are now witnessing as a result, to not recall and point to something Lincoln said in his First Inaugural Address: "While the people retain their virtue and vigilance, no administration, by any extreme of wickedness or folly, can very seriously injure the government in the short space of four years." Fondly do we hope, fervently do we pray, that he is right!

Koppelman poignantly relies upon a line of Lincoln's that he hopes will comfort those who might well be appalled by and worried about the prospective damage that their president might do in a single term. It is, however, presented cautiously, for the times have indeed changed and unlike Lincoln's days, everything moves at lightning speed today and the tools and instruments on hand can do so very much damage, so very, very fast. In the unacceptable extreme, for instance, they include the truly alarming prospect of either wiping out life on this planet or of incapacitating the planet's very ability to sustain us.

While neither is imagined nor foreseen, it is the awful specter of the possible that haunts us when reason fails and we let our fears prevail.

He also calls to mind Lincoln's 1838 *Lyceum Address,* which certainly spoke to Lincoln as he ascended to the White Houseouse and and to us today. and still speaks to concerned Americans today.

In it, he addressed a growing spirit of vigilantism and lawlessness and the threat to the civil order and the stability of society. He had been moved by the recent and violent assault of a mob that attacked an outspoken, brave and free African American proponent of abolition, newspaper editor, Elijah Lovejoy in the autumn of the previous year. While Lovejoy was brutally murdered, that wasn't enough as this mob symbolically destroyed his printing press as well, the mouthpiece of his undying cry for freedom.

While Lincoln suggested that it was "useless to recount the horrors" of so many like incidents across the country, he did indeed reference quite a number of them, the all of which bore witness to a dangerous spirit of lawlessness. It begged the question of whether or not our government itself might be threatened by that same spirit, a question that Lincoln addressed accordingly. He wrote, "I *answer, if it ever reach us, it must spring up amongst us. It cannot come from abroad. If destruction be our lot, we must ourselves be its author and finisher."*

And then he proceeded to explain how:

It's helpful and instructive to reflect upon Lincoln's extraordinary Young Men's Lyceum of Springfield Address on January 27, 1838. Entitled the *Perpetuation of our Political Institutions* Lincoln continued, here is one telling passage:

> *I know the American people are much attached to their government. I know they would suffer much for its sake. I know they would endure evils long and patiently, before they would ever think of exchanging it for another. Yet notwithstanding all this, if the laws be continually despised and disregarded, if their rights to be secure in their persons and their property, are held by no better tenure than the caprice of a mob, the alienation of their affections from the government is the natural consequence; and to that, sooner or later, it must come.*

Towering genius," he said, *"disdains a beaten path. It denies that it is glory enough to serve under any chief. It thirsts and burns for distinction; and, if possible, it will have it. It will have it, whether at the expense of emancipating slaves, or enslaving freemen. Is it unreasonable then to expect, that some man possessed of the loftiest genius, coupled with ambition sufficient to push it to its utmost reach, will, at some time, spring up among us? And when such one does, it will require the people to be united with each other, attached to the government and laws, and generally intelligent, to successfully frustrate his designs." ---"Distinction will be his paramount object; and although he would as willingly, perhaps more so, acquire it by doing good as harm; yet, that opportunity being past, and nothing left to be done in the way of building up, he would set boldly to the task of pulling down.*

And this was his proposal for guarding against it.

Let every American, every lover of liberty, every well-wisher to his posterity, swear by the blood of the Revolution, never to violate in the least particular, the laws of the country; and never to tolerate their violation by others.

There we have it, as Lincoln argued that the United States can never be destroyed by a foreign power and that any dissolution of the American form of self-representative government could only come from within. Then, still relying upon his faith in the *"virtue and vigilance"* of the people, who will protect what is the precious legacy and blessing of being a free and empowered people, he rejected the specter of it.

He argued for *"Reason, cold calculating reason, intelligence, morality and a reverence for the Constitution and laws."*

And yet today, his words haunt us and make us take a hard look at where we are, in a place where our self-proclaimed "Genius" of a president indeed unequivocally and harshly wars against his own justice department and FBI and intelligence community and the Constitution itself. Consider again the Paris Climate Accords, environmental regulations, the Iranian Nuclear Disarmament deal, the hit on Iran's celebrated General, fealty to our allies, our relationship with the United Nations, foreign aid, our helping hand to refugees and legitimate seekers of asylum, voting rights, school lunch programs, the arbitrary and capricious implementation of tariffs largely inflicted upon our friends, the Executive Order driven attack upon the Affordable Care Act, the elimination of federal aid to Sanctuary Cities, the Muslim Ban, unleashing off-shore gas and oil drilling, opening up the Artic to it and certain National Parks as well, the bogus Election Integrity Commission, undermining the right to collective bargaining, the rejection of globalism, the embrace of despots, no action whatsoever on poverty or the raising up" of the people, racial, ethnic and political divisiveness and the latest declaration that he intends to use the military to put down public protest and dissent, and the ignoring of the emoluments clause of the Constitution. There's more, of course, and indeed the beat goes on.

The Constitution and Trump clashed in an Impeachment Trial and the verdict was alarming.

Reasonable, no. Intelligent, no. Moral, no. Reverent, no. Alarming, yes.

Picking up on the above, *Edna Greene Medford* responded to our final question in an illuminating way. She wrote:

The greatest overall issue we face today, in that it affects everything, is the role of government and what it should do to improve the lives of Americans. One of my favorite quotes from Lincoln comes from his speech to the special session of Congress convened on July 4, 1861. Lincoln takes the opportunity to explain the reason for the government's duty to quash the rebellion.

He said,

> *This is essentially a people's contest. On the side of the Union, it is a struggle for maintaining in the world that form and substance of government whose leading object is to elevate the condition of men, to lift artificial weights from all shoulders, to clear the paths of laudable pursuit for all, to afford all, an unfettered start, and a fair chance in the race of life.*

If we all embraced that assertion, America would truly be the land of opportunity that we historically have claimed it to be. That exceptionalism we are so fond of celebrating would be a reality for all Americans, not reserved for the most privileged."

It is an assertion that we ought to be aspiring to and living but we are not. For Trump's *America First* is not about 'We the people' and nor is it about the future. It is about the success of enterprise and of America's contemporary robber barons. It is about their winning in the now and the people and the future and our inherent and debilitating problems be damned. Trump has made straight the path for the fossil fuel, oil, coal and gas companies, without understanding that countries all over the world, like Ireland, which will no longer be dependent on fossil fuels at all in a few more years, are reaching for the sun and the wind and the waters and alternatives and tomorrow. They are passing us by. To go the way we are is not the way of the future. So too, on infrastructure and public transit and our ports and our airports and beating back pandemics with monsters like Covid-19. Our systems are dying or suffering, while Europe and China and even India are, often against great odds, looking to tomorrow.

America First is not American Exceptionalism. What makes us exceptional is not that we are the mightiest with the fastest planes and the finest weapons of destruction. It is our history, our legacy, our once goodness and that once open door. It is not in walls or in barriers but rather in our embrace of our fellow nations and our willingness to stand together with them to resolve the overarching and common denominator challenges of all mankind, beginning with the saving of the planet, the source of the all of life. It is about giving the poor and everyone access to health care as a right, which is the only path to beating back future pandemics.

As to the exceptional, the current administration engages none of the above and truth is, while Lincoln was certainly bogged down in a devastating war, free from its tentacles, there is no idea aimed at the betterment of people that he would not have explored.

MIchelle Krowl, like all of our collaborators, responded quite some time ago, early in the Trump administration days, so I am increasingly amazed at just how timeless was their commentary. Erudite and poignant, this is Michelle's contribution to this dialogue:

> Perhaps the easier question would be what did Abraham Lincoln do or say that is not relevant in some way to the challenges of our own time. On one level, this is the case because the nation continues to confront challenges of how to reconcile different opinions in a democratic republic that encompasses a geographically broad land inhabited by a diverse society. While Lincoln's world may have been a little less diverse than our own in some ways, the issues of equality, inclusion, fairness, security, the limits of basic freedoms, federal versus state supremacy, economic opportunity, immigration, voting rights, media biases, infrastructure, banking regulation, and a host of other subjects have been debated for generations and continue to be debated today.
>
> That politicians and pundits on both sides of the political spectrum can look to Abraham Lincoln and find relevance in his words speaks to that continuity in our history and the variety of related issues Lincoln faced in his own time.

Had you asked this question a year or two ago, the specific words or actions of Lincoln's that resonated most powerfully for me might have been different. But now that we seem to be living in another time when feelings and public statements run so deep and so divisively, we may profit from remembering Lincoln's attempts to understand the people with whom he did not agree. A passage from Lincoln's February 22, 1842 address to the Springfield Washington Temperance Society remains true today:

> *To have expected them to do otherwise than as they did---to have expected them not to meet denunciation with denunciation, crimination with crimination, and anathema with anathema, was to expect a reversal of human nature, which is God's decree, and never can be reversed. When the conduct of men is designed to be influenced, persuasion, kind, unassuming persuasion, should ever be adopted. It is an old and a true maxim, that a 'drop of honey catches more flies than a gallon of gall.' So with men. If you would win a man to your cause, first convince him that you are his sincere friend. Therein is a drop of honey that catches his heart, which, say what he will, is the great high road to his reason, and which, when once gained, you will find but little trouble in*

convincing his judgment of the justice of your cause, if indeed that cause really be a just one. On the contrary, assume to dictate to his judgment, or to command his action, or to mark him as one to be shunned and despised, and he will retreat within himself, close all the avenues to his head and his heart; and tho' your cause be naked truth itself, transformed to the heaviest lance, harder than steel, and sharper than steel can be made, and tho' you throw it with more than Herculean force and precision, you shall no more be able to pierce him, than to penetrate the hard shell of a tortoise with a rye straw.

One can appreciate Michelle's point of view, which given the unraveling of Trump's administration, likely shifted some, for forging understanding, given the rigid divisiveness, enhanced by the manipulator who feeds on it, is increasingly difficult.. The quote she pulls from Lincoln's 1842 *Temperance Society Address* is a wonder, one that so defines Lincoln's temperament and way of being. Fight for the right and hold tight to it, while being respectful and empathetic and considerate of those who hold a different point of view. But this can only be the handiwork of one with a moral center, of one who is grounded and civil and aware of the duty, responsibility and accountability that is owed to all, even those who may vehemently disagree with one's course of action.

Lacking the ability to be persuaded by facts, by truth, by the cries of his people or by righteousness, our President today does not aspire to this so very rational notion of Lincoln's. His end game is ever and always to win, to defame those who think differently, to punch and keep on punching, to decimate and to roll over and forward. With guns blazing, from one crisis in a news cycle to the next and with an arrogance and disdain for those who dare call him out in the process, the embattlement and the destruction is at the heart of his new reality show. The people and their nation's needs are but pawns on the playing field.

The pawns in his game plan also include his base, his most volatile supporters, the ones to whom he gives the privilege of wallowing in his greatness. That's all he has got and all they truly get.

Matt Lakemacher had no problem demonstrating just how deep that passion runs in responding to our query about 'Lincoln in our own time.' Here, his words:

Lincoln still speaks to our troubled times, not only in his deep and growing faith in God, not only in his ability to change on issues of religion and race, but also in his undying belief in the American Experiment. Lincoln was not an originalist when it came to the Declaration of Independence. Clearly Jefferson did not intend to include "all men," let alone the fairer sex, in his statement on unalienable rights. Nor did the Founders interpret that document as such when they wrote the Constitution.

But Lincoln viewed both documents as living things that could change with the times and speak to higher truths. Since immigration is such a hot-button topic today, it was instructive to listen to Harold Holzer speak at the 2016 Lincoln Forum on the Sixteenth President's views on that issue. As a wave of Nativism washes once again over the U.S. today, it is revealing to read Lincoln's 1855 letter to Joshua Speed, in which he writes: '*As a nation, we began by declaring that 'all men are created equal.' We now practically read it "all men are created equal, except negroes.' When the Know-Nothings get control, it will read 'all men are created equal, except negroes, and foreigners, and Catholics.' When it comes to this I should prefer emigrating to some country where they make no pretense of loving liberty—to Russia, for instance, where despotism can be taken pure, and without the base alloy of hypocrisy.'*

Although those words were never meant for public consumption, it does give us insight into Lincoln's private position on the topic at that time. Also by the 1850s, the time had come for America to address its original sin of slavery. Lincoln the fatalist was unusually optimistic when it came to America's promise and the unending work of making a 'more perfect union.' We so desperately need that optimism today, especially when the Party of Lincoln has moved so far from its original creed. Most Americans, on both sides of the aisle, look at politics as being a dirty thing, yet Lincoln viewed it as a positive good and a means to a better end. We need the next generation to view politics in this way. We need to move past the malaise of the 1960s and the Culture Wars of the 1980s. We need to embrace compromise, the founding principle of the American Experiment and the Grand Consensus that marks a straight line from Alexander Hamilton to Henry Clay to Abraham Lincoln to Theodore Roosevelt to Ronald Reagan to Barack Obama.

As Thaddeus Stevens said of the passage of the 13th Amendment in Steven Spielberg's film "Lincoln," which presidential candidate Hillary Clinton made reference to in 2016 while defending her having both a public and a private position in politics, it was '*The greatest measure of the Nineteenth Century. Passed by corruption, aided and abetted by the purest man in America.*' We need that unfading light, now more than ever. It's in Abraham Lincoln that we find it."

To think of politics as an instrument of the good and as a reaffirmation of all that we hold dear in America, to think of the prospective good that may come from honorable compromise rather than stalemate and, Lord above, to utter the word consensus that has long been lost in a whirlwind of dissension, vituperation and even downright hatred.

But if not today, Matt, and I sadly see no path to it today, why not next year or the year after that. Why not begin electing leaders who will be dedicated to forging it and not these singers of the same old familiar songs that please the base and their financiers alone, why not lay the swords down and begin again. Why not pure unadulterated truth and a holistic reaffirmation of Lincoln's ideals.

"Hope is a good thing. Maybe the best of things," Andy Dufresne said to Red in *Shawshank Redemption*. I'll take a flyer on hope.

The former curator of the Lincoln Museum in Illinois, *Anne Moseley*, spends her days with Lincoln and presents him to the public, in ever changing ways. She taps her intimacy with Lincoln to present him in so many different lights. In our effort to shed that light, here, her contribution:

> Abraham Lincoln's election in 1860 marked the first time a Republican was elected president. Having no experience in national affairs and facing a crisis of enormous proportions, Lincoln strategically filled his cabinet with the men who had opposed him for the nomination and who were his political rivals. Formed from a disparate coalition of Whigs, Democrats, Free Soilers, easterners, westerners, northerners, radicals, and conservatives, the new Republican political party mirrored the men who served in Lincoln's cabinet.
>
> Every president since George Washington has selected a cabinet to assist and advise him. But not every president knowingly selects cabinet ministers who will freely disagree. A variety of factors determine why someone is selected for a cabinet post including ability, political compatibility and geographical considerations. Lincoln, extremely self-confident, selected a team of political adversaries who were regularly at odds with each other. However, Lincoln looked beyond each man's foibles and competing egos and saw the talent and intelligence each man brought to his administration. Cabinet members were free to disagree with each other and Lincoln's unique personality ensured balance within his cabinet. Lincoln recognized the risks of having conflicting opinions in his cabinet, but he chose them because they were the best individuals for the job.
>
> *In all our rejoicing let us neither express, nor cherish, any harsh feeling towards any citizen who, by his vote, has differed with us. Let us at all times remember that all American citizens are brothers of a common country, and should dwell together in the bonds of fraternal feeling.* —A. Lincoln, November 20, 1860

Ideally, there is no doubt about this, no doubt about being open to and accepting of all, no doubt about being respectful of divergent opinions, no matter your view, no doubt about doing that which you believe to be right, each and every time. But Trump sees neither the need to listen to divergent points of view and nor does he appreciate the value of fair consideration. In fact, our Commander in Chief today will have none of it. He suffers no dissension, but even worse, neither does he suffer any exploration, which is the most devastating consequence of his governance, wherein there is no search for truth or any analysis of just how egregiously each executive order or each rewriting of federal regulatory rules hurt. Deep seeded conservative ideology alone would be one thing, but he is not an ideologue. Hinged only to winning, there is no counting the cost or assessment of the damage done.

Recently, for instance, I discovered that they are moving to narrowly define gender as a biological, immutable condition determined by genitalia at birth, which is nothing more and nothing less than a drastic move in a government wide effort to roll back recognition and protections for transgender people under federal civil rights law. The aim is simply to eliminate existing protections and open them up to overt discrimination.

Why, because the Evangelicals, who long ago stopped communicating with Christ and his commandment to love, don't like them. This under the radar regulatory move is born of hate and ignorance and it is unacceptable in that there is nothing immutable about sex, as so many precious babies are born both male and female and parents make choices on the fly that more often than not, lead those they love to be understandably conflicted. The science has long told us that there are more than two sexes.

But our leaders today refuse to look upon the naked truth and prefer to look out upon the world that exists only in their biased and bigoted heads and in the name of the imaginary, strike out against the innocents.

Just to think that their Jesus explicitly suggested that they ought to stop worrying about the splinters that they see in the eyes of those who bother them and first take the prodigious logs out of their own. Blind to that which is real and right, they keep tightening the screws of ignorance.

As long as the base keeps cheering and as long as the prodigious forces of greed, callousness and indifference stay the course and prop our president up, this beat goes on. In all of its ugliness and reprehensibility, discrimination plays well for Trump. A winner for him, he revels in it, no matter the years he is setting us back nor the enormity of the damage being done.

So many of our collaborators, like Anne, wonderfully channeled Lincoln in the hope that Candidate Trump would not become President Trump, but he did; and we are here and we go to Lincoln in order to hold on to the faith that we might, once again, rise from the ashes of this dustup and reclaim the soul of America.

And not for nothing but the truth is that there is little to no Christianity in the Christian right, for the New Testament proclaims the God of love and forgiveness and not the God of hellfire, damnation and justice. A radical love is celebrated and not a God who dares discriminate against his own creation.

Douglas Egerton, next on our Collaborator "hit parade." As to what Lincoln did that relates to our moment in time, his response comes with a rich and haunting pathos, for oh how very different, it once was. Just imagine, amiability, kindness and honesty as opposed to "Lock Her Up," "Throw him out" or "He's a lowlife and a moron."

The exhaustive research he did for his *Year of Meteors,* I believe, enabled him to so easily reference a couple of incidents along the campaign trail in 1858, where Douglas went out of his way to defend the character of his opponent. Maybe because we are so far removed from that kind of high honor, civility and courtesy in our politics, each struck me as powerfully moving.

Here, Egerton's response:

Clearly, the challenges of leading a society as rich and complicated as ours, especially when it comes to race and ethnicity, are only marginally less today than they were in Lincoln's time. In some ways, thanks to the tide of immigration at the dawn of the twentieth century, our society is even more diverse than his.

But what may be missing the most now in modern politics is Lincoln's empathy and humanity. Even before the guns of Sumter, of course, Lincoln's era was angry and fractured, as Congressman Preston Brooks' assault on Charles Sumner indicated. But in a time when politicians shout "you lie" or "wrong" during speeches and debates, Lincoln's 1860 campaign and that of his longtime foe, Stephen Douglas were unique in how charitable they were toward one another. When Douglas was speaking in New Hampshire, the Illinois Democrat reflected that Lincoln was "a very clever fellow, a kindhearted, good natured, amiable man." They simply disagreed on policy, Douglas added. When a Democrat in the audience shouted that Lincoln was good for little besides splitting rails, Douglas defended his rival, saying that as a young man, he too had worked with wood, "constructing bureaus and secretaries" at a carpenter's shop. That sort of pleasant, polite disarmament of tensions seems sadly absent in today's Washington.

"Sadly absent" is to put it mildly and oh how much we long for it and how poorer we are for the lack of it.

I can pull a little tale out of my back pocket that speaks to this as I, given the business and community organization I once served in the Jersey Meadowlands, had the opportunity to introduce Vice President George Herbert Walker Bush at a breakfast meeting during his 1988 presidential run.

I briefly related a tale of being with my Grandfather, stuck in a traffic jam in a construction zone, when he said, "Oh, It would be a great country if we ever got it finished." I then went off on a brief philosophical musing as to the fact that it never is and never will be and that there is always great work to be done. Given the weight of that work and the awesome responsibility of the office, the willingness of those who look to dedicate themselves to bearing the burden of it all for us, commanded respect. It was a high minded kind of back door, Teddy Roosevelt 'The Man in the Arena" musing. Then honestly reflecting upon his own lifetime of service, with particular focus upon his role in World War II, I added that his life had been one of honor. But I fell short of endorsement and there was no rousing, "I give you the next president of the United States."

I gave them an honorable man and "The Vice President of the United States of America."

He was very gracious, we warmly shook hands and he thanked me and said that my introduction "was among the most gracious and moving endorsements he had yet received," only to pause, look at me and, with voice lowering, smilingly say, "Come to think of it, Rich, that wasn't quite an endorsement, was it"? The crowd haltingly but loudly laughed and he graciously and kindly smiled at me all the more.

I loved that smile of his and can picture it still and I knew then that I was looking at a very good and gentle man, my problems with Reagan's economics notwithstanding.

The upside of this tale is that his first debate with the Democratic nominee, Governor Michael Dukakis of Massachusetts, followed shortly thereafter, at which the final question from the moderator was prefaced with a commentary about the denigration and escalating mean-spiritedness of our presidential politics, followed by a "Therefore, what can you tell us of the good in your opponent." I remember only that Dukakis disingenuously tripped all over himself and that George Herbert Walker Bush smoothly applied the sum and substance of my recent introduction.

Right down to his own version of my, "It would be a great country if we ever got it finished."

Inadvertently, I felt that I had given him quite a gift and oh the weight of the responsibility I came to carry, one so deep that G.W. and his weapons of mass destruction and Cheney and Rumsfeld and all their varied and sundried barbarians at the gates were part of the package.

But a weight that was innocent, largely imagined and, in retrospect, my liberal politics and the war notwithstanding, not all that terrible, because they were both good and caring men who were faithful to both their high office and our country. Neither of them ever tossed dignity or high honor to the vagaries of the wind as does Donald trump.

Egerton uses Lincoln's renowned opponent to remind us of something so simple, yet so important, that all too many politicians, Democrats and Republicans alike, have long lost sight of. Something that all must admit is not in Trump's toolkit, in that what was once ugly has grown monstrous, mean-spirited, racist and intolerable.

"Civility, Pass it on," the billboard I passed in South Dakota read. But with Trump, there is nary a shred of it.

Karen Hawbecker submitted this:

If we look at what Lincoln said about the importance of Union and unity to the country's survival and success, his words are just as instructive for us today as they were when he spoke them.

> As early as 1843, in a Whig campaign circular, Lincoln wrote, "*That 'union is strength' is a truth that has been known, illustrated and declared, in various ways and forms in all ages of the world.*" Certainly, he wrote his famous House Divided speech to address the polarizing issue of slavery, but the principle applies to all points of political polarization. In stating that a '*House divided against itself cannot stand,*' Lincoln recognized that polarization endangers its continuity.

In his First Inaugural, he tried to bridge the divide and remind the whole country of unifying principles. He stated, '*My countrymen, one and all, think calmly and well upon this whole subject. Nothing valuable can be lost by taking time.*' Identifying commonalities, he said that '*Intelligence, patriotism, Christianity, and a firm reliance on Him who has never yet forsaken this favored land are still competent to adjust in the best way all our present difficulty.*' He made a final appeal to attempt to salvage the country: '*We are not enemies, but friends. We must not be enemies. Though passion may have strained it must not break our bonds of affection.*'

In my view and based on my perspective of working as a government lawyer in Washington, D.C., for over 25 years, we are becoming more and more polarized as a people today. The electorate is divided on every issue and almost equally matched in number on both sides of those issues in both local and national elections. Sometimes, the issues under debate are silly and sometimes momentous, but all too often, we exhibit a willingness to take sides just to take sides. Too many of us grasp political party talking points like a club to brandish against our political opponents. We talk past each other and demonize each other to justify our mistreatment of each other. We even celebrate violence against and injury to those political opponents. Too many view all aspects of life only through the lens of party politics. No topic seems safe from this seeping political polarization.

While Karen's conclusion seems, in many ways, to be both rugged and sad, there is a bitter truth to it.

Cryptic, thought provoking and challenging as ever, *Richard Brookhiser* again submitted the shortest response of all. He simply wrote, "*Charity for all is impossible. Malice toward none is hard enough.*"

As elusive as it was pointed, Brookhiser again prodded me. I understood what he meant and on a visceral level, I agreed, while at one and the same time, doing so just didn't sit well.

For the heart longed for it to be different.

The heart longs for "Love one another as I have loved you" and "Whenever you do these for the least of my brethren, you do them also for me" and "If a man asks you to go one-mile, go with him two," and "Give them your coat as well" and "Be perfect as your Heavenly Father is perfect." Why not charity—Why not make gentle the life of the world—Why not human kindness—Why not mutual respect—Why not compassion and empathy—Why not love and not hate, we wonder.

All faiths aspire to the same core beliefs, the same prescriptions for living, the same Golden Rule. What they herald also is found in the plays of Shakespeare, the novels of Dickens, the best of our literature and poetry. And while the romance fades with the literature of the Realists and certainly in the modern era and even, I sadly recall, in the latter works of my great friend, Mark Twain—that even he, in his final two short stories, *The Man that*

Corrupted Hadleyburg and *The Mysterious Stranger,* went dark on us, But the mystics, poets and saints never quite give up on us.

And so the battered and tamed idealist in me struggles with reality and proffers his wide array of "Why Nots," only to have them fiercely buffeted by the winds of ego and greed that leave us all wallowing in the brackish waters of selfishness and indifference.

I so want it to be different but I lose.

As the political divide today is fever pitched and for so long as President Trump is empowered, any path or door to charity is closed.

But still, we remember that Lincoln said, "Why not" often and, however rough-hewn the road he traveled, he never lost faith in his "*Last Best Hope of Earth*" and his "*Raising them all up.*" In the burying of the dead and in the laying of the weapons down and in the bitter mourning, he aspired to hope and called us to charity.

After all, "If we have not charity," then what, then why?

David Sullivan has a rich reverence for legacy, for the ties that bind and for that which we owe our forefathers and posterity. This was his response:

> Abraham Lincoln just happened to live during one of the most challenging times for our young nation, which was still in the throes of establishing its own national identity. Lincoln was also a loving father, a devoted husband and a true friend. Sure, Lincoln had strengths and weaknesses like we all do. However, throughout his life and his presidency, he lived by what he believed and that was that all men are created equal.
>
> Lincoln had the common sense mentality of I give, you give, we get. He believed "*Right makes might*" and he stuck to his principles under the most extraordinary circumstances and pressures throughout his presidency. Still, Lincoln listened to and accepted the opinions of others. He knew how to work with people to accomplish his goals which were always for the greater good of the nation and democracy itself. He understood and skillfully practiced the art of compromise. It is sad that our government leaders have strayed so far from Lincoln's principles and teachings to the point where we no longer function as a governing body should. They have what is called a "me, mine and my" mentality under the guise of "it's what the American people want."
>
> I believe Doris Kearns Goodwin's book *Team of Rivals, The Political Genius of Abraham Lincoln* ought to be a reading prerequisite for each incoming President, Senator and Congressman to read before taking the oath of office as well as memorizing the *Gettysburg Address . . . that all men are created equal . . . and that government of the people, by the people, for the people, shall not perish from the earth.*

The takeaways, for me, include Sullivan's point that our leaders, and most especially this president, do not listen to the people, do not work with the people; and are sadly, as we've noted again and again, beyond persuading and fixed. Once the goal is fixed, no matter the practical or moral consequences and no matter a bolt of lightning from the heavens saying stop, our president today, as ever devoted to winning, will never reconsider. Should he have to lie through his teeth to do so makes not one iota of difference! Well practiced in the art of doing so, he'll sell the lies with bombast and fury.

Beyond Goodwin's book, we'd do well to add a great deal more to a mandatory reading list. How about the Constitution and the *Declaration of Independence,* most of the major speeches, key Messages to Congress and letters of Lincoln's and a good taste of the Jefferson-Adams Correspondence and *Washington's Farewell* and Thoreau's *Essay on Civil Disobedience* and Emerson's *Self-Reliance* and Shaara's *Killer Angels* and primers on both Teddy and Franklin, the two Roosevelt's and Kershaw's *The Longest Winter* about the Battle of the Bulge. How about Eisenhower's last presidential address and a good bit of Martin, John and Bobby and even bits of *Malcolm X's Autobiography* and selected speeches of Reagan's and Harvey Milk's and *To Kill a Mockingbird* and O'Brien's *The Things We Carried* and Abdo's *Main Street and Mecca: Muslim Life in America After 9/11* and excerpts from Oswalt's *This Land Was Theirs*. Oh what the hell, we can go on and on as I could well add some 50 other books on Lincoln, largely from our contributors and yes, Burlingame, Cawardine, Goodwin, and, and…but this would be a good beginning.

The above and more before the policy papers and the contemporary issues and party platforms and their National Security briefings. Like Lincoln, leaders ought to know something of the great challenges we've faced, many of which continue to fester, and they ought to know who contributed to meeting the great crises and to forging real change and to inspiring. They ought to listen to the pulse of America's beating heart and swim around in its soul. They ought to immerse themselves in the sufferings and dreams of its people and to feel the pain that has afflicted and made heavy the lives of tens upon tens of millions. After all, there is oh so much that has been left undone for oh so long.

Paula Hopewell, one of our many Lincoln presenter collaborators wrote:
Considering this subject, my first thought is the *Gettysburg Address*. We are still testing today whether this nation might live. In the big scheme of history, we remain a still new experiment in self-government. Will government *"of the people, by the people, for the people"* perish from the earth? I don't know. We are on the battleground right now.
An attorney friend of mine, a Civil War buff himself, once remarked to me that the Civil War had settled the matter of whether states could secede. I disagree. It only settled the matter over slavery in 19th century America. We have evolved into a country with problems far more complex than the Founding Father's or Lincoln's. We are living in an age of warp-speed communication, the internet, social media, etc., etc.

Paula's right, to a degree but despite our brave new world and our having piled on magnificently, it is the great unresolved problems of the 19th and 20th centuries that continue to haunt, and most dramatically, impinge in the 21st as well. We are, for instance, still living what Lincoln looked to resolve

Oh yes, "We must continue to 'strive on,' and to 'finish the work we are in.'"

As to Lincoln, the crisis was thrust upon him, while Trump is the wizard who has fashioned a crisis all of his own making.

He attacks and eats his own—he expresses racist sentiments—and the hell with voting rights and Muslims and Mexicans and the Transgender community and the freedom of the press. He castigates his Justice Department, his Federal Bureau of Investigation, the Environmental Protection Administration. He defies the science of climate change and gravely imperils the life of the earth. He stands with Putin rather than his own Intelligence community and ignores their warnings. He diminishes his allies, breaks treaties and says why not immigrants from Norway rather than those "shit counties." It is as if entities like Health and Human Services and Housing and Urban Development and the Urban Mass Transportation Administration and the like have no standing whatsoever anymore. He usurps the continued will of the majority and via Executive Order bleeds the life out of the Affordable Care Act. As to the emoluments clause, the co-equal branches of Congress and the Judiciary and interference in foreign affairs for political benefit, he is the Criminal in Chief, who unchecked by Congress sees it all there for the taking.

The beat goes on and on and the truth is that outside of the tools of war, security, finance and economy, he has little love for all other departments and agencies. Deregulate, denigrate, dissolve, dismiss.

Our friend, *Kathryn Harris* wrote, "As we are living in a time of polarization, particularly in politics, and at a time that is rife with racial bigotry and hatred that I perceive to be coming from the top Republican in our nation today, i.e. the President, I know that Lincoln would attempt to unify rather than divide. I believe that he would admonish us to seek out our common "better angels"—that's all of us or as many of us as possible. A divided nation was not good in the 1860's and it is certainly not good for us today.

Troubled indeed, Karhryn reminded us that W. E. B. DuBois insisted that the 20th century's great problem would be the color line and so it is in the 21st and not just black and white, for there are disparities and inequalities that affect all people of color (Hispanics, Asians, Native Americans), leaving Kathryn to say, "I believe that Lincoln would weep if he were to see where we have come on so many fronts today."

We must start anew. We must begin again. We must begin today. And tomorrow and the day after that and next month and next year and then the day after that and the next year. New leaders, new champions, new Kings, new Milks, new Bobbys and new Lincolns until, until, until . . . and for as long as it takes . . . until that happy day.

On the night before he died, Martin Luther King told an emotionally charged audience in Memphis that "He may not get there with them," but that the Good Lord had given him the chance to "Go up to the mountaintop." And then the richly reverberating affirmation of his "I have seen the Promised Land." Indeed he had and then he promised every one of them that one day they too will get to the Promised Land." 52 years ago, he had that vision. "Mine eyes have seen the glory of the coming of the Lord," he cried out as his words soared until he was emotionally spent and could say no more. He sat down and he just cried, for he knew how long the road ahead and "how difficult the days ahead." It is a sacred duty of all Americans today to stand before the prodigious mountain that still stands in the way of fulfilling that promise—to stand before it and to together pick up our damn shovels and start digging.

Steve Raymond added, "The present great divide among our people is sadly reminiscent of the situation confronting Lincoln when he became President. Even the immortal words he uttered then could not prevent the fiery trial that was to come. And words may not be enough to quell the present unrest. But they are still surely worth repeating: *"That we are not enemies, but friends; that though passion may have strained, it must not break our bonds of affection; that surely the better angels of our nature"* will yet prevail.

Then he shared a personal note: "The most moving moments I've experienced in my pursuit of Lincoln were at Ford's Theatre. I think a visit to that sacred venue would inspire almost anyone to study Lincoln."

Sadly, the words Raymond so understandably intoned are, as he admits, likely to fall on the same deaf ears, but hell, it can't hurt to shout them from the rooftops. Then too, we all know how locked in the base and the resistance are and one can't help but think that all the therapy in the world won't make a damn bit of difference. But why not try? Again the thought, why don't our great Universities and the national media advance some form of ongoing National Communal Therapy sessions at venues like Ford's Theatre or the Old Statehouse in Springfield that both FOX and CNN and all will agree to televise? Why not an airing out of our grievances, *mano a' mano*, with fact checking? Why not see if we can't hone down to the common denominators or the nubs and have a conversation, devoid of hate? Why not debate and analyze and puzzle our puzzlers as Lincoln did? Why not try? Why not get out of our boxes and holes and begin by shaking hands.

Like me and like you, *George Buss,* renowned Lincoln impersonator, calls upon Lincoln. He wrote, "We are a greatly divided nation. When I appear across the country, the reoccurring comment from people is, 'We need you back, Abe.' And they mean it. We've lost the middle and we've lost the great American spirit of compromise. We defeat incumbents who reached across the aisle (for the sin of not being partisan enough). Whenever I deliver the '*House Divided Speech,*' which I just did yesterday, there is a palpable response from the listeners. Their cerebral response says it all."

Moving and haunting, for the divide is so very stark today. Lincoln, of course, immediately suggested that it would either be all slave or all free. Likely, he would ask us just that again. Will we be free? So free as to welcome all into the tent, all factions, all races, all faiths, all honorable seekers of asylum, all sexual orientations, so free as to celebrate genuine liberty and the pursuit of happiness for all, so free as to embrace the concept of 'one man-one vote' again where each and every voice might again be as empowered and loud as any other? Or will we, under the auspices of Citizen's United, remain enslaved?

Or will we say, as so many and for so long and so miserably and vilely have, that "I've got the power and I hold on to it by limiting yours." 13th,14th and 15th amendments be damned and there, in a nutshell, the great sin and stain of racism.

THE STARK AND TELLING CONTRAST

Trump is no Lincoln and we need Lincoln. Truly we do, but wishes are wishes and reality is harsh. One grew up dirt poor and one with a golden spoon in his mouth, one lived the short and simple annals of the poor" and one grew up in luxury and received more than $450 million from his father, one was self-taught and the other graduated from the acclaimed Wharton School of Business at Penn, one was steeled in the ways of politics and had often served in office and one had virtually no political or governmental experience at all, one was steadfast and true to principles and policy positions as to the evil of slavery and raising up all in the race of life and the other held to vague, confused, and often conflicted positions, one used self-deprecating humor and joked about everything from his looks to his failings to his losses and the other was all boast and brag and 'big-better-best,' one held tight to values that rendered him saint-like and the other was without a moral center, one went to the White House to serve and the other to rule.

THE LIES

In his 1848 *Spot Resolutions* speech on the floor of Congress, Lincoln, among a distinct minority, opposed the War with Mexico and asked President Polk to inform the people where the exact spot of the first battle was. Certain, as he was, that America incited the battle on Mexico's sovereign land and not 'they upon ours,' he said,

This strange omission, it does seem to me, could not have occurred but by design. I have sometimes seen a good lawyer, struggling for his client's neck, in a desperate case, employing every artifice to work round, befog, and cover up, with many words, some point arising in the case, which he dared not admit, and yet could not deny. Party bias may help to make it appear so; but with all the allowance I can make for such bias, it still does appear, that just such, and from just such necessity, is the President's struggle in this case to me." And so he will not define the spot wherein it all began – because it is a lie.

Later in this speech, he added,

First he takes up one, and in attempting to argue us into it, he argues himself out of it; then seizes upon another, and goes through the same process; and then, confused at being able to think of something new, he snatches up the old one again, which he has some time before cast off. His mind, tasked beyond its power, is running hither and thither, like some tortured creature, on a burning surface, finding no position, on which it can settle down, and be at ease.

Note that Lincoln here unpopularly allied himself with the abolitionists and those who argued that Polk was serving the interests of Manifest Destiny and opening doors up to the further expansion of slavery. At his own political peril, Lincoln loudly told the truth when the people of his district were all high on the fight with Mexico. However unpopular, he did what conscience demanded and the politics be damned.

Now neither is Trump Polk, but he gets caught in lies every day and he just keeps lying on. As I noted earlier, the *Washington Post*, one of those "Enemies of the People" reported that he surpassed the documented 17,000th lie. In fact, he has told so very many more during the coronavirus crisis alone and set the healing and the atonement back, it's likely moving beyond 18,000 by now and by the time this is read, who knows. One of his grandest is that he dares to maintain that we the people believe him to be greater even than Lincoln, whose teeth would have fallen out if he told one lie.

Trump's old whoppers include the Inaugural crowd size—Obama's having tapped his office—the massive voter fraud without which he would have won the popular vote—that Obamacare is an abomination—that global warming was invented by the Chinese—that he did all he could for Puerto Rico—that the social safety net is too costly—that all the people he ridicules are what he suggests they are—that he didn't know that his attorney had paid off Stormy Daniels—that Mexico will pay for his Wall—that our free press is the enemy of the people—that the FBI investigation proved the innocence of Brett Kavanaugh—that reducing emission standards on automobiles, gutting more than one-half of all EPA regulations, opening up drilling and mining opportunities and doing the bidding of the fossil fuel industry is needed and justifiable—that climate change and the clock that's ticking on the death of Mother Earth are mythological—that the Mueller Report completely exonerated him—that his interventions in Ukraine were all perfect—that the World Health Organization failed—and so on and on . . .

ON DUMBING DOWN & OBFUSCATING INFORMATION

Back in Lincoln's day, the people would listen to debates of 3 to 4 Hours. Towards the end of one of them with Stephen Douglas in 1858, Lincoln said, "*I have quoted so much at this time merely to show that according to our ancient faith, the just powers of governments are derived from the consent of the governed.*"

True, but? That was absent apathy, absent the manipulation, distortion, lies, misinformation, absent Citizen's United and the bought elected officials, absent the big money, the anonymous PACs and the egregious self-interest. In Lincoln's day, it was just newspapers and plenty of them, but today newspapers are dying. So there is far less exploration and the Broadcast News cycle is daily reinvented and the bloggers and podcasters are everywhere. Yesterday's news is tossed out with the trash, We do not investigate—we do not go long—we so easily forget and Trump plays this like a fiddle. There is little depth and no finality. All of the bells and whistles of our technology, of our cells and our social media have, in the end, serve only to dumb down the dissemination of truth. Worst of all, there is no search for truth, no sustainable follow-up. Out of our "Oh so very much more," we get so very much less.

In that same speech. Lincoln also said, "*Who is responsible for this? Is it those who resist the measure, or those who, causelessly, brought it forward and passed it through, having reason to know, and, in fact, knowing it must and would be resisted so.*"

Consider how we obfuscate and demonize process in Washington today. There is little examination or genuine truth seeking today as democracy itself also is everywhere dumbed down. Bills, i.e. the attempts to bury the ACA, are moved on the fly without examination, without hearings, without process, without any serious debate. The all of which is praised by a president whose only true goal is always and everywhere to win. An impeachment trial with no witnesses, no testimony, no submission of evidence is, of course, 'dumbed down on steroids.

Lincoln added,

Fellow countrymen—Americans south, as well as north, shall we make no effort to arrest this? Already the liberal party throughout the world, express the apprehension 'that the one retrograde institution in America, is undermining the principles of progress, and fatally violating the noblest political system the world ever saw.' That is not the taunt of enemies, but the warning of friends. Is it quite safe to disregard it—to despise it? Is there no danger to liberty itself, in discarding the earliest practice, and first precept of our ancient faith? In our greedy chase to make profit of the negroe, let us beware, lest we "cancel and tear to pieces" even the white man's charter of freedom.

Our Charters of Freedom, our Declaration, our Bill of Rights, our Constitution have all been threatened by our president today, who likes the sound of 'lifetime president' and sees no need for term limits and prefers to go around and defy Congress and demean and denigrate their status as a co-equal branch and who regularly threatens the freedom of our own citizens and of our free press.

And rather than communicate with our allies, he threatens them.

ON RIGHTS AND BIGOTRY

An August 15, 1855 letter from Lincoln to George Robertson of Lexington, Kentucky was extraordinary. It included this famous passage:

On the question of liberty, as a principle, we are not what we have been. When we were the political slaves of King George, and wanted to be free, we called the maxim that 'all men are created equal' a self-evident truth; but now when we have grown fat, and have lost all dread of being slaves ourselves, we have become so greedy to be masters that we call the same maxim a 'self-evident lie.' The fourth of July has not quite dwindled away; it is still a great day—for burning fire-crackers.

Ever so much more today, we fail, for the president looks to tear down every social safety net program—and he lambasted the NFL for not firing players who freely and respectfully protested on behalf of Black Lives Matter. And no, it is not about the flag or our military but rather and only a harsh truth about the murders of black citizens that continue to be ignored. And then there's the Muslim Ban and the Wall that targets those Mexicans, asylum seekers and those longing to escape what for them has grown intolerable.

On August 24, 1855. Lincoln wrote an equally famous letter to his closest friend, Joshua Speed. Well noted already, it focused on the Know Nothings, bigotry, our progress in degeneracy and the base alloy of hypocrisy.

Much later on December 8 1863, he issued a *Proclamation of Amnesty and Reconstruction* in the heart of the Civil War. Imagine that Lincoln was willing to give amnesty to and forgive those who went so far as to betray their own country, forgiving rebels who waged war against their own, and yet we can't find the way forward to give illegals who took great risks to find a better life here a way forward to citizenship, something all presidents before Trump saw as the honorable way forward.

In another April 4, 1864 letter to Alfred Hodges, a Kentucky newspaper editor who had met Lincoln and was satisfied with a response that he asked Lincoln to put into writing or this:

> *I could not take the office without taking the oath. Nor was it my view that I might take an oath to get power, and break the oath in using the power. I understood, too, that in ordinary civil administration, this oath even forbade me to practically indulge my primary abstract judgement on the moral question of slavery.*

The oath matters – to preserve, protect and defend. It is the all of the Constitution, separation of powers, limitations upon powers, Bill of Rights, etc., In it, the sacredness of a free press and the right to free speech and protest, however distasteful it may be to him, and then, there are the due process issues surrounding our treatment of illegals and the veritable incarceration of their children that are being wholly ignored . . .

THE 45TH PRESIDENT OF THE UNITED STATES OF AMERICA

What follows is extremely brief. An earlier draft was loaded with outrageous and frightening and egotistical quotes. In them, a picture of a bully and a brute without bounds or borders. No more, just these few. A few is more than enough.

> *The line of 'Make America great again,' the phrase, that was mine, I came up with it about a year ago, and I kept using it, and everybody's using it, they are all loving it. I don't know, I guess I should copyright it, maybe I have copyrighted it.* (Actually, it was Ronald Reagan's.)
> *I'm intelligent. Some people would say I'm very, very, very intelligent." I'm a very stable genius—I am the greatest president—greater even than Abraham Lincoln.*
> *Show me someone with no ego and I'll show you a big loser.*

Two final maddening cries. Some time ago, without expressing any sympathy whatsoever for the victims of rape in the military, he placed the blame on those governmental "geniuses" who integrated the military in the first place, rather than the men who actually and criminally assaulted their fellow service-members. As if it was only natural that rape must be the consequence of men and women working together.

Of the hundreds of things said or done that drive me inside out and upside down, this is the most appalling.

Then there is what we're living now as I submit this manuscript.

Trump tragically and long ignored the warnings and the reality of the Covid-19 pandemic. There was no preparation, no plan, no pre-emptive measures, a daily dose of lies and misinformation along with virtual campaign ads, the usual self-adulation and praise, the daily demeaning of Democratic Governors and any, even his own, who dared demand truth. This dereliction of duty was criminal. What was ever and only at issue for him was how he looked and what the polls suggested. Honesty, duty, responsibility be damned.

As to its end, all I know, at this juncture is that leaders across the country, health care professionals and the American people are tirelessly working to see us through and, when safe, turn America back on. Trump will, of course, be busy blaming everybody else from the World Health Organization, the Governors, the reporters and lying often enough to leave the 17,000 lies told mark in the dust. Maybe even 18,000. More?

CLOSING THOUGHTS

His features would transform and his face would light up and his voice would grow more pleasant as he warmed up to the words at hand. He would, from his perch at the podium, embrace the crowd, mesmerize the crowd, become one with them. He would gain their trust and their faith and once he reeled them in, they were loath to let go. Words would soar and content would claim. And from the words and the clarity of thought, the substance and the lyrical persuasion and the buying in and the conviction. With truth and high ideals and high purpose in tow, each speech became a sacred endeavor and he would reap what he sowed.

A politician by choice and a public servant by choice, he honored this calling and devoted himself to the betterment of the lives of those he served.

He gave thought to each word, each step, each action and accomplishment. A friend's friend, a generous lawyer, a good partner, the most inspiring of writers, a remarkable student of and leader of men, an impassioned advocate for freedom and justice, a haunted Commander and Chief, a tireless believer, a gentle and generous soul, ever faithful, compassionate and fiercely devoted president.

He bled with every soldier who fell, he was tortured by migraines and misgivings, as he strolled over to the Telegraph office in the War Department to get the latest news from the front. That's how to picture him. See him pacing the cold floors of the White House in his robe in the dead of night. See him despondent over Willie or playing with Tad in his office. See him telling his stories to Hay and Nicolay late on a winter's evening in his cold office with his feet up on his desk in his nightgown. See him waking them in the dead of night to ask a question or to relate the latest quip he read by Artemus Ward or his old friend, Petroleum V. Nasby.

See him walking with and cheering for and honoring his soldiers. See him visiting them in the Hospital wards in D.C. See him with the mothers and the daughters and the widows, ever pardoning their own to the dismay of his commanders. See him kneeling with them and praying on the floor of his office for their loved ones and all of his soldiers. See him carrying Tad on his back or flailing those long arms, as he affirms a point in a meeting with his Cabinet. See him sitting with a soldier on the park bench, arm around his shoulder. See him free, with face transfixed and beaming, as he smiles and laughs in Secretary Seward's parlor. See him with a comforting arm draped across Mary's shoulders and with his firm, strong right hand extended out to greet the next of the thousands upon thousands of visitors.

Then just listen to these few words:

- My childhood home l see again—And gladden with the view—And still as memories crowd my brain—There's sadness in it too . . . The very spot that grew the bread—That formed my bones I see—How strange, old friend, on thee to tread—To feel I'm part of thee . . .
- But we have forgotten God. We have forgotten the gracious hand which preserved us in peace, and multiplied and enriched and strengthened us; and we have vainly imagined, in the deceitfulness of our hearts, that all these blessings were produced by some superior wisdom and virtue of our own. Intoxicated with unbroken success, we have become too self-suffi-cient to feel the necessity of redeeming and preserving grace, too proud to pray to the God that made us"
- I pray that our Heavenly Father may assuage the anguish of your bereave-ment, and leave you only the cherished memory of the loved and lost, and the solemn pride that must be yours to have laid so costly a sacrifice upon the altar of freedom.
- The will of God prevails.
- I am not a great man.

To your show me someone with no ego and you'll show me a loser. Mr. President, I give you Abraham Lincoln. No ego. No loser. Fully 155 years later, as revered and honored as ever.

As to your legacy, I shudder to think.

Figure 5.1.   In that it is in the earliest of years that personalities and dispositions and ways of being are forged, that which made Lincoln so extraordinarily humble, compassionate, empathetic and true enough to save his "Last best hope of earth" manifested here. *Source:* Seated Lincoln, Hodgenville, Kentucky - by Adolph Weinman 1909. Photographed by Dave Wiegers.

Conclusion

And in the End

Upon visiting the site of Abraham Lincoln's birthplace at Sinking Springs Farm and boyhood home at Knob Creek where he lived to 7 years of age in Hodgenville, Kentucky on one hot and late, June 18' afternoon, we were surprised—my son, Bill and I—to find ourselves utterly alone. There we were on the sacred terrain where he first drew breath and took his baby steps, where he first ran and played and tackled the kind of chores that would forever render frontier farming distasteful to him—and, oh yes, where he would have drowned that one fine summer afternoon, had Austin Gollaher not been there to jam that stick into his hands.

As it has run dry, there is no Knob Creek to either see or swim in today, so it is strange to imagine that once upon a time, its waters raged wildly enough to threaten to take him from us prematurely, something that the heavens would not abide. When we visited, the air was so soft and still that I could, in my own spirited imaginings, have sworn that I heard both his infant cry and the primal cry that he let loose when he slipped off that log into the raging creek and struggled to grab the branch that Austin pressed into his flailing hands.

The hard, dark wood of the cabins conspired with the lush green of the forest and a bright blue sky to remind me that this once frontier, first laid claim to and shaped and steeled him for what would be his life abundant, one in which he reclaimed a nation and forever inspired generations of its citizens to hold tight to its history and its ideals. On its rolling and undulating grounds, however altered by time and tide they may have been, the all of one of the greatest of American stories was set in motion.

Given my lot in life, there was to be no ascension to the Greco-Roman palace commemorating what the forest and the once spring and the green leaves ever so much more beautifully proclaimed. Profoundly aware of the fact that we were standing upon, what is for the American Republic, holy ground, I so wished that the rocks and the wood and the dirt could speak and tell tales that have never been told of him or of his Father, Thomas, with whom he became estranged or of his mother, Nancy and sister, Sarah upon whom he then depended so.

We know, truly know, that the disposition, basic mindset and personality is forged in the earliest of years and thus the humility, kindness, devotion and courage of Abe Lincoln, who would hold firm, as if '*with a chain of steel,*' were forged right there. There, right there, no matter how much we discern and study and write, lies what will always remain the impenetrable wonder and mystery of 1809 through 1816 and Hodgenville, Kentucky and the magic in the moonlight there that miraculously rendered our Lincoln—Lincoln.

There was peace to be found in this private and personal communion with him. And so too in simply basking in the warmth of that afternoon and the living hope that his life and legacy and words might continue to help America strive to be the better America that he devoted the all of his life to fashioning in the first place.

Indeed, it was an odd day, for upon later visiting Hodgenville's humble, downtown square where presidential Abe and boyhood Abe stare each other down, there was, once again, nary a living soul to be seen on the streets. Literally no one. *Twilight Zone* like, it was.

Notably, I was moved, as I am so easily moved by any and every image of him, by the raw power of the Adolph Weinman sculptures which were first unveiled there in 1909 to commemorate the then centennial of Lincoln's birth.

Again and not to overstate this, but alone as we were, it was as if the fates had conspired to grant us a private audience with young Lincoln that day. It was a cosmic mystery and blessing as no room, literally no room, was left for distraction; and nary a shop or a business, at roughly 4:00 p.m., was open either. None that was until my eyes witnessed the "Closed" sign in the small *Lincoln's Loft Bookstore* door flip to "Open."

As if on cue, it did this.

Anticipating it to be 'chock full of' rare finds, I was, at first, disappointed to discover that it was just a very small and ordinary shop replete with books of all genres. As to the town's celebrated icon, there was little. Little on the Civil War or on A. Lincoln himself. In fact, I remember only Foote's *Shiloh*, Foner's *Fiery Trial*, Shaara's *Killer Angels* and Holzer's *Lincoln President-Elect*. It did not appear to be a place that could afford either volume or discount buys or one that was able, in any way, to keep up with contemporary Lincoln scholarship.

But what the shelves may have lacked, its engaging and aging proprietors more than compensated for with a transcendent goodness and grace. They offered us free books or what they described as publisher's promotions and they gave us *Lincoln's Loft* pens that I will treasure and crushed Lincoln pennies and homemade cookies that I ate, Doctor's orders notwithstanding. They were of the "restore your faith in human nature" class, worthy of the town and of its Lincoln. Like the druggist in Wilder's *Our Town* or the proprietors of the *Bailey Brothers' Building & Loan in Bedford Falls* or as I like to believe the Lincolns' Hodgenville neighbors may have been, they were the epitome of the good neighbor, of those rare entrepreneurs who are remarkably more interested in giving than receiving.

So very kind as Lincoln was kind, I thought.

Suddenly, I spotted it, one lonely, soft cover book, published in 1954, the title was *River Road – A Story of Abraham Lincoln*, by Meribel LeSueur. Never before heard of, it was buried behind other books on a low-lying shelf, the surprise, the gem that I was to extract from *Lincoln's Loft Bookstore*. Its cover and the image of a strapping, young boy who would be a man suggested children's book while the wordsmithing and metaphorical imagery within would later suggest otherwise.

Originally born in 1900, I soon learned that LeSueur led a storied life of 96 years, championing everything from populism to communism, from the rights of migrants, laborers, the impoverished, Native Americans and women. She set the tone for the no-holds barred activism of the Sixties. It was no small thing, after all, to have written stories worthy of today's *'Me-Too'* movement and *'Resistance'* 80-odd years ago, or to have long lived among the Navajo with whom she became one, or to have been blacklisted during the McCarthy era. Worthy of her own biography, this Hollywood extra and stunt woman who helped make movies like the famous and celebrated *The Perils of Pauline* in her youth was the real deal.

While she wrote a wide array of stories, of particular and added interest to me was her *Nancy Hanks of Wilderness Road: A Story of Abraham Lincoln's Mother*.

I found myself taken, both by the author and by her story and wondered what my collaborators, who graciously forged this effort with me, would think of this little tome, one which I consequently determined, on a whim, to briefly reflect upon in tying the ribbon around and here placing the bow upon our *Unfading Light*.

Bound as we all are by this love of Lincoln, why not?

While a 1954 *New York Times Review* suggested that the writing in *River Road* "rose to the level of prose poetry," contemporary critics might be less forgiving, as she romanticizes and nigh on deifies him. Laudatory, overstated, hyperbolic but wonderful, she gives her strapping, 19-year old Abe the proverbial wisdom of the ages and conjures up ways to have him voice and bear witness to the quotes that were to later comprise many of his *greatest hits*.

Yes, she was over the top, but what the hell, so am I.

We are introduced to a tortured, introspective young Lincoln, who is determined to escape and take flight, a young man who longed "to know things" and to embrace the fullness of life. A seeker of knowledge, full of questions, he was desperate for more, desperate to matter, desperate to live so as to honor the memory of his Mother, desperate for purpose and oh so ready to escape and "hightail it" out of Pigeon Creek. It is on the flatboat manning the long paddles or broad horns, somewhere on the Ohio or the Mississippi, in port in Natchez, Baton Rouge or New Orleans or anywhere along that 1276 mile trek downriver fighting the tides, where a measure of peace and perspective were to be found.

Along the way, he speaks to many casual acquaintances of democracy and service and slavery and the eternal verities and truths. On any ordinary day, from April 18 or 19 of 1828 when they left Rockport, Indiana until June 21 when they returned, her young Lincoln kept weighing in on the great issues of the age, returning to freely embrace his circumstances and, be it 'slavery' or not to him, fulfill his obligation to his family, both to his Step-mom and his Father.

And make no mistake, with '*Me-Too*' in mind, Nancy Hanks and Sarah Bush Johnston Lincoln are as wildly celebrated in *River Road* as is its young protagonist.

Sure, the tale is familiar, especially the fact that it was to be his first encounter with slavery in the chains, the fields, the flesh and the mind, the harsh, red-hot, searing reality of it, something that he would wrestle and struggle with for all the days of his life. Boring into his personal struggle with his lot in life and his hunger for ever so much more, LeSeuer's telling of the tale, poetic imagery and musings prove penetratingly moving.

As to being a success, he rejects the very notion of it, for devoid of contribution or goodness or service, success is of nothing. however rational he tried to be, the right hand of God took hold of him and the very fire of the "*Spirit of Jehova trembled within him*," however rational he tried to be, the right hand of God took hold of him and the very fire of the "*Spirit of Jehova trembled within him*," No, it must rather save them from avarice and greed and indifference and denial.

Success for its own sake is the great trap, the great void and LeSueur's Lincoln, like Merton, determines to suffer none of it.

Devoid of selfishness, a life must count. To young Lincoln, to succeed is to matter and to serve, to fulfill his duty to others and in so doing, "leave his mark."

I was most moved by her impassioned metaphorical use of the natural elements that shaped him, the trees and wood and wind of the frontier forests that embraced him as he grew, the very trees that he climbed and communed with, the trees that he felled and cleared for planting seeds, the trees with which he built cabins and coffins and cradles and mean sticks of furniture.

Oh, she insists that he well knew and was one with the wood of the forest. He grew as it grew and he was shaped as it was shaped.

Its heartwood and his were of one and the ultimate strength of his heartwood would, after all, make all the difference.

"The seed of man is carried over time," she suggested. His seed, of course, was watered by tears and loss and sorrow and not just by the loss of his own, but of others who lived in these forests with him, old and young, sudden, surprising, long anticipated, neighbors and passersby. There was the Kickapoo Indian who was alleged to have drafted this incredibly introspective and simple verse, a sentiment first believed to have been expressed in an earlier George MacDonald story and a sentiment to which Lincoln would attach himself:

Here lies Johnny Kongapod—Have mercy on him, Gracious God—As he would do if he was God—And you were Johnny Kongapod.

Oh, what this simple ditty suggests of the great soul that was rising up in this young boy, who would dare to join others in advising God how it is that he ought to behave. And oh what it foretells of the lifelong shadow-boxing match that Lincoln was to have with God.

The all of this work, especially the great goodness that she wraps Lincoln in struck me as the portal with which to make our end.

For Johnny Kongapod, *Emancipation Proclamation*, the "Last best hope of earth" and the Thirteenth Amendment are of one.

I loved Le Sueur's contention that it was the frontier and the trees and the wood of the forest and the elements and the unknown and the unexpected in it and the wonder of it all that, more than anything else, shaped and steeled Lincoln for the great challenges he was to confront.

For he was a "tall timber," whose "grain was straight" and whose wood had attained the "bearing strength."

The tree could take it and so could he.

In and through 45 collaborators who have all written here of what drew them to become so invested in the life of Abraham Lincoln, of the character traits in him with which they most identified, of the conversations they would most have liked to have had, of the words of his that they hold most dear and, oh yes and most importantly, of why he and his legacy and his light continue to matter so in the life of our distressed America today.

It is with a final expression of thanks to each of them that I close, for they rendered this work possible. I am in awe of them and I so deeply respect and admire what each of them do to bring Abraham Lincoln, who was as good as it has ever gotten for America, to people today. In tireless research and scholarship and books and presentations and photographs and paintings and displays and animations and performances, they do this and they will continue to do so, ever hoping to teach and to elevate and to inspire and shine a bright light upon what America once strived to be and what we may yet be.

Yes, "Slowly, slowly, the sapwood turns to heartwood," LeSueur wrote, "slow in a man as in a tree and the bending strength is made, and the bearing strength. And the straightness of the grain."

Her young Abe, she again and again insisted, knew the wood, knew both its strength and the trajectory of its fall. He could take the measure of a tree as he later took the measure of a man and the measure of a republic.

He knew that it was "The heartwood of men, of the plain people in the long struggle, carrying upon their shoulders the great and durable questions of all ages" that move nations and people forward.

Her story captured but "a few months in the life of a boy becoming a man. Men and nations are made in the firing of such days." She would have us believe that he, who became "*Father Abraham,*" was honed by the very wood of the trees that he felled and the forests he knew, honed by its darkness and the sun that filtered through its leaves, honed by its shadows and its majesty, tall, firm, giving, nurturing, what a person ought to be, what a president ought to be.

In the end, she quotes his Herndon. "Abe was like those that lean like grand old towers, with lights on their brows, almost dipping in the deep, the unknown, the unknowable and unfathomable deeps of the future. We thus come and go and in the comings and the goings, we have moved forward."

The light was indeed in him, as his heartwood still shines and still dips in the deep. Forward, indeed, both then and now, illuminating the path.

Bibliography

Abdo, Genevieve, *Mecca and Main Street: Muslim Life in America after 9/11* , Oxford University Press, New York, 2006.

Angle, Paul, *The Lincoln Reader*, Kingsport Press, Kingsbridge, Tenn., 1947.

Barton, William Eleazer, *The Women Lincoln Loved,* The Barton Collection Research Center at the University of Chicago Library, Chicago, Illinois, 1927.

Bassuk, Daniel, *Abraham Lincoln and the Quakers*, (Pendle Hill Pamphlet #273/p 16) Wallingford, PA, 1987.

Bishop, Jim, *The Day Lincoln was Shot*, Harper & Collins, New York, 1955.

Boritt, Gabor, The Gettysburg Gospel: The Lincoln Speech That Nobody Knows, Simon & Schuster, New York, 2006.

Boritt, Gabor, *The Lincoln Enjgma: The Changing Faces of an American Icon,* Oxford University Press, New York, 2001.

Brewster, Todd, *Lincoln's Gamble: The Tumultuous Six Months that Gave America the Emancipation Proclamation and Changed the Course of the Civil War*, Simon & Schuster, New York, 2014.

Brewster, Todd, with Jennings, Peter, *In Search of America*, Hyperion, New York, 2002.

Brookhiser, Richard, *Founders' Son - A Life of Abraham Lincoln*, Basic Books, New York, 2014.

Brookhiser, Richard, *What Would the Founders Do - Our Questions-Their Answers*, Perseus Books, New York, 2006.

Burton, Orville Vernon, *The Age of Lincoln*, Hill & Wang, New York, 2007.

Carnegie, Dale, *Lincoln the Unknown*, Dale Carnegie & Associates, Inc. Garden City, New York, 1979.

Carroll, James *A Terrible Beauty: Conversions in Prayer, Politics, and Imagination*, Paulist Press, Mahwah, NJ, 1970.

Carwardine, Richard, *Lincoln: A Life of Purpose and Power,* Vintage Books, New York, 2007.

Current, Richard Nelson, *The Lincoln Nobody Knows,* the First American Century Series, Hill & Wang, New York, 1999.

Donald, David Herbert, *Lincoln,* Simon & Schuster, New York, 1995.

Dueholm, James, *Lincoln's Suspension of the Writ of Habeas Corpus: An Historical and Constitutional Analysis*, the Journal of the Abraham Lincoln Association, Volume 29,Issue 2, Summer 2008, Springfield, Illinois, 2008.

Egerton, Douglas, *Thunder at the Gates*: *The Black Civil War Regiments That Redeemed America* . New York: Basic Books, NY, 2016. (Co-winner Gilder-Lehrman Lincoln Prize.)

Egerton, Douglas, *Year of Meteors: Stephen Douglas, Abraham Lincoln, and the Election that Brought on the Civil War* . Bloomsbury Publishing, New York, 2010.

Egerton, Douglas, *He Shall Go Out Free: The Lives of Denmark Vesey*, Rowman and Little-field, Lanham, MD., 1999.

Egerton, Douglas. *Gabriel's Rebellion: The Virginia Slave Conspiracies of 1800 & 1802*, University of North Carolina Press, Chapel Hill, N.C., 1993.

Epstein, Daniel Mark, *Lincoln and Whitman: Parallel Lives in Civil War America*, Ballantine Books, New York, 2004.

Epstein, Daniel Mark, *The Lincolns: Portrait of a Marriage*, Random House, New York 2008.

Fritzky, Richard, *What Must Needs Come - A Legacy of Gettysburg*, Tate Publishing, Oklahoma, 2015.

Gerry, Margaret Spalding, *Through Five Administrations: Reminiscences of Colonel William H. Crook*, (Body-Guard to President Lincoln), Open Road-Integrated Media, North Carolina, 1910.

Gerson, Michael, *What Good Friday Teaches Us about Cynicism*, the Washington Post April 13 2017, Washington D.C., 2017.

Goodwin, Doris Kearns, *Team of Rivals*, Simon & Schuster, New York, 200.

Gramm, Kent, *Gettysburg: A Meditation on War & Values*, Southern Illinois University Press, Carbondale, Illinois, 1999.

Gramm, Kent. *Gettysburg: The Living and the Dead*, Southern Illinois University Press, Carbondale, Illinois, 2019.

Gramm, Kent, *November: Lincoln's Elegy at Gettysburg*, Indiana University Press, Bloomington, Indiana, 2005.

Grinspan, Jon, *The Stephen Colbert of the Civil War (Petroleum Vesuvius Nasby)*, The New, York Times, June 11, 2012, New York, 2012.

Guelzo, Allen C., *Abraham Lincoln: Redeemer President*, William B. Eerdmans Publishing Company, Grand Rapids, Michigan, 1999.

Haley, Alex, with Malcolm X, *The Autobiography of Malcolm X*, Penguin Modern Classics, New York, 2001.

Hicks, Robert, *The Widow of the South*, Warner Books, New York, 2006.

Holzer, Harold, with Horrocks, Thomas, *The Annotated Lincoln,* Harvard University Press Cambridge, Mass., 2016.

Holzer, Harold, with Cuomo, Mario, *Lincoln on Democracy*, HarperCollins, New York, 1990.

Holzer, Harold, *The Lincoln-Douglas Debates: The First Complete, Unexpurgated Text,* Harper Collins, New York 1993.

Holzer, Harold, *Lincoln Revisited: New Insights from the Lincoln Forum* (co-edited with John Y. Simon and Dawn Vogel), Fordham University Press, New York, 2007.

Holzer, Harold, co-edited with Horrocks, Thomas A. & Williams, Frank J., *The Living Lincoln*, Southern Illinois University Press, Carbondale, Illinois, 2011.

Holzer, Harold, with Garfinkle, Norton, *A Just and Generous Nation: Abraham Lincoln and the Fight for American Opportunity*, Basic Books, New York, 2015.

Holzer, Harold, *The 2016 Presidential Election*, The Huffington Post, October, 16, 2016 Judson, Clara Ingram, *Abraham Lincoln: Friend of the People*, Voyageur Press. Minneapolis, 2016.

Kershaw, Alex, *The Longest Winter: the Battle of the Bulge and the Story of World War II's Most Decorated Platoon,* De Capo Press/Perseus Books, New York, 2004.

King Jr., Martin Luther, *Where Do We Go From Here, Chaos or Community*, Beacon Press, Boston, 1968.

Koppelman, Steve, Editor, *The Wide Awake* (the annual newsletter of The Lincoln Group of New York), 2004---2018.

Krowl, Michelle,*Women Who Dare: Women of the Civil War,* Donning Co. Pub, Virginia Beach, Virginia, 2004.

Lapsley, Arthur Brooks, *Writings of Abraham Lincoln*, 8 volumes with an introduction by Theodore Roosevelt, P.F. Collier & Son, New York, 1905–1906.

LeSueur, Meribel, The *River Road – A Story of Abraham Lincoln,*Holy Cow Press, Duluth, Minn., 1994.

Lincoln, Abraham w/Basler, Roy et al, *The Collected Works of Abraham Lincoln*, Rutgers University Press, New Brunswick, NJ, 1953–1955.

Masur, Kate, *The African American Delegation to Abraham Lincoln: A Reappraisal,* Kent State University Press, Kent, Ohio, 2012.

McClure, A. K., M. D., *Lincoln and Men of War Times,* True Publishing Company, Philadelphia, PA, 1892.

McElroy, John Harmon, *The Sacrificial Years, A Chronicle of Walt Whitman's Experiences in the Civil War,* David R. Godine Publishers, Boston, MA, 2000.

McPherson, James M., *Abraham Lincoln as Commander in Chief,* Penguin Group, New York, 2008.

McPherson, James, *Tried by War,* Penguin Group, New York, 2008.

Medford, Edna Greene, *Lincoln and Emancipation,* Southern Illinois University Press, Carbondale, Illinois, 2015.

Medford, Edna Greene, with Holzer, Harold & Williams, Frank, *The Emancipation Proclamation: Three Views,* Louisiana State University Press, Shreveport, LA, 2006.

Medford, Edna Green, editor & contributor, *The Price of Freedom - Slavery and the Civil War,* Cumberland House Publishing, 2000.

Miers, Earl Schenck, *Abraham Lincoln in Peace and War,* The American Heritage Junior Library Series, Rutgers University Press, NJ, 2011.

Morris, Rebecca, *A Low Dirty Place: The Parole Camps of Annapolis, MD 1862–1865,* The Anne Arundel Historical Society, Maryland, 2012.

Newfield, Jack, *RFK: A Memoir,* Dutton Books, New York, 1969.

Obama, Barack, *Audacity of Hope: Thoughts on Reclaiming the American Dream,* Crown Publishing Group, New York, 2006.

O'Donnell, Kenneth P & Powers, David F., *Johnny We Hardly Knew Ye,* Open Road - Integrated Media, New York, 1972.

Owen, Frederick, *Abraham Lincoln: The Man & His Faith,* Tyndale House Publishers, Carol Stream, Illinois, 1981.

Patch, Eileen, *This from George—The Civil War Letters of Sergeant George Magusta Englis 1861–1865,* (Company K, 89th New York Regiment of Volunteer Infantry or the Dickinson Guard), Broome County Historical Society, Binghamton, NY 2001.

Pattersen, Richard North, *The Loss of Bobby Kennedy Has Never Felt Greater,* Huffington Post Column, *June 2018 Power, J. Tracy, Lee's Miserables: Life in the Army of Northern Virginia from the Wilderness to Appomattox,* Civil War America Series, University of North Carolina Press, Chapel Hill, North Carolina, 1998.

Powers, John, The Kennedy Mystique, Vogue Magazine, November 11, 2013, New York

Pryor, Elizabeth Brown, *Brief Encounter: A New York Cavalryman's Striking Conversation with Abraham Lincoln,* Journal of the Abraham Lincoln Association, (Volume 30, Issue 2), 2009, Springfield, Illinois, 2009 . . . (also see the Lucien P. Waters Papers/the New York Historical Society).

Raab, Nathan, *This is an Abraham Lincoln Revival,* Nathan's Blog, Forbes Magazine, May 1, 2013.

Rice, Allen Thorndike, Ed., *Reminiscences of Abraham Lincoln by Distinguished Men of His Time,* (Schuyler Colfax, p 342–343, Speaker of the House when Lincoln served as President), North American Publishing Company, New York, 1886.

Sandburg, Carl, *Abraham Lincoln the Prairie Year,* New York, Charles Scribner & Sons, New York, 1926.

Sandburg, Carl, *Abraham Lincoln the War Years,* Charles Scribner & Sons, New York, 1939.

Sarna, Rabbi Jonathan, with Shappel, Benjamin, *Lincoln and the Jews: A History,* Thomas Dunne Books/St Martin's Press, New York, 2015.

Sarna, Rabbi Jonathan, with Mendelson, Adam, *Jews and the Civil War: A Reader,* NYU Press, New York, 2010.

Shaara, Michael, *Killer Angels,* Random House Publishing, New York, 1974.

Shenk, Joshua Wolf, *Lincoln's Melancholy: How Depression Challenged a President and Fueled His Greatness,* Houghton Mifflin Company, New York, 2005.

Shi, David & Tindall, George, *America: A Narrative History,* W.W. Norton & Co., New York, 2010.

Sorensen, Theodore, Abraham *Lincoln, a Man of His Words - Lincoln Had the Best Speechwriter –Himself,* Smithsonian Magazine, October 2008, Washington D.C.

Staib, Justine, The Political and Constitutional Thought of John Archibald Campbell , Ph.D. Dissertation, the University of Alabama, Tuscaloosa, Alabama, 1966.

Staudenraus, PJ, ed., *Mr. Lincoln's Washington: The Civil War Dispatches of Noah Brooks,* Kent State University Press, Kent, Ohio, 1966.

Starobin, Paul, *Madness Rules the Hour: Charleston, 1860 and the Mania for War,* Perseus Books, New York, 2017.

Wagenknecht, Edward, ed., *Abraham Lincoln, His Life, Works and Character,* Creative Age Press, New York, 1947.

Waugh, John C., *Lincoln and McClellan: The Troubled Relationship between a President and His General,* Palgrave MacMillan, NY, 2010.

Waugh, John C., *One Man Great Enough: Abraham Lincoln's Road to Civil War,* Harcourt,Books, NY, 2009.

Waugh, John C, The Class of 1846—From West Point to Appomattox: Stonewall Jackson, George McClellan and their Brothers, with Foreword by James McPherson, Warner Books, 1994 & Ballantine Books, 1999.

Washington, John E, *They Knew Lincoln,* Oxford University Press, New York, 2018.

White, Ronald Jr., *Lincoln's Greatest Speech: The Second Inaugural,* Simon & Schuster, New York, 2002.

White, Theodore H., *In Search of History: A Personal Adventure,* Harper & Row, New York, 1978.

Williams, Frank J., *Lincoln as Hero* (Concise Lincoln Library), Southern Illinois University Press., Illinois, 2012.

Williams, Frank, J., with Holzer, Harold, *Judging Lincoln* Southern Illinois University Press, Carbondale, Illinois, 2007.

Williams, Frank J., with Holzer, Harold & Medford, Edna Greene, *The Emancipation Proclamation: Three Views,* Louisiana State University Press, Louisiana, 2006.

Wills, Gary, *Lincoln at Gettysburg: The Words that Remade America,* Simon & Schuster, New York, 1992.

Woodward, Bob, *Fear: Trump in the White House,* Simon & Schuster, New York, 2018.

Index

Index

About the Author

Rich Fritzky is a 70-year-old quadruple amputee and survivor of neisseria meningitis, cancer, end stage renal disease, multi pneumonias, CDIF, mercer, diabetes and ever so much more. In fact, he wrote this book with the stub of the one finger left to him.

He has devoted his life to public and community service and education.

He worked for the first African American Mayor of Newark, NJ and was with the Mayor of Boston during the forced bussing to achieve racial integration years. He long served the Meadowlands Regional Chamber of Commerce, contributing to tremendous economic expansion and environmental reclamation. Forged many non-profits focused upon job development, job training and job placement, transportation, education, affordable housing, adult literacy, youth services and more. He long fought for the Meadowlands Rail Station and helped bring it to fruition, co-founded Meadowlink, NJ's first transportation management association which today serves tens of thousands of commuters daily and long worked with the Sisters of Saint Joseph of Peace to open the Kenmare Alternative High School for Unwed Mothers and the Saint Joseph's Transitional Housing Complex in Jersey City.

Appointed by both Democratic and Republican Governors as a State Planning and Workforce Development commissioner and as the chairman of State Task Forces on Adult Literacy and Gender Equity and by United States Senator Bill Bradley to the Northeast-Midwest Leadership Coalition. Also long served on the boards of many charitable and community service organizations in northeast Jersey.

At times, he taught at Seton Hall Prep, Felician College, Bergen Community College and for more than 35 years at Fairleigh Dickinson University. He now serves his alma mater, as a member of the Adjunct Faculty of Seton Hall University.

Previous books include *A Pilgrim's Song: Mary Varick and her Theology of Suffering, Tidings of Great Joy: Keeping Christmas Well, It Isn't Cheaper by the Dozen Anymore* and *What Must Needs Come: A Legacy of Gettysburg.*

He lives in Stanhope, NJ with his wife, Maggie. His 12 children and 22 grandchildren are all within striking distance.